GEOGRAPHIES OF GENDER-BASED VIOLENCE

A Multi-Disciplinary Perspective

Edited by
Hannah Bows and Bianca Fileborn

BRISTOL
UNIVERSITY
PRESS

First published in Great Britain in 2022 by

Bristol University Press
University of Bristol
1–9 Old Park Hill
Bristol
BS2 8BB
UK
t: +44 (0)117 374 6645
e: bup-info@bristol.ac.uk

Details of international sales and distribution partners are available at bristoluniversitypress.co.uk

© Bristol University Press 2022

British Library Cataloguing in Publication Data
A catalogue record for this book is available from the British Library

ISBN 978-1-5292-1449-9 hardcover
ISBN 978-1-5292-1450-5 paperback
ISBN 978-1-5292-1451-2 ePub
ISBN 978-1-5292-1452-9 ePdf

The right of Hannah Bows and Bianca Fileborn to be identified as editors of this work has been asserted by them in accordance with the Copyright, Designs and Patents Act 1988.

Cover design: Nicky Borowiec
Front cover image: YiuCheung
Bristol University Press use environmentally responsible print partners.
Printed and bound in Great Britain by CMP, Poole

Contents

List of Figures, Tables and Boxes

Figures

Tables

Boxes

List of Abbreviations

CAM	community asset mapping
CMCoord	civilian–military strategic coordination
CNN	convoluted neural network
DCVAW	Directorate to Combat Violence Against Women
DV	domestic violence
DVA	domestic violence and abuse
EUCAP	EU Capacity Building Mission
FDS	Forces de Défense et Sécurité (Security and Defence Forces)
GBI	gender-based inequalities
GBV	gender-based violence
GRC	Plan India International Gender Resource Center
INGO	international non-governmental organization
KRG	Kurdistan Regional Government
LGBTQIA+	lesbian, gay, bisexual, transgender, queer and/or questioning, intersex, and asexual and/or ally including all people who have a non-normative gender identity or sexual orientation
LSOAs	lower super output areas
NGO	non-governmental organization
NN	neural networks
NTE	night-time economy
NUDM	Non Una di Meno (Not One Less)
VAW	violence against women

Notes on Contributors

Kristine Anderson is a researcher and humanitarian worker specialized in gender-based violence. She has worked extensively in fragile and conflict-affected settings in the Middle East and West Africa conducting research and implementing gender-based violence response and prevention programmes. She has authored and co-authored a number of research reports on gender-based violence and gender justice for the United Nations High Commissioner for Refugees, the United Nations Population Fund and several international non-governmental humanitarian organizations. She holds a master's in Middle Eastern Languages and Cultures from the University of Texas at Austin.

Jane Anyango is a well-known urban-grassroots woman living and working in Kibera, the biggest slum settlement in sub-Saharan Africa, in Nairobi, Kenya. She organizes women from different communities in response to cases of sexual manipulation and violence towards adolescent girls, and has mentored thousands of girls through her 'GPende' [Love Yourself] campaign. She is the Founding Director of Polycom Development Project, and has received numerous awards and accolades. She met President Obama in 2015 as one of the ten most influential Kenyan women, and featured in the award-winning documentary *I Will Not Be Silenced* in 2014.

Chiara Belingardi is Senior Research Fellow at the Italian National Research Council. She holds a PhD in Urban and Regional Planning from Florence University. She is on the editorial boards of IAPh Italia and *Scienze del Territorio*, and is editor-in-chief of the 'Conversation in Planning' booklet series. She is the author of *Comunanze Urbane: Autogestione e cura dei luoghi* (FUP, 2015) and co-editor with Federica Castelli of *Città: Politiche dello spazio urbano* (IAPh Italia, 2016) and *La libertà è una passeggiata: Donne e spazi urbani tra violenza strutturale e autodeterminazione* (IAPh Italia, 2019) with Federica Castelli and Serena Olcuire.

Giada Bonu is a PhD candidate in Political Science and Sociology at the Scuola Normale Superiore in Florence. She is currently conducting research on the production of feminist safer spaces in urban context between Italy and Spain, through participatory action research (PAR). She is editor of the feminist journal *DWF-DonnaWomanFemme*. She collaborates with Atelier Città (IAPh Italia) and with the independent research group on postcolonial studies in Sardinia, Filosofia de Logu.

Hannah Bows is an Associate Professor in Criminal Law at Durham University. Her research to date has focused on different forms of violence and abuse against adults, with the bulk of her work examining older adults as victims and perpetrators. More recent projects have examined sexual violence at festivals and the so-called 'rough sex defence' to murder that has been observed in homicides of women.

Anja Bredal holds a PhD in Sociology from the University of Oslo, Norway and is a senior researcher at the Centre for Social Research (NOVA) at the Oslo Metropolitan University. She has done extensive research on families of immigrant background with a focus on gender and generational conflict and abuse, including studies on public policies and service provision. She is part of the leadership of the NOVA's Research Programme on Domestic Violence (2014–2024). In 2019–2020 the Norwegian government appointed her leader of an expert group on children and young people who are left abroad against their will.

Frederica Castelli is a Postdoctoral Fellow in Philosophy of Politics at Roma Tre University, and supervisor and coordinator for the I level master's in Gender Studies and Policies. She is editor of *DWF-DonnaWomanFemme*, and on the editorial board of IAPh Italia. Recent publications include: *Il pensiero politico di Nicole Loraux* (IAPh Italia, 2016), *Spazio Pubblico* (Ediesse, 2019), *Comunarde: Storie di donne sulle barricate* (Armillaria, 2021), *Città: Politiche dello spazio urbano* (IAPh Italia, 2016, edited with Chiara Belingardi) and *La libertà è una passeggiata: Donne e spazi urbani tra violenza strutturale e autodeterminazione* (IAPh Italia, 2019, edited with Chiara Belingardi and Serena Olcuire).

Hugo d'Arbois de Jubainville worked as a research officer at the French Observatory of Crime and Criminal Justice (ONDRP) from 2015 until its closing down in 2020. During this period, he participated in several international projects, including Transit Safety Among College Students. His main areas of work are fear of crime and transit safety. He holds a master's in Public Affairs from the Institut d'études politiques de Paris and three university degrees in criminology from the Institut de criminologie et de droit pénal de Paris.

Walter DeKeseredy is Anna Deane Carlson Endowed Chair of Social Sciences, Director of the Research Center on Violence and Professor of Sociology at West Virginia University. He has published 27 books, over 120 scientific journal articles and 90 scholarly book chapters on violence against women and other social problems. He holds many awards, most recently the Critical Criminal Justice Scholar Award (2014, Academy of Criminal Justice Sciences' Section on Critical Criminal Justice), the Career Achievement Award (2015, American Society of Criminology's Division on Victimology) and the Impact Award and Robert Jerrin Book Award (both 2017, ASC's Division on Victimology).

Corinna Di Niro is a leading expert of Commedia dell'Arte in Australia. She holds a PhD in Commedia dell'Arte and runs her own theatre company, Stage Secrets, combining cutting-edge technology with theatre to create performances that address social issues. In 2019, she directed *Bone Cage* by Geoff Gillham for the '(In)Visible Violence Towards Women and Their Resistance' conference. She is co-editor of *Commedia dell'Arte for the 21st Century: Practice and Performance in the Asia-Pacific* (Routledge, 2022), has published widely, is a Guest Lecturer at National Institute of Dramatic Arts and a sessional academic at the University of South Australia.

Elsa D'Silva is the Founder of Red Dot Foundation in India and President of Red Dot Foundation Global in the US. Its platform, Safecity, crowdsources personal experiences of sexual violence and abuse in public spaces. Elsa holds several fellowships, and she co-founded the Gender Alliance, a cross-network initiative bringing together feminists from a range of fields. She is listed as one of BBC Hindi's 100 Women and has won several awards. She is a co-editor and author of *The Demographic Dividend and the Power of Youth* (Anthem Press, 2021) and writes and speaks widely.

Alexandra Fanghanel is Senior Lecturer in Criminology and Co-lead of the Gender, Deviance and Society Research Group at the University of Greenwich. Her research focuses on fear of crime, security, sexuality, rape culture and public space. She is the author of *Disrupting Rape Culture: Public Space, Sexuality and Revolt* (Bristol University Press, 2020), and the winner of the 2020 British Society of Criminology Women Crime and Criminal Justice Network paper prize.

Bianca Fileborn is Senior Lecturer in Criminology and DECRA Research Fellow in the School of Social and Political Sciences at the University of Melbourne. She lives and works on the unceded lands of the Wurundjeri people. Her work explores the interplay between space/place, identity, culture and sexual violence, and innovative justice responses to sexual violence. Her current research examines victim-centred justice for street harassment, sexual violence at music festivals, and sexual violence and LGBTQ+ communities. She is the author of *Reclaiming the Night-Time Economy* (Palgrave, 2016) and co-editor of *#MeToo and the Politics of Social Change* (Palgrave, 2019) with Rachel Loney-Howes.

Suzanne Goodney Lea is CEO of Red Dot Foundation Global, which strives to make public spaces safer using crowd mapping and community engagement. She is Assistant Professor of Crime, Justice and Security Studies at the University of the District of Columbia. Her research explores place as a unit of analysis for understanding crime, gender-based violence, police use of deadly force, and ways of engaging communities to enhance their safety and the effectiveness of their governance policies. She is an adviser for #DontMuteDC and is co-author of *Let's Talk Politics: Restoring Civility Through Exploratory Discussion* (with Adolf Gundersen, CreateSpace, 2013).

Sarah Hewitt is a Teaching Fellow at the University of Southampton, in the Faculty of Engineering and Physical Sciences, and is Senior Tutor for a range of computer science modules. Her main area of interest is how the Web is used by professional bodies, for example by teachers to form communities and make their voices heard. She taught English and Media in a large secondary school for over ten years and is late to the world of computer science, where she is an advocate for mature students of any gender, and particularly supportive of women in science.

Haje Keli obtained her PhD in Gender Studies in 2018 from SOAS University of London. Her topic was the continuum of violence against women in the Kurdistan Region of Iraq, focusing on female genital cutting, forced marriage and structural violence. She has taught at SOAS and the University of Exeter, worked at women's rights NGOs in Iraq and held a weekly feminism class at Women for Refugee Women in London. She has extensive fieldwork experience and keeps an active social media presence, where she is engaged in online activism to raise awareness on violence against women in Iraqi Kurdistan.

Debbie Kilroy is a settler on unceded lands. She was first imprisoned at age 14, spending the subsequent 20 years moving in and out of women's and children's prisons in Queensland, Australia. After her final release from prison in 1992, she established Sisters Inside, which advocates for the human rights of women and girls affected by the criminal legal system. In 2007, she was the first person in Australia with serious convictions to be admitted to practise law by the Supreme Court of Queensland. Debbie continues to lead Sisters Inside as CEO and is Principal of Kilroy & Callaghan Lawyers.

Tabitha Lean is a Gunditjmara woman and a storyteller, poet and freelance writer. She is also a lived experience abolitionist having spent almost two years in prison, and two years on home detention in Adelaide, South Australia. Tabitha is committed to elevating the voices of those with lived prison experience in order to expose carceral state-sanctioned violence in an effort to stop the brutalizing and killing of her own people in the colonial frontier that is the criminal injustice system. She is a member of the recently formed National Network for Incarcerated and Formerly Incarcerated Women and Girls.

Jade Levell is Lecturer in Criminology and Gender Violence at the School for Policy Studies at the University of Bristol. She researches the relationship between masculinities, violence and vulnerability, using music elicitation as a narrative research tool. She currently leads a research team in a study on domestic violence and abuse perpetrator interventions, with partners in UK, Cyprus, Greece, Romania and Italy; she is in an international team using music elicitation in an Albanian project to divert young men from serious organized crime; and she has worked in a variety of roles for charities aiming to end gender-based violence.

Claire Loughnan is Lecturer in Criminology at the University of Melbourne. She researches the modes, practices and effects of living and working in carceral and confined spaces, whether immigration detention, youth detention, prisons, or aged and disability care. Her work explores how ethical relations of responsibility are conducted in institutional and social life, including through place as a site of memory. Claire is a member of the Carceral Geography Working Group of the Royal Society of Geographical Society. She lives and works on the land of the Wurundjeri and Boon Wurrung peoples of the Kulin Nation.

Cat Morgan is Postdoctoral Research Associate based in the Centre for Employment, Work and the Professions at Heriot-Watt University. Her research investigates feminist activists' use of Twitter for political communication, connection and action. She has an interdisciplinary research approach that encompasses the fields of computer science, social media, feminism, gender studies and ethnography. She is a member of the Feminist Studies Association (FSA), promoting feminist research in the UK and Ireland.

Emily Nicholls is Lecturer in Sociology at the University of York. Her research interests and expertise include gender and identity (specifically femininities); the sociology of consumption (specifically alcohol and sobriety); risk; and the night time economy. Recent work includes a project funded by the Institute of Alcohol Studies on the marketing and consumption of alcohol-free drinks. Emily is co-convenor of the Sobriety, Abstinence and Moderation research cluster (part of the international Drinking Studies Network) and author of *Negotiating Femininities in the Neoliberal Night-Time Economy: Too Much of a Girl?* (Palgrave Macmillan, 2019).

Serena Olcuire is Postdoctoral Fellow in Urban Planning at the DICEA Department in the Sapienza University of Rome, focusing on artistic practices as tools for the activation of territorial transformations. Her PhD research concerned the interweaving of street sex workers' geographies and urban policies for the management of public space, demonstrating how these are contributing to processes of exclusion. She collaborates with the Environmental Humanities Master at Roma Tre University and the Atelier Città at IAPh Italia. She is also part of the editorial board of the scientific journal *Tracce Urbane*.

Suzi Quixley is a settler, activist, academic, practitioner and consultant. She has specialized in work with community-driven social justice organizations throughout Australia for over 35 years. Suzi met Debbie Kilroy shortly after her release from prison and has periodically worked alongside her ever since. She continues to contribute to Sisters Inside, mainly through research, writing and organizational development, and has recently enjoyed the privilege of co-writing with Tabitha Lean.

Amelia Walker is a creative writing researcher who uses and investigates methods and methodologies for conducting inquiry and generating new knowledge via writing and arts-based practices. She holds a PhD in creative writing and currently lectures at the University of South Australia. Much of her work involves small or large group collaborations. Across 2019–2020 she co-facilitated an Indian–Australian online literary exchange to produce a special issue of *Text* (#60) featuring Indian and Australian poets in dialogue exploring issues of gender, culture, ecological sustainability, social inequality and the challenges of COVID-19, among others. She has published widely.

Ruth Weir is Senior Research Fellow at the Violence and Society Centre, City University, London. Her research expertise is in the geographic and quantitative analysis of crime and her PhD focused on individual, family and neighbourhood-level predictors of domestic abuse. Prior to working at the university, she held a number of research and policy positions in local and central government. She has also worked as a consultant and has carried out evaluations for a number of public sector and third sector organizations.

Acknowledgements

Hannah: I am grateful to the contributors in this collection and to my co-editor, Bianca, for helping to bring this collection together. It is my hope that this collection contributes to the small but growing work in this area and will be useful to feminist scholars, students and, importantly, activists and practitioners.

Bianca: I would like to thank all the authors for their contributions, which were written during what can only be described as challenging times. I'd also like to acknowledge those who were unable to take part in this collection due to the impacts of the COVID-19 pandemic. My thanks to my friends and family (you know who you are!), colleagues at the University of Melbourne and all of the wonderful scholars I've collaborated with over the years. Extra thanks and love to my partner, Grant, fur babies Sapphire and Ruby, and in memory of Bella. I live, work and benefit from land stolen from the Wurundjeri people, and acknowledge that sovereignty was never ceded.

Introduction

Hannah Bows and Bianca Fileborn

Background

Spaces – physical and digital, public and private – are gendered. Conceptually, symbolically and physically, women, men and gender-diverse folk access, use and experience spaces differently. For example, the private sphere of the home has traditionally been constructed as safe, but this construction predominantly applies to (White, cis-gender, heterosexual and able-bodied) men, who are most likely to be victims of violence or other crime in public places (ONS, 2020). For women, the home is frequently not a haven, but instead a site where, globally, at least one in three women will experience some form of physical, sexual, emotional or financial abuse by a partner or family member (WHO, 2021), and around two women are killed each week (ONS, 2020; Femicide Census, 2018).

Contemporary evidence shows the routine, commonplace occurrence of physical and sexual violence against women and LGBTQ+ people in public places; four out of five women in the UK have been sexually harassed in a public place (UN Women UK, 2021). Research from the US shows that LGBTQ+ people and people of colour also routinely experience harassment in public spaces (Stop Street Harassment, 2014). LGBTQ+ people also face heightened risk of domestic and family violence at rates similar to, if not higher than, cis-gender heterosexual women (LGBTIQ Domestic and Family Violence Interagency and CSRH, 2014). Yet, the home can also be a sanctuary or space of safety and belonging in a world that is too often heterosexist, homophobic and transphobic, while some public spaces can be sites of queer community, transgression and disruption to the heterosexist norm (Valentine, 1996; Duncan, 1996b; Corteen, 2002). These tensions point to the complex, fluid, relational and temporal nature of spaces as sites of safety or harm – they require us to ask safe or dangerous for whom, and in what contexts?

As we began preparing this collection, the COVID-19 pandemic swept the globe, fundamentally shifting our relationships to and uses

1

of space – often in ways that heightened and brought to the fore pre-existing inequalities (Kay, 2020; Young, 2021; Bonu et al, Chapter 1). Of relevance to this collection, the pandemic has exacerbated gendered (and other) inequalities, while increased rates of gender-based violence (GBV) in the home have been recorded across the world, leading to what the United Nations for Women have termed the 'shadow pandemic' (UN Women, nd). 'Home' was portrayed as the safest place to be to avoid the virus, but for those experiencing domestic violence 'home' is often the riskiest place to be (see Kay, 2020; Young, 2021; Levell, Chapter 3). Those most at risk of domestic violence faced heightened rates and/ or severity of violence, as illustrated by spikes in calls to helplines and, in the UK, a doubling of fatal violence against women (Boxall et al, 2020; Kay, 2020). However, while the pandemic has shone a light on violence experienced in the home, 'the realities of women's experiences of urban public spaces have been relegated to the backburner' (Bharadwaj and Mahanta, 2021: 1). Increased racist harassment of Asian people was also documented during the pandemic, with the bulk of this occurring in public and semi-public spaces (Asian Australian Alliance, 2020). The experiences of Asian women documented in work by the Asian Australian Alliance (2020) demonstrated that this harassment and abuse could be *both* racist and sexist in nature.

These examples raise the centrality of undertaking a spatial analysis of GBV. Even across these brief snapshots, we can see that GBV occurs across different spaces in different forms. Moreover, this discussion begins to evidence how the social and cultural production of space is implicated in the occurrence of GBV. Gender-based violence can represent a means of (re)producing spaces in particular ways (for example, as the domain of men and whiteness, as heteronormative), while the social and cultural production of space may in turn normalize and facilitate the occurrence of some forms of violence. Our discussion suggests that GBV may be understood differently depending on where it occurs – in the 'private' space of the home, for instance – with subsequent implications for what 'counts' as 'real' or 'serious' violence, and what is deemed worthy of intervention (Bows and Fileborn, 2020). Likewise, we begin to see different patterns emerging in terms of the temporal and geographical specificities of violence. In short, we contend that space must be taken seriously as a point of analysis in understanding, conceptualizing and intervening in GBV. Contributions to this collection aim to foreground the role of space and place in GBV from different perspectives. In this Introduction, we aim to provide readers with a snapshot of key debates, developments and concepts relating to gender, space and place, and GBV.

Conceptualizing gender and gender-based violence

This collection foregrounds space and place in the analysis of GBV. It is important to unpack the terms and concepts that are central to our endeavour. We adopt the definition of GBV established in the Istanbul Convention (Council of Europe, 2011: para 44): 'Gender-based violence refers to any type of harm that is perpetrated against a person or group of people because of their factual or perceived sex, gender, sexual orientation and/or gender identity'. Our approach to GBV draws heavily on Kelly's (1988) concept of the continuum, which has influenced much of the work on GBV over the last three decades and provides the framework for many of the chapters in this collection (such as DeKeseredy, Chapter 6). Accordingly, we see GBV as ranging in behaviours (from non-physical abuse including the male gaze, unwanted attention, verbal harassment and abuse, to physical assaults and rapes) and contexts, time and place, but always with the same purpose – to maintain the patriarchy (and, we would add, heteronormativity, White supremacy, colonialism, ableism and so forth).

Although gender is the distinguishing feature of GBV, this category cannot be viewed as wholly separate to or distinct from other categories of identity and relations of power. It is co-constructed in and through categories such as race, sexuality and class. This collection draws on an intersectional lens in understanding GBV (Crenshaw, 1994). Further, while gender is central to any understanding of violence, we do not suggest that gender is the only structural or systemic factor at play, or that it is *always* the most significant factor underpinning violence. Likewise, when we say 'gender-based violence', we do not *only* refer to men's violence against women, though this is of course a core focus throughout this volume. Thus, when we talk about gender, GBV and gendered space, we come from the perspective that 'gender' cannot be disentangled from race, sexuality, class, (dis)ability and other power structures. Indeed, as several chapters in this collection show, violence is situated at the intersections of gender, race and colonialism (see Kilroy, Lean and Quixley, Chapter 11). We also take this term to encompass how the social production and performance of gender is tied up with lived experiences of violence: who harms, who is harmed, and how we individually and collectively come to understand and make sense of both violence and gendered identity. Drawing on post-structuralist contributions (for example, Butler, 1990), 'gender' must be understood as multifaceted, relational and fluid.

Space, place and power

Since the early 1990s there has been a shift to recognizing not only the physicality of space, but also the social, cultural and temporal features and constructs of different spaces which (re)produce gender inequality within different sites. Aitchison (1999) notes that space was previously viewed as absolute and material, but it is now widely recognized as relative and symbolic, providing new ways of seeing and understanding leisure spaces. The contributions of de Certeau (1984) were central to driving this shift: his conceptualizations of space/place differentiated between a geographical, material location (place) and space as constituted through the practices, discourses and symbolic meaning associated with a given place. That is, *'space is a practiced place'* (de Certeau, 1984: 117, original emphasis). This marks a clear shift from seeing space as purely physical, to instead recognizing space as sociocultural and relative in nature.

Consequently, the synergies between gender relations and spatial relations began to be explored (Aitchison, 1999). Early feminist geographers (for example, Valentine, 1990; Pain, 1991; Duncan, 1996a; McDowell, 1996, 1999) provided foundational research into the gendered nature of spaces, from their design to their function, which were built, constructed and maintained within the wider patriarchy. For example, traditional gender roles assigned the home and domestic realm as women's domain, as a space free from state interference and, paradoxically, as a space in which men retained control as 'head of the household', collectively contributing to the existence yet invisibility of domestic violence (Valentine 1992; Duncan, 1996a; Wesely and Gaarder, 2004). In saying this, it is important to consider for *which* women this was the case. As Black feminist and critical scholars have pointed out, women of colour and socio-economically marginalized women participated in the public sphere and paid employment by necessity (Beck, 2021). The notion that women were relegated primarily to the private or domestic sphere reflects the experiences of White, middle-class women (though, they too resisted and contested this – Kern, 2021), while home for Black women could also be an important site of political organizing and resistance, *as well as* a space of patriarchal oppression (see Duncan, 1996b, drawing on hooks, 1990 and Crenshaw, 1994). This example again illustrates the importance of employing an intersectional analysis, demonstrating the *gendered* reproduction of spaces, but also the ways in which the category of gender and gendered space is shaped through power relations of (in this case) race and class (and see Valentine, 1996, 1997 in relation to sexuality). As McDowell (1999: 4) explains, 'places are contested, fluid and uncertain ... with multiple changing boundaries, constituted by social relations of power and exclusion'. As such, we should be wary of analyses that attempt to render space in any singular, coherent or universal way.

Spaces, particularly public spaces, are (White, heterosexual, able-bodied) masculine territories (Duncan, 1996a, 1996b; Valentine, 1996; Fanghanel, 2019; Kern, 2020) which restrict women's access, regulate their behaviour and expose them to risks that are not experienced in the same way, or to the same extent, as men. Feminist scholars have argued that space is constructed in a binary way, whereby patriarchy assigns space as masculine or feminine and 'in doing so, society retains control of the subordinate group by restricting movements, behaviour and activities' (Pain, 1991: 422; see also Duncan, 1996b). Space is thus of critical importance in 'asserting, maintaining and reinscribing binary gender norms', though this manifests in different ways across different spaces, contexts and times (England, 2021: 1; see also Duncan, 1996a; McDowell, 1996; Valentine, 1997). Several chapters in this volume attend to the social and cultural production of space and its role in gender-based violence. For instance, DeKeseredy (Chapter 6) examines how rural spaces facilitate what he terms woman abuse, while Morgan and Hewitt (Chapter 7) consider how digital space is produced as masculine space, which is in turn implicated in digital harassment. Alexandra Fanghanel's analysis of Brexit (Chapter 8) shows how constructions and representations of the White victim and Black 'other' in the context of sexual violence are drawn on in producing an imagined national identity in need of protection. Turning to the Sahel region of West Africa, Kristine Anderson (Chapter 10) outlines the implications that the militarization and 'NGO-ization' of space has for GBV.

Feminist scholars such as Duncan (1996a, 1996b) worked to destabilize and expose the artificial construction of space as a public/private binary. While this construction is popularly perceived as 'natural', Duncan (1996b: 127) shows how this divide is instead 'deeply rooted in political philosophy, law, popular discourse and recurrent spatial structuring practices'. This work is taken up by Haje Keli's contribution to this volume (Chapter 12), as she illustrates the ways in which the public and private blur into one another in institutional spaces. The organization of space as public/private has also been implicated in the construction of GBV (for example, Duncan, 1996b; Stanko, 1985), working to occlude and normalize violence. Violence against particular bodies in particular spaces come to be positioned as 'acceptable' and as 'non-violence' (Fanghanel, 2019). This is clearly illustrated through the historic (and contemporary) failure of the state to intervene in men's violence against women in the 'private' or domestic sphere (though the state has been all too willing to intervene in the 'private' affairs of others, as illustrated through the surveillance and regulation of homosexuality, or those dependent on the state for support − Duncan, 1996b). The spatial organization of 'acceptable' violence is apparent in Kilroy and colleagues' analysis of state-sanctioned violence against women in prisons (Chapter 11), where the use of sexually violent practices such as strip searches are constructed as normal and *necessary* 'procedures' against women. Given that women in Australian prisons are disproportionately Indigenous, the spatial isolation and perpetration of state-sanctioned violence must also be understood as a tool of colonization.

More recent work drawing on conceptual contributions such as assemblage thinking (Deleuze and Guattari, 1987; Grosz, 1995; Duncan, 1996b; Fanghanel, 2019), critical materialism and posthumanism further complicate our understandings of space. In relation to the city, for example, Alison Young (2021: 20) posits that 'we must think it as a space characterised by multifarious moments of collision between the multiple bodies, or legal subjects, human and non-human, that inhabit its spaces'. Such approaches ask us to move beyond viewing the material elements of space as simply the 'inert background' on which human interaction happens to instead recognize how material spaces (and other non-human elements) can themselves be productive forces (Fileborn, 2016; Fileborn et al, 2020). As Fileborn et al (2020: 72) explain, this line of thinking requires us to consider how 'cultural, discursive, spatial, material and human elements come together in fluid and temporally specific ways to generate incidents of sexual violence'. Moreover, the idea that the materiality of space plays a role in shaping how and whether GBV occurs is something that has less commonly been considered in research and scholarship on GBV. The role of material space and, in this case, transnational mobility, is brought to the fore by Anja Bredal in Chapter 9. Bredal's contribution demonstrates how perpetrators' control over space and movement through space – in addition to a host of other factors – plays a role in enabling their actions.

Space and fear

Public spaces have long been linked to fear of crime, particularly for women, LGBTQ+ communities and other marginalized groups (Vera-Gray, 2018; Berry et al, 2021). Early feminist geographers and sociologists, particularly Valentine (1989) and Pain (1991, 1995) documented the spatiality of women's fear, and experiences, of crime in public places. From an early age, women are told that public spaces are dangerous and the possibility of sexualized threats from men in these spaces means that accessing them carries with it responsibility for managing risk. Women are consequently held accountable for the violence they experience in public spaces as a form of contributory negligence (Burt and Estep, 1981).

It is therefore no surprise that women do not believe they have a right to public spaces; a 2016 Australian study reported that a third of young women surveyed did not believe they should be in public space at night at all and a quarter said that young women should never travel alone on public transport (Plan International and Our Watch, 2016). Arguably, the ongoing COVID-19 pandemic has resulted in a collective discomfort of public spaces, providing a taste of what women and LGBTQ+ communities have always experienced. As Bharadwaj and Mahanta (2021: 1) argue, 'it has to be recognized that the heightened sense of fear and distrust we experience on the street in the present underlines how women have always experienced the city – as a hostile, unsafe and potentially violent space'. However, women's fear of crime in public spaces – or more specifically, their fear of sexual violence, has to some extent been accepted and taken for granted while simultaneously positioned as irrational. This is because, according to official crime statistics and surveys, men are much more likely to experience violence victimization in public spaces.

Women are required to have the 'right amount of panic' when occupying public spaces (Vera-Gray, 2018). They must engage in an 'appropriate' amount of safekeeping work to 'stay safe', while simultaneously avoid being 'hysterical' or as overreacting to a 'non-existent' threat. The use of safekeeping strategies, which themselves manifest in spatially specific ways, further contributes towards the production of public spaces as masculine and heteronormative in nature (Pain, 1999; Fileborn, 2021a). As Lea and colleagues' chapter illustrates (Chapter 13), safekeeping strategies can greatly restrict women's access to public spaces. However, research since the 1990s has confirmed that women are not irrational in their fear of public spaces, nor 'hysterically overreacting to a "non-existent" threat' (Gilchrist et al, 1998: 285). In fact, women continue to face high levels of physical and sexual violence in public spaces – streets, public transport (see d'Arbois de Jubainville, Chapter 5), at university, at work, in gyms and in nightlife venues (see Nicholls, Chapter 2) as well as the home. Women's fear is therefore well placed and reflects the everyday reality.

However, we must also recognize the differential levels of privilege experienced by women. Different women will experience fear to different extents, and in different temporal, geographical and relational contexts. Women who enjoy greater levels of privilege may be more able to experience a sense of safety, ease and belonging in the world, or to possess the resources needed to avoid sites of unsafety (Kern, 2005, 2020). Indeed, women's fear can at times perpetuate other structural inequalities such as classism and racism (Kern, 2020; Phadke, 2013). This is seen in Emily Nicholls' work (Chapter 2), where women's fear on a night out was associated with the spaces occupied by working-class men.

Moreover, scholars have argued that, although men experience violent assaults at higher rates than women in public spaces, it is men who perpetrate this violence and thus violence against men and women in public spaces, although manifesting in different ways, can be understood through the (spatial) lens of hegemonic masculinity (Connell, 2005). As England (2021: 2) summarizes, 'Hegemonic masculinity idealises and empowers a cultural ideal of masculinity as brutal, violent and dominant, demanding subordination from women and problematisation of non-hegemonic masculinities – for instance, trans, queer, racialised and economically marginalised men'. Spaces, particularly public spaces, thus offer a location 'where hegemonic masculinities are enacted, maintained and legitimised' (2021: 2), a point that is taken up by Levell in Chapter 3 on the experiences of men who experienced domestic abuse as children and their lives 'on road' as adult men. Experiences within public spaces differ accordingly. As Vera-Gray and Kelly (2020: 265) point out, 'belonging in public space is both different for women and differs between women: for example, the possibility of not being observed/judged is accentuated if you are minoritized or gender non-conforming'. England (2021: 2) argues that 'the presence of women, trans and queer people in public space is tolerated contingent upon how they behave, and how they are constructed, within the space'.

Space and justice

The work in this volume shows that we need to take space seriously as a (literal and figurative) site of justice in relation to GBV. While our discussion in this collection focuses on space and justice in relation to GBV, it is essential to state that such conversations cannot be disconnected from the return of stolen lands to First Nations peoples and that, ultimately, no justice can be achieved without land justice. As mentioned earlier, spatial practices in relation to GBV are themselves inherently intertwined with processes of colonization and oppression (see Kern, 2020; Kilroy et al, Chapter 11). Leslie Kern (2020: 4) recently observed that 'the degradation and stigmatization of Indigenous women were part of the urbanization process', a legacy she argues continues to be reflected in the disproportionately high rates of GBV against Indigenous women and girls. While we are only able to touch on this point briefly, it is one that requires ongoing conversation, and needs to be centred in future discussions on spatial justice. We aim here to outline some of the ways in which space has been approached as a site of justice in relation to GBV to date.

Speaking to the spatial inequalities rendered more visible throughout the COVID-19 pandemic, and the assumption that the home represents a space of safety, Kay (2020: 888) suggested that 'while we are staying the fuck at home, we should also be imagining how much fucking better home could be, and fighting to make it so'. Achieving justice and rectifying intersectional inequality requires us to fundamentally transform the gendered meanings attached to and reproduced through space. Further, justice requires us to undo the organization of space. As Duncan (1996b: 142), drawing on Deleuze and Guattari, articulated over two decades ago, we require a 'spatial revolution that would conceive of physical and political or discursive space as less clearly divided between publicly recognized territories of formal power, depoliticized spaces of urban spectacle and protected spaces of uneven privatized power relations', to be replaced by 'open-ended, proliferating and inclusive sites or empowerment and resistance'. In her earlier work, contributor Alexandra

Fanghanel (2019: 3) defines spatial justice 'as a forging of a mode of living outside of the constraints of exclusions and marginalisations that compose public space'. Across each of these approaches, there is a call to reimagine how spaces are conceived, used, experienced and designed.

A cohort of feminist scholars have begun to think through what spatial justice might involve in relation to GBV (see, for example, Phadke, 2013; Antonsdóttir, 2019; Fanghanel, 2019; Kern, 2020; Fileborn, 2021a). Reclamation of space has featured in several accounts, as well as being a focus of feminist activism. Giving the examples of SlutWalk and Take Back the Night, Antonsdóttir (2019: 721) describes such activism as a form 'of collective spatial resistance where women claim the public space'. However, as Kern (2020: 17) warns us, this discourse of 'reclaiming' space reproduces colonial processes and may impede 'the efforts of Indigenous people to reclaim lands taken and colonized'.

For the victim-survivors interviewed in Antonsdóttir's (2019: 731) research, survivors' '(re)claiming of space' after experiencing sexual violence was 'about changing power relations to be able to exercise ... the right to everyday life'. However, the ability to reclaim space from perpetrators often hinged on survivors' access to resources and support systems. Nonetheless, by refusing to delimit their access to different social and civic spaces in the aftermath of sexual violence, these women asserted what Antonsdóttir (2019: 737) terms a 'just claim to space'. Shilpa Phadke (2013: 50) has similarly argued the need to shift focus away from women's safety in public space towards 'women's right to access public space' (see also Phadke et al, 2009). The practice of loitering in public spaces, according to Phadke (2013: 51), offers one avenue for 'rewriting the city as a more inclusive, diverse and pleasurable city', on the provision that loitering is an activity available to *all* marginalized groups. Lea and colleagues (Chapter 13) provide some practical examples of how this reclamation of public spaces can be achieved through their activist work in India and Kenya.

Other forms of activism, such as the use of crowd mapping by anti-street harassment groups, function to disrupt and challenge the dominant construction of public space by making an often-hidden form of violence visible (Fileborn, 2021b). Both Claire Loughnan (Chapter 14) and Walker and Di Niro (Chapter 15) consider the potential for different spaces – namely, sites of public memorialization and creative arts respectively – to function as sites of resistance and transformation in relation to GBV.

Gender and queer-sensitive and social justice-oriented approaches to design, mobility and access to resources also have a role to play in creating spaces that foster a sense of belonging and reflect the needs and uses of diverse groups (Phadke, 2013; Low and Iveson, 2016; Enright, 2019; Kern, 2020; Berry et al, 2021). In this volume, for example, Ruth Weir (Chapter 4) uses community asset mapping (CAM) to demonstrate the role that access to community resources can play in (under)reporting domestic and intimate partner violence. Space, then, is fundamentally intertwined with questions of justice in relation to GBV. One aim of this volume is to encourage scholars in the field of GBV to heed the role of space in achieving justice to this harm, alongside an acute awareness of the possibility for spatial responses to perpetuate other forms of marginalization and exclusion.

Structure of the volume

This volume comprises 15 chapters examining GBV in different spaces, organized into five parts. Part I includes four chapters examining GBV in urban and community spaces. In the first chapter, Bonu and colleagues examine the physical and symbolic potential of a 'feminist city'. Using Italy as a case study, the authors examine how the traditional framing of GBV in cites was both sexist and racist, depicting the White woman as a passive victim of the ethnic male 'other' who was responsible for sexual and physical violence in public spaces. This framing justified a securitization approach, where public spaces and the women within them were 'protected' through expulsion of foreign citizens. However, an alternative framing emerged through feminist activism in Italy which focused on the structural nature of GBV. The authors argue for a new approach, which centralizes collective feminist practices of self-determination that have the potential to shape the city into a feminist one.

The second chapter is also concerned with the city, looking specifically at the phenomenon of the 'Girls' Night Out', drawing on Nicholls's research with 26 young women from Newcastle-upon-Tyne in the UK on their management and production of 'appropriate' femininity within the night-time economy (NTE). Nicholls's contribution considers how the NTE represents a space where sexual violence and harassment are a seemingly ever-present risk to be managed, with this risk actively produced through the social and cultural norms and spatial design of licensed venues. At the same time, participants constructed the risk of sexual violence in bounded and relational ways, with women designating venues associated with working-class male patrons as spaces to avoid at all costs.

In the third chapter, Levell provides insights into how men who have experienced domestic violence and abuse (DVA) negotiated the spaces of home and being 'on road', and the ways in which these spaces were related to their production of masculinity. Her chapter touches on an often-overlooked element of gender-based violence by focusing on the spatialized coping strategies of boys and men experiencing DVA. Drawing on the Welsh concept of 'hiraeth', Levell destabilizes distinctions between the home and public/private space – 'home' became a place to avoid, a site of harm and isolation for the men she spoke with. Instead, her participants turned 'on road' to find a sense of home, belonging and control.

The final chapter in this part comes from Weir, who demonstrates the importance of considering geographic variation in the reporting of domestic violence, and the extent to which the features of a community, such as social capital, collective efficacy and the ready availability of resources, may be predictive (or not) of rates of domestic violence. Utilizing CAM as a method – an approach that has rarely, if ever, been adopted before in research on domestic violence – Weir's work demonstrates the importance of examining domestic violence at the local community level.

Part II moves on from urban space to consider how gender-based violence manifests across a range of 'local-level' and transitionary spaces, from public transport to rural and digital spaces.

The first chapter in this part, from d'Arbois de Jubainville presents findings from the French component of a larger study examining sexual violence on public transport. Unlike previous studies, they adopt a whole of journey approach and present a comparative analysis of journeys on rail and bus transport, as well as the journey taken *to* and *between* public transport, including walking to and waiting at railway stations and bus stops. They report high levels of sexual harassment, particularly on trains, with variation in the prevalence and nature of harassment and assault reported on bus versus trains. Overall, the findings chime with previous research on sexual violence on transport but advance our understandings of the continuum of sexual violence experienced across the entire journey a woman takes from A to B. This has implications for transit design and monitoring, which the authors suggest may benefit from more use of potential formal 'guardians' (bystanders) which are valued by women and may explain lower rates of sexual violence on buses.

Walter DeKeseredy (Chapter 6) moves on to examine the features of woman abuse in rural spaces, specifically the role that male peer support (in the form of the good ol' boys network), patriarchal organization, attitudes and beliefs, and pornography consumption play in legitimizing and facilitating violence against women in rural environments. Moreover, the geographical isolation that often attends rural spaces can increase the risks that rural women face, while reducing their access to support services. DeKeseredy's chapter attends to the importance of considering *both* the social and cultural production of space as well as the physical features of space.

The final contribution in this part, from Morgan and Hewitt, considers how Twitter as a virtual geographic space reinforces gendered stereotypes and enables online misogyny and gendered cyberhate aimed at women. The authors show that the rules, algorithms and policies that govern these spaces shape women's experiences and reinforce gender inequalities. They argue that the anonymity provided by the platform enables individuals to perpetrate online abuse:

> Women are still not the 'full participants' in digital spaces that they imagined. It is mostly men who shape the system and the rules, determining how women are treated and how full their membership of digital space. If cyberspace is constructed using language and language is inherently patriarchal ... power is inherently directed towards men. (p 128, this volume)

They suggest that, to reduce abuse, Twitter should be more inclusive in terms of their staff (employing more women, ethnic minorities and diverse communities) as well as educating moderators and engineers in ethics to minimize privilege and bias.

Part III of this volume moves from the urban and local to the transnational and political. Alexandra Fanghanel (Chapter 8) considers how sociopolitical discourses concerning a series of highly publicized attacks on women in Cologne in 2015 and the separate Brexit referendum and subsequent decision to leave the European Union can be analysed and understood through the spectre of the rape of the nation and the latent menace of the body of the Black 'other'. Specifically, the author argues that a spatialized and sexualized understanding of the nation-as-territory, through which the White female body is symbolically mobilized as needing protection from the Black other, advance our understandings of rape culture.

Anja Bredal, in Chapter 9, develops the concept of the 'transnational regimes of violence' as a lens for understanding domestic and family violence that occurs across borders. Drawing on interviews with women survivors whose experiences contained transnational elements, as well as Norwegian case law, Bredal's analysis deftly illustrates how perpetrators were able to draw on transnational space as a tool of abuse. Transnational mobility can be utilized by perpetrators in and of itself as a form of control and abuse, for example through forced movement across countries. Bredal's work brings a new perspective to understanding abuse experienced by migrant women through emphasizing the roles that space and mobility play in enabling violence.

The third chapter in this part, from Kristine Anderson, examines the role NGO-ization and militarization have played in shaping gender-based violence in Niger. Anderson suggests that the NGO-ization and militarization of spaces in Niger produces these spaces in a way that circumscribes the ability of women and girls to participate in civil and political life, while privileging neoliberal and Western notions of rights and civic participation. Simultaneously, the increased militarization of spaces contributes to their production as masculine and patriarchal spaces which (re)produce gendered inequalities and increase the prevalence of gender-based violence.

Part IV moves on to consider the role of institutional spaces as sites of violence. While institutional settings are popularly viewed as sites of 'justice' and protection from gender-based violence, the two chapters in this part challenge this perspective by showing how institutional settings are instead *sites* of violence. Kilroy, Lean and Quixley (Chapter 11) – examine violence *by* institutions, specifically violence against incarcerated women, sanctioned by the state. They argue that women in prison are subject to humiliation, control and shame – tactics that are routinely used by perpetrators of domestic abuse, and in fact prisons replicate women's past experiences of violence. The authors powerfully argue that this is intentional and is a core feature of the spatial design and geographic isolation of prisons.

Continuing the focus on institutional violence, in Chapter 12 Haje Keli explores the role of government institutions in Iraqi Kurdistan in perpetuating and reinforcing the structural and spatial conditions for domestic violence. Drawing on interviews with survivors and experts, and observation in institutional settings, Keli unpacks the ways in which the very institutions designed to 'protect' women instead function as sites of violence. She argues that government institutions can work to protect and reproduce patriarchal family structures, thus blurring and destabilizing the boundaries between public and private spaces.

The fifth and final part in this volume consists of three chapters examining how we might respond to and/or achieve a sense of justice in relation to gender-based violence in ways that are attentive to the roles of space and place. In Chapter 13, Suzanne Goodney Lea, Elsa D'Silva and Jane Anyango provide reflections on the Safecity reporting platform and subsequent interventions to sexual harassment and violence in public spaces, drawing on case studies from New Delhi and Mumbai in India, and Nairobi, Kenya. Their work draws attention both to the extent of sexual violence and harassment that women and girls can face in public spaces, illuminating 'how the location and the cultural context contributes' (p 216, this volume) towards these experiences. Importantly, the authors detail the interventions they have developed across these locations and provide reflections on the successes achieved and challenges faced across each location. While gender-based violence is undoubtedly a 'wicked problem' that is challenging to address, Lea and colleagues' experiences show that tangible change is possible at the local level through some simple yet effective interventions.

Claire Loughnan, in Chapter 14, considers the memorial for Eurydice Dixon who was sexually assaulted and murdered in 2018 in a public park in Melbourne, Australia. Loughnan analyses the messages left at the memorial and argues that the memorial became more than just a place to pay respects to Eurydice; it revealed, as she describes it, 'a localized politics of resistance to the ongoing violence against women' (p 232, this volume). Loughnan proposes that, rather than simply seeing spaces as sites of gendered violence, they hold the transformative potential to operate as alternative sites of justice.

Finally, Walker and Di Niro examine in Chapter 15 how creative arts practices and can offer spaces for dialogues about GBV and potential strategies via which to reduce it. Through autoethnographic accounts of burlesque and performance poetry, the authors observe that both of these creative performance spaces exist and function as masculine spaces. They identify three contributing factors: binary gender, commodification and aesthetic conventions.

References

Aitchison, C. (1999) 'New cultural geographies: the spatiality of leisure, gender and sexuality', *Leisure Studies*, 18(1): 19–39.

Antonsdóttir, H.F. (2019) 'Injustice disrupted: experiences of just spaces by victim-survivors of sexual violence', *Social & Legal Studies*, 29(5): 718–744.

Asian Australian Alliance (2020) *COVID-19 Coronavirus Racism Incident Report: Reporting Racism Against Asians in Australia Arising Due to the COVID-19 Coronavirus Pandemic*, np: Asian Australian Alliance.

Beck, K. (2021) *White Feminism: From the Suffragettes to Influencers and Who They Leave Behind*, New York: Simon & Schuster.

Berry, J., Moore, T., Kalms, N. and Bawden, G. (2021) 'Introduction: contentious cities', in J. Berry, T. Moore, N. Kalms and G. Bawden (eds) *Contentious Cities: Design and the Gendered Production of Space*, Abingdon: Routledge, pp 1–9.

Bharadwaj, G. and Mahanta, U. (2021) 'Space, time and the female body: New Delhi on foot at night', *Gender, Place & Culture*, ahead of print. Available from: https://doi.org/10.1080/0966369X.2021.1916447 [Accessed 15 April 2022].

Bows, H. and Fileborn, F. (2020) 'Space, place and GBV', *Journal of Gender-Based Violence*, 4(3): 299–307.

Boxall, H., Morgan, A. and Brown, R. (2020) *The Prevalence of Domestic Violence Among Women During the COVID-19 Pandemic*, Statistical Bulletin 28, July, Canberra: Australian Institute of Criminology.

Burt, M. and Estep, R. (1981) 'Apprehension and fear: learning a sense of sexual vulnerability', *Sex Roles*, 7: 511–522.

Butler, J. (1990) *Gender Trouble: Feminism and the Subversion of Identity*, New York: Routledge.

Connell, R.W. (2005) *Masculinities* (2nd edn), Cambridge: Polity Press.

Corteen, K. (2002) 'Lesbian safety talk: problematizing definitions and experiences of violence, sexuality and space', *Sexualities*, 5(3): 259–280.

Council of Europe (2011) *Explanatory Report to the Council of Europe Convention on Preventing and Combating Violence Against Women and Domestic Violence*. Available from: https://www.coe.int/en/web/conventions/full-list?module=treaty-detail&treatynum=210 [Accessed 15 April 2022].

Crenshaw, K.W. (1994) 'Mapping the margins: intersectionality, identity politics, and violence against women of colour', in M.A. Fineman and R. Mykitiuk (eds) *The Public Nature of Private Violence: The Discovery of Domestic Abuse*, New York: Routledge, pp 93–118.

de Certeau, M. (1984) *The Practice of Everyday Life*, Berkeley: University of California Press.

Deleuze, G. and Guattari, F. (1987) *A Thousand Plateaus: Capitalism and Schizophrenia*, Minneapolis: University of Minnesota Press.

Duncan, N. (1996a) 'Introduction: (re)placings', in N. Duncan (ed) *BodySpace: Destabilizing Geographies of Gender and Sexuality*, Abingdon: Routledge, pp 1–10.

Duncan, N. (1996b) 'Renegotiating gender and sexuality in public and private spaces', in N. Duncan (ed) *BodySpace: Destabilizing Geographies of Gender and Sexuality*, Abingdon: Routledge, pp 127–145.

England, E. (2021) '"This is how it works here": the spatial deprioritisation of trans people within homelessness services in Wales', *Gender, Place & Culture*, ahead of print. Available from: https://doi.org/10.1080/09663 69X.2021.1896997 [Accessed 15 April 2022].

Enright, T. (2019) 'Transit justice as spatial justice: learning from activists', *Mobilities*, 14(5): 665–680.

Fanghanel, A. (2019) *Disrupting Rape Culture: Public Space, Sexuality and Revolt*, Bristol: Bristol University Press.

Femicide Census (2018) '*UK Femicides 2009–2018*'. Available from: https://www.femicidecensus.org/wp-content/uploads/2020/11/Femicide-Census-10-year-report.pdf [Accessed 15 April 2022].

Fileborn, B. (2016) *Reclaiming the Night-Time Economy: Unwanted Sexual Attention in Pubs and Clubs*, London: Palgrave Macmillan.

Fileborn, B. (2021a) 'Embodied geographies: navigating street harassment', in J. Berry, T. Moore, N. Kalms and G. Bawden (eds) *Contentious Cities: Design and the Gendered Production of Space*, Abingdon: Routledge, pp 37–48.

Fileborn, B. (2021b) 'Online activism and street harassment: critical cartographies, counter-mapping and spatial justice', *Oñati Socio-Legal Series*, 11(5): 1198–1221.

Fileborn, B., Wadds, P. and Tomsen, S. (2020) 'Gender, transgression and sexual violence at Australian music festivals', in L. Platt and R. Finkel (eds) *Gendered Violence at International Festivals: An Interdisciplinary Perspective*, Abingdon: Routledge, pp 69–85.

Gilchrist, E., Bannister, J., Ditton, J. and Farrall, S. (1998) 'Women and the "fear of crime": challenging the accepted stereotype', *British Journal of Criminology*, 38(2): 283–298.

Grosz, E. (1995) *Space, Time and Perversion: The Politics of Bodies*, St Leonards, NSW: Allen & Unwin.

hooks, b. (1990) *Yearning: Race, Gender and Cultural Politics*, Boston, MA: South End Press.

Kay, J.B. (2020) ' "Stay the fuck at home!": feminism, family and the private home in a time of coronavirus', *Feminist Media Studies*, 20(6): 883–888.

Kelly, L. (1988) *Surviving Sexual Violence*, Cambridge: Polity Press.

Kern, L. (2005) 'In place and at home in the city: connecting privilege, safety and belonging for women in Toronto', *Gender, Place & Culture*, 12(3): 357–377.

Kern, L. (2020) *Feminist City: Claiming Space in a Man-Made World*, London: Verso.

LGBTIQ Domestic and Family Violence Interagency and the Centre for Social Research in Health (2014) *Calling It What It Really Is: A Report into Lesbian, Gay, Bisexual, Transgender, Gender Diverse, Intersex and Queer Experiences of Domestic and Family Violence*, Sydney: CSRH, UNSW.

Low, S. and Iveson, K. (2016) 'Propositions for more just urban public spaces', *City*, 20(1): 10–31.

McDowell, L. (1996) 'Spatializing feminism: geographic perspectives', in N. Duncan (ed) *BodySpace: Destabilizing Geographies of Gender and Sexuality*, Abingdon: Routledge, pp 28–44.

McDowell, L. (1999) *Gender, Identity and Place: Understanding Feminist Geographies*, Cambridge: Polity Press.

ONS (Office for National Statistics) (2020) 'Crime in England and Wales: year ending March 2020'. Available from: https://www.ons.gov.uk/peopl epopulationandcommunity/crimeandjustice/bulletins/crimeinenglanda ndwales/yearendingmarch2020 [Accessed 15 April 2022].

Pain, R. (1991) 'Space, sexual violence and social control: integrating geographical and feminist analyses of women's fear of crime', *Progress in Human Geography*, 15(4): 415–431.

Pain, R. (1995) 'Elderly women and fear of violent crime: the least likely victims? A reconsideration of the extent and nature of risk', *British Journal of Criminology*, 35(4): 584–598.

Pain, R. (1999) 'Women's experiences of violence over the life-course', in E.K. Teather (ed) *Embodied Geographies: Spaces, Bodies and Rites of Passage*, London: Routledge, pp 126–141.

Phadke, S. (2013) 'Unfriendly bodies, hostile cities: reflections on loitering and gendered public space', *Economic and Political Weekly*, 48(39): 50–59.

Phadke, S., Ranade, S. and Khan, S. (2009) 'Why loiter? Radical possibilities for gendered dissent', in M. Butcher and S. Velayutham (eds) *Dissent and Cultural Resistance in Asia's Cities*, Abingdon: Routledge, pp 185–203.

Plan International and Our Watch (2016) *Right to the Night: Australian Girls on Their Safety in Public Places*. Available from: https://www.plan.org.au/wp-content/uploads/2020/08/a-right-to-the-night-australian-girls-on-their-safety-in-public-places-2016.pdf [Accessed 15 April 2022].

Stanko, E.A. (1985) *Intimate Intrusions: Women's Experience of Male Violence*, Abingdon: Routledge & Kegan Paul.

Stop Street Harassment (2014) *Unsafe and Harassed in Public Space: A National Street Harassment Report*, Reston, VA: Stop Street Harassment.

UN Women (nd) *The Shadow Pandemic: Violence Against Women During COVID-19*. Available from: https://www.unwomen.org/en/news/in-focus/in-focus-gender-equality-in-covid-19-response/violence-against-women-during-covid-19#facts [Accessed 15 April 2022].

UN Women UK (2021) *Prevalence and Reporting of Sexual Harassment in UK Public Spaces*, London: APPG for UN Women. Available from: https://www.unwomenuk.org/site/wp-content/uploads/2021/03/APPG-UN-Women-Sexual-Harassment-Report_Updated.pdf [Accessed 15 April 2022].

Valentine, G. (1989) 'The geography of women's fear', *Area*, 21(4): 385–390.

Valentine, G. (1990) 'Women's fear and the design of public space', *Built Environment*, 16(4): 288–303.

Valentine, G. (1992) 'Images of danger: women's sources of information about the spatial distribution of male violence', *Area*, 24(1): 22–29.

Valentine, G. (1996) '(Re)negotiating the "heterosexual street": lesbian productions of space', in N. Duncan (ed) *BodySpace: Destabilizing Geographies of Gender and Sexuality*, Abingdon: Routledge, pp 146–155.

Valentine, G. (1997) '(Hetero)sexing space: lesbian perceptions and experiences of everyday spaces', in L. McDowell and J. Sharp (eds) *Space, Gender, Knowledge: Feminist Readings*, London: Arnold, pp 284–299.

Vera-Gray, F. (2018) *The Right Amount of Panic: How Women Trade Freedom for Safety*, Bristol: Polity Press.

Vera-Gray, F. and Kelly, L. (2020) 'Contested gendered space: public sexual harassment and women's safety work', *International Journal of Comparative and Applied Criminal Justice*, 44(4): 265–275.

Wesely, J.K. and Gaarder, E. (2004) 'The gendered "nature" of the urban outdoors: women negotiating fear of violence', *Gender and Society*, 18(5): 645–663.

WHO (World Health Organization, on behalf of the United Nations Inter-Agency Working Group on Violence Against Women Estimation and Data) (2021) *Violence Against Women Prevalence Estimates, 2018.* Available from: https://www.who.int/publications/i/item/9789240022 256 [Accessed 15 April 2022].

Young, A. (2021) '"Stay safe, stay home": spatial justice in the pandemic city', *Legalities*, 1(1): 19–43.

PART I

Gender-Based Violence in Urban and Community Spaces

1

Gender-Based Violence and Urban Spaces: From Security to Self-Determination – Insights from the Italian Debate

Giada Bonu, Chiara Belingardi, Federica Castelli and Serena Olcuire

Introduction

In recent years, feminist movements from all over the world have gathered in a shared struggle against violence against women (both cis and trans), speaking out against the patriarchal system that precludes women's freedom and self-determination (Cirimele and Panariello, 2018; Chironi, 2019). Women have gathered in a wave of protests, sharing experiences, practices and reflections on violence against women (such as the #MeToo and Ni Una Menos movements). Following this new international feminist wave (Gago et al, 2020), in Italy – the context that we write from – the Non Una di Meno (Not One Less, NUDM) movement arose as a national network of feminist groups, associations and individuals. This movement drove the collective writing of *We Have a Plan: Feminist Plan Against Male Violence over Women and gender Violence*, which has opened up the possibility of identifying violence in every area that hampers freedom in women's lives. As feminist movements claim, patriarchal violence is structural, not just physical, and today more pervasive than ever – due to neoliberal policies, austerity, precarity and border proliferation (Non Una di Meno, 2017; Belingardi et al, 2019; Cavallero and Gago, 2019).

In the light of the transnational feminist struggle against men's violence, the political urgency of rethinking forms of structural violence arising from urban space becomes apparent. From the feminist walk at night, to the opening of women's houses, to marches and public protests, urban space has been a primary target for the feminist movements since the 1970s (Roberts, 2016; Spain, 2016). Drawing on this genealogy, as feminists and urban scholars, we acknowledged that spaces where our lives take place play a role in creating the terms and conditions of our freedom. From this urgency, we felt the need to discuss the structural violence arising from urban spaces. Going beyond the identification of the role they play in contributing to episodes of physical violence, we argue there is a need to recognize the implicit violence disposed by and through the ways space(s) are imagined, organized, designed and governed.

Many mechanisms produce the expulsion of women from public space and their confinement in domestic, private space (Cirillo, 2018). Such mechanisms include victimization discourses reducing women to potential objects of violence, securitarian discourses and policies, the populist rhetoric on urban decay and urban decency, and the dynamics of fragmentation and privatization marking neoliberal cities (Simone, 2012; Hanhardt, 2013; Pisanello, 2017; Olcuire, 2019). Additionally, the absence of spaces for women to meet, share and participate in political struggle makes political organization challenging for women, and contributes towards increased isolation, despite the growing proliferation of digital and online spaces. Self-determined spaces created and run by women are today made precarious and under threat in Italy (Paoletti, 2018). For example, the lack of local services makes it difficult for women to have multifaceted lives, forcing them to be 'just' mothers, or workers, or activists – one thing at a time (Saraceno, 1984). 'Reconciliation' policies are deemed 'good practices' oriented to 'the reconciliation of work, family and private lives' (EIGE, 2015). However, these policies do not always simplify everyday tasks, and do not question from a gender perspective the division of productive and reproductive labour (Macchi, 2006).

In the light of all these factors the urban environment appears to be another element underpinning gender-based violence (Belingardi et al, 2019). Fortunately, cities are not homogenous; they are constructed through the different practices and uses of those who live within, reshaping the city according to their desires, and reinventing the city through everyday practices in creative and expressive ways (Kern, 2020). So, the city can also be a space of reappropriation, legitimization and freedom. Urban space can be considered a battlefield, where different visions of politics and relationships confront each other (Pisanello, 2018; Belingardi et al, 2019).

This chapter recollects and refines the results of an ongoing debate started in Italy in 2017 within the movement NUDM, and pursued through the creation of a research space (Atelier Città). Our reflection had a pivotal moment with a public seminar (*La Libertà è una passeggiata* – Freedom is a stroll) and continued in Helsinki with a workshop at the Gender Studies Conference 2019: On Violence. The aim of this path was (and still is) to open up a collective debate, rooted in a critical approach to urban policies and with a focus on women's spatial practices for self-determination. The collective aim is for new and shared visions and narratives of the city that may go beyond victimizing and objectivating paradigms, which are normative and frequently oppressive.

We outline some Italian feminist reflections and practices relating to the link between urban space and gender-based violence, focusing on the shift from an idea of security towards one of self-determination in public space. In order to map the Italian debate through our theoretical and empirical work, we will sketch out three meaningful dimensions. First, we outline the shift in the literature on women and LGBTQIA+ (lesbian, gay, bisexual, transgender, queer and/or questioning, intersex, and asexual and/or ally including all people who have a non-normative gender identity or sexual orientation) subjectivities and the city from an understanding of security to self-determination, by redefining the notion of gender-based violence. Then, we will describe certain feminist and transfeminist movements' activities in urban spaces as an example of self-determination from below. Finally, we will propose some emerging insights from the contemporary pandemic context. By combining the experiences and contributions that we collected, we aim to provide a picture of a feminist city.

Is 'security' enough? Redefining gender-based violence

From a historical point of view, Italian feminist movements have engaged with the notion of gender-based violence, in order to make it visible and, eventually, political (Bracke, 2019). Up to a point, gender-based violence did not exist, because no one named it. Feminists' efforts in the 1960s and 1970s forced this topic to become a priority in public debate and policies, by challenging some slippery assumptions. First, that violence only comes from the outside and from foreigners, or those perceived as such (Simone, 2012). The nasty entanglement of sexism and racism often hides the 'reality' of gender-based violence, by dislocating responsibility to 'the other'. This was illustrated more recently in Italy, where national debate was prompted by the rape and femicide of Giovanna Reggiani, a middle-class and middle-age woman murdered by a Romanian man in the suburbs of Rome in 2007 (Peroni, 2012). While the public debate targeted foreigners as the source of gender-based violence, a huge feminist and separatist demonstration on 25 November 2007 claimed that 'the killer has the key to the house', by drawing attention to the prevalence of domestic violence compared to other types of gender-based violence (Fusani, 2007). Despite this feminist resistance, the Italian government enacted the so-called *Pacchetto Sicurezza* (Security Decree) as a consequence of Reggiani's case, which pinpointed the expulsion of Roma people as the solution for the supposed increasing problem of urban violence due to the presence of illegal immigrants.

The second element highlighted by the feminist movements is the structural dimension of gender-based violence. By challenging the interpretation of the phenomenon as a deviation from the ordinary or as an exceptional occurrence, feminist movements outlined the ways in which violence shapes and produces our understanding of reality, interpersonal relationships and, more generally, the social world (Cavallero and Gago, 2019). Triggered by the Argentinian movement against gender-based violence Ni Una Menos (Cirimele and Panariello, 2018), Italian groups, collectives and individuals gathered together in 2016 with the collective name of Non Una di Meno (Barone and Bonu, forthcoming). The movement promotes an understanding of gender-based violence as a structure which shapes people's everyday life. With the 'Feminist Plan Against Male Violence on Women' (NUDM, 2017) the movement aimed to point out all the situations where violence takes place: in interpersonal relationships; at work; on national boundaries; in institutions; in the educational field and so on. Moreover, the Plan enlarges the scope of subjectivities which are affected by gender-based violence, including all those people 'on the margin' according to minoritized race, gender, class, age and so on. By redefining gender-based violence, NUDM singles out an innovative repertoire of action: for instance the global feminist strike of productive and reproductive work each 8 March; walks at night; and the reappropriation of feminist spaces in urban settings as a response to urban violence.

However, NUDM draws attention to another challenging issue: the structural violence of urban settings, which affects personal experiences within, and collective perceptions of, urban space. Not only does gender-based violence *occur* in urban settings, but urban settings are also a *source* of gender-based violence. Thus, we conceptualize violence as being in and of urban spaces (Belingardi et al, 2019). The way urban spaces are designed and inhabited affects women and LGBTQIA+ people's urban experiences: sometimes inducing them to avoid certain areas more than others, only accessing the city during the daytime, in turn restricting people's access to services, work and leisure spaces, and so on (Valentine, 1989; Borghi and Blidon, 2010). Moreover, these subjects are not often taken into account in the design of public space (Irschik and Kail, 2016). It is this strong impact on women's behaviours that allows us to consider urban spaces as a source of violence, according to the understanding of violence as structural, as already mentioned.

Several studies have highlighted the dimension of fear as a typical gendered emotion in public space (Valentine, 1989; Pain, 1991). Fear is also transformed and enacted by collective actors in order to make their lives liveable:

> The turn that the fear/urban spaces node takes is often that of paternalistic protection, victimization, and disempowerment. ... Many

feminist reflections have instead made fear an active and generative passion, removing it from the victimizing and deadly tradition elaborated by Western patriarchal culture. ... Playing on the political character of emotions and their transformative potential, feminist movements impose a reversal of fear as a device of control and gender violence. Fear, like anger, is understood as generating other possibilities of crossing and inhabiting public space, and consequently one's own existence. (Belingardi et al, 2019: 29–30, our translation)

Too often, the institutional response to the perception of fear is the implementation of securitarian discourses and policies. The extensive use of security as a rhetorical justification of urban governance, by marginalizing or expelling those subjects who are considered 'deviant' according to race, sexuality, gender, class and so on, requires a deep and situated feminist critique. Institutions and policies have adopted a victimizing paradigm in order 'to protect' women in public spaces, more than working for their empowerment (Olcuire, 2019). The security lens is not only insufficient, but often misleading in order to frame the experience of women and LGBTQIA+ people in urban space. Neoliberal political actors have instrumentalized gender-based violence in an exclusionary manner, by 'cleaning' cities and neighbourhoods from 'undesirable' subjects. Despite feminist engagement with the terrain of 'safety', by claiming safe spaces in the urban setting, the concept opens up a contested field that need to be readdressed through the lens of self-determination. Women and LGBTQIA+ subjectivities are not claiming to be protected; instead, they aim to develop agency in urban settings (NUDM, 2017).

Urban space as a battlefield: self-determination from below

The city is not only power that becomes stone, walls, fences and monuments ... but also a place of reappropriation, invention, legitimization and liberation. It is the practices, relations, actions and discourses of the everyday political dimension that produce new visions, open up new spaces and redefine places. Uses, desires and everyday practices can overturn the organization and underlying logic of the existing configuration, creating new senses.

Castelli, 2019: 65

As security is not enough to prevent gender-based violence, we need to rethink feminist responses to gender-based violence through the lens of self-determination. According to the feminist concept of situated knowledge

(Rich, 1984; Haraway, 1988), we acknowledge our positionality as White women and scholars, but also as feminist activists. Thus, we write from within and from without the field, avoiding a supposed neutrality that can never be achieved in the field of social sciences. Moreover, we develop insights through the relationships we have established with local groups, spaces and feminist movements, with whom we collaboratively pursue a situated production of knowledge.

In this section, we aim to develop the concept of self-determination from below, through feminist movements' engagement with/within urban settings. To begin with, we go back to Pain's reflection on fear, security and public space:

> There is scope to widen consideration of threat and space within geography: just as the threat of rape deters some women from being out on the streets at night, sexual harassment at work functions to deter some women from the public domain. Domestic violence takes place almost exclusively within the home, but still may affect the broader spatial experiences and choices of women affected by or threatened by it. ... While sexual violence occurs mainly in private space, women tend to fear it far more when they are in public space. This has implications for the usefulness of the precautions they take to avoid sexual violence, and for their ultimate safety. (Pain, 1991: 417)

Why do women and LGBTQIA+ people tend to fear violence more in public space? And how do they, through collective organization, challenge that fear? In order to address these questions, we refer to the wide range of feminist movements and organizations in the Italian context, and look closely at their practices. First, movements tend to blur the dichotomous separation between private and public spaces. In the 1970s, feminists emphasized women's exit from the house (as a site of women's subjugation) – towards public space (as a site of politics). Their claim that 'the personal as political' was a way of disentangling the spatialization of gender inequalities (Bracke, 2019). However, nothing is purely private or public: these two dimensions always interplay. In fact, consciousness-raising groups usually took place in private homes, while at the same time huge demonstrations occurred in urban settings, but the two experiences were inherently part of activists' empowerment (Willson, 2010). Moreover, as Black feminists highlighted, the home is not merely a site of women's subjugation, but it is also the place where community is established and nurtured, and where Black women and men cultivate resistance (hooks, 1991; Lorde, 1984).

Starting from this blurred understanding of private and public space, we look at how gender-based violence has been addressed and challenged by feminist movements on the ground of the city. As Kern explains:

A geographic perspective on gender offers a way of understanding how sexism functions on the ground. Women's second-class status is enforced not just through the metaphorical notion of 'separate spheres', but through an actual, material geography of exclusion. Male power and privilege are upheld by keeping women's movements limited and their ability to access different spaces constrained. ... As feminist geographer Jane Darke says: 'Any settlement is an inscription in space of the social relations in the society that built it. ... Our cities are patriarchy written in stone, brick, glass and concrete.' This simple statement of the fact that built environments reflect the societies that construct them might seem obvious. ... What sometimes seems even less obvious is the inverse: that once built, our cities continue to shape and influence social relations, power, inequality, and so on. Stone, brick, glass, and concrete don't have agency, do they? They aren't consciously trying to uphold the patriarchy, are they? No, but their form helps shape the range of possibilities for individuals and groups. Their form helps keep some things seeming normal and right, and others 'out of place' and wrong. In short, physical places like cities matter when we want to think about social change. (Kern, 2020: 42–44)

Following Kern's concerns, we consider the question: can agency occur in this inextricable structure? According to feminist movements yes, it can. In this section, we address the repertoire of action of feminist movements, which highlight the shift from a neoliberal understanding of security to a politicization of the concept of safety through the lens of self-determination.

The repertoire of action of feminist movements, developed from the 1970s onwards, includes the space of the city as a purposive site of social change. While rape culture and the fear of sexual violence limited women's movements within the city, feminist groups organized walks at night, and creatively reply when violence happens (such as the Take Back the Night marches and Marches de Nuit [Spain, 2016]). Marches, protests and demonstrations have used public spaces to advance feminist movements' claims on issues ranging from health, social reproduction as a women's function, violence and so on. Some of the practices that bring sexual bodies and public spaces into play originated in the US in the early 1990s: the march, the collective walk, went from being demonstrations of dissent, solidarity and claim to a deeper meaning of putting one's sexuality 'in the public square' and reappropriating certain spaces (Custodi et al, 2020). Being in the streets is the practice of 'stasis' that creates space for revolt and simultaneously arranges an affective, collective way of experiencing public space. During these moments, corporeality is exposed in all its passionate intensity, and this new centrality of bodies allows us to grasp the relationship that these moments weave with urban spaces, and the new sense of politics that they propose (Castelli, 2015, 2019).

Another relevant practice that sheds light on the shift from security to self-determination is the opening of safer spaces. In response to the lack of women's spaces for change, feminist movements opened spaces, libraries, health centres and so on. The existence of women's spaces is one of the most interesting in the Italian context for several reasons. From the 1970s, women's collective action has been oriented towards opening women's houses: the first one, in 1976 in Rome, hosted the creation of a feminist radio station, a health centre, a university for women and one of the first women's shelters (Oddi Baglioni and Zaremba, 2003). By challenging a private issue – domestic violence – through the reappropriation of public space, feminist movements provide an example of self-determination from below. Women formed alternative publics, or what Nancy Fraser calls 'subaltern counterpublics'. 'Subaltern counterpublics function as spaces of withdrawal and regrouping, and they are training grounds for political activities directed toward wider publics' (Spain, 2016: 18). From then on, women's houses and centres proliferated. We refer here to the International House of Women, and to the House of Women Lucha y Siesta, in Rome. Both the spaces were originally occupied by feminist activists, and are now negotiating with institutions for their survival. Both the spaces have opened the perimeter for a new type of politics and well-being. As already mentioned, the collective response of feminist activists to violence is based on independence and self-determination. Within these spaces, cis and trans women can meet and discuss, create new projects, develop a situated culture and politics, provide education on feminist politics, and continue the memory of women's genealogy. The entanglement of bodies, spaces and politics reshapes the surface and purpose of the city, by broadening the scope of what can be done and felt.

> The concept we started from is that safety is not provided by the army, not by security packages, but by women who organize themselves. Above all, safety should be understood as social security, which is what is missing in the Italian political discourse: there is no longer any talk of income, work, the right to housing, the right to health, which are exactly the things we are dealing with here. The establishment of a women's group was also born out of the idea that security is not only physical or social, but also that it should be a security of closeness and relationships. It is clear that you can never feel safe alone. The idea with which we occupied this place seven years ago, and which continues, is that security is also given to you by your roommate, by whoever is next to you, because at the moment when you are a little less secure, maybe the other one is, therefore an idea that is a little more circular

and shared. With all its facets. In short, creating a community security, between women who help each other, support each other. (Belingardi, 2016: 185–186)

By challenging discourses that construct women as passive victims, feminist movements are engaging on urban ground in two directions: first, by disentangling the conventional notion of 'security', towards an intersectional and grassroots understanding of safer spaces (Roestone Collective, 2014); then, by reshaping the urban setting through collective practices of self-determination. To this effect, we define the urban space as a battlefield, where women and LGBTQIA+ subjects are not closing down defensively but actively engaging with the change of urban structures.

Questioning the pandemic

All the experiences and reflections on gender-based violence and feminist movements' actions that we have discussed so far need to be reframed in the light of the coronavirus pandemic.[1] The emergence of the pandemic opened up new ways of understanding the shift from security to self-determination enacted by feminist movements in the Italian context. From a feminist viewpoint, the concepts of safety and security have broader meaning than is typically acknowledged. As we outlined earlier, the concept of 'security' has been expanded by feminist activism to encompass health and survival, for example. Despite the contingent and unforeseen developments of the pandemic situation, we will try to sketch out some reflections on the way the pandemic affects women, LGBTQIA+ and feminist movements.

In the last year, as we write, we have been trapped by the spread of the pandemic from COVID-19 on a global scale. As much as individual movements, transnational feminist movements, but also goods and financial capital, spread globally, so did the virus. The pandemic radically changed our everyday life, our behaviour and our relational patterns. How did the pandemic intervene on the intersection between urban space, gender-based violence and feminist movements?

The virus called into question a primary dimension: the body. We have been made acutely aware of the vulnerability of bodies through the day-by-day confrontation with illness and death. Under the risk of being infected or infecting others with the virus, we have seen the spaces of our lives become narrower and narrower. Several lockdowns, depending on the country, have been imposed in order to contain the spread of the virus. Thus, the main space of our lives has become, more than ever, the private space of the home. We have still impressed on our eyes the images of empty streets and squares. Paradoxically, the retreat of the human has allowed non-human animals to take back space, and we have seen unexpected subjects – such as rabbits, boars and geese – going around cities. However, the emptying of urban space from humans dramatically impacted on collective action. While we can rejoice in this as ecofeminists, we also keep questioning how this shift affects the lives of women and LGBTQIA+ people.

In the wake of the pandemic, public debates constantly call care into question. However, they do not refer to the long-standing tradition of feminist thought on care, but rather reproduce a gendered and neoliberal understanding of care. However, feminists are inevitably involved in the debate, as they always focused on the (largely unpaid) reproductive work of women as a space of subjugation. The horizon of meaning of care is not limited to maintenance. It is not a matter of 'cleaning up', but of recognizing the complex meaning of care as an action aimed at improvement, at the unfinished, at work-in-progress, in a space in continuous evolution, in a continuous adaptation to the needs that from time to time should arise (Belingardi, 2015: 32).

While lockdowns bound people at home, women and LGBTQIA+ subjects were – again – the ones charged with a double shift: productive and reproductive. Recent data shows how an overwhelming majority of people who became unemployed were women (Mastrodonato, 2021). While children were home from school, it became increasingly difficult for women to keep their job, as they were expected to manage paid employment with the unpaid, full-time care of their children. The increased burden of care work risked reproducing a gendered division of labour, something that feminists have long sought to disrupt and reimagine. As the Care Collective claims, care should become the heart of the state and the economy, by promoting 'the collective joy' rather than old inequalities (Care Collective, 2020). In relation to care work during the pandemic, we can see the dichotomy between private and public space strengthening, despite feminist efforts blurring this line.

Arguably, the most common experience of public space during the pandemic has become one of loneliness and fear. Fear has a changing nature: others are a threat because of the invisible presence of the virus. This period has been marked by two main spatial concepts: social distancing and the notion of 'essential'. The only spaces that remained opened were those considered 'essential', such as large-scale distribution and food commerce. A key public health strategy for reining in the pandemic was to reduce our social lives as much as possible by constantly narrowing down what (and *who*) is essential at the individual level.

Despite the limits placed on the physical dimension of life, physical social interaction remained more crucial than ever. Increasing rates of domestic violence emerged as a result of lockdowns, through which women had been locked up with their abusers. The four walls of the house, which are supposed to be the only safe space in the pandemic, became a cage for countless women and LGBTQIA+ people. As a result, anti-violence centres increased their capacities and creativity in order to support as many women as possible, despite the lack of public funding, interest and space.

Despite the rarefaction of our presence in public space, violence keeps persisting, often exacerbated by increasing social inequalities. By multiplying their resourcefulness, feminist movements tried to keep their presence alive in both private and public spaces. In Italy, several initiatives flourished, such as a canteen for trans sex workers'[2] efforts to strongly denounce the increase of femicides relating to lockdown policies;[3] and the provision of 'everyday' support to people in need.

> Something is moving in the rubble of the pandemic. We are separated, but today more than ever united by the desire to change everything. A devastating event like COVID-19 requires powerful responses and boundless ambition. The epidemic has revealed that the reproduction of life is incompatible with the neoliberal project of extending the logic of the market to every sphere of existence. Let us start again from feminist and transfeminist knowledge and practices, which have made social reproduction their priority area of conflict. Let us start again from a collective and situated fabric, changing in the transversal alliances in which it always takes a new shape. Because if the present is catastrophic, the future is not yet written and our struggles will have to determine the forms of coexistence after the pandemic. (Non Una di Meno's blog[4])

As an example of the intersection between violence, urban space and movements during the pandemic, NUDM called for the reinstatement of a place in the city where activists gathered each time a femicide occurred. Thus, renamed NUDM squares appeared, where, by keeping a safe distances from one another, activists could gather, bound together by their rage and pain, to call for social change.

In order to propose an opening for further discussion rather than a conclusion to the debate, we argue that the pandemic sheds light on already crucial nodes, such as the body, relationships, the provision of care and the need to reorient spaces towards the needs of *all* people. These nodes remain open, and further analysis is needed in order to more fully address the topic. However, the feminist lens allows for a deeper understanding, since now, more than never, we cannot think about a duality between body and mind, nature and culture, private and public, safe and unsafe, and complete autonomy or interdependency.

Conclusion

We started with the assumption that in recent years global feminist movements have gathered in a shared struggle against violence against women (both cis and trans), speaking out against the patriarchal system that precludes women's freedom and self-determination. In order to provide a comprehensive approach to gender-based violence, we established the structural dimensions of the phenomenon, which includes urban settings as a stage shaping the conditions for gender-based violence. Drawing on examples from Italian feminist activism, we examined the idea of self-determination from below, which does not come from an external actor or a 'saviour', but rather occurs through collective action and self-consciousness raising. Finally, we proposed some insights on the consequences of the pandemic, which strongly influenced our lives on an individual and collective level. In closing, we reflect briefly on why we consider the shift from security to self-determination so relevant.

In her work on women's houses in North America, Daphne Spain argues for a 'constructive feminism':

> Women in feminist places could respond to, or withdraw from, gender discrimination and interaction with men in order to form their own identities. Such places were created primarily by radical feminists, but they emerged in the context of major legal victories won by feminist reformers. ... Feminist places were 'free spaces', environments in which women learned a new self-respect and asserted a group identity based on the values of democratic cooperation. According to the historian Sara Evans, voluntarily established free spaces are 'settings between private lives and large-scale institutions where ordinary citizens can act with dignity, independence, and vision'. The political scientist Margaret Kohn calls them 'radical democratic spaces', political sites where marginalized groups can claim their rights. Radical spaces are essential if social movements are to expand the meaning of citizenship to include the previously disenfranchised. (Spain, 2016: 13)

By adopting the definition of constructive feminism, we referred to the agency and capacity of feminist groups to engage, elaborate and subvert urban space. Where securitarian discourses have always targeted fragile subjectivities, minoritized subjects are currently gaining their own voice and space, changing the nature of the city itself. We analysed this movement, from the margin and in the margin, as a vital energy toward the creation of autonomous, liberated and empowered subjectivities and spaces. By combining these experiences and examples, we argue the result is the picture of a feminist city.

Notes

[1] Some insights on the Italian feminist debate can be found here: https://femministerie. wordpress.com/category/prossimamente

[2] https://nudmfirenze.noblogs.org/cosa-bolle-in-pentola-la-solidarieta-transfemminista-sto
ria-di-pop-wok-mensa-popolare-femminista/
[3] https://radiosonar.net/sul-ponte-giorgiana-masi-contro-i-femminicidi-e-le-narrazioni-
tossiche/
[4] https://nonunadimeno.wordpress.com/2020/04/28/la-vita-oltre-la-pandemia/

References

Barone, A. and Bonu, G. (forthcoming) 'Ni Una Menos / Non Una di Meno', in D. Snow, D. della Porta, B. Klandermans and D. McAdam (eds) *The Blackwell Encyclopedia of Social and Political Movements* (2nd edn), Oxford: Blackwell.

Belingardi, C. (2015) *Comunanze urbane: Autogestione e cura dei luoghi*, Florence: FUP.

Belingardi, C. (2016) 'Alcune riflessioni sulla sicurezza da una prospettiva di Lucha e di Siesta', in C. Belingardi and F. Castelli (eds) *Città: Politiche dello spazio urbano*, Rome: IAPh Italia.

Belingardi, C., Castelli, F. and Olcuire, S. (eds) (2019) *La Libertà è una Passeggiata: Donne e spazi urbani tra violenza strutturale e autodeterminazione*, Rome: IAPh Italia.

Borghi, R. and Blidon, M. (2010) 'Generi urbani', in P. Barbieri (ed) *E' successo qualcosa alla città: Manuale di Antropologia urbana*, Rome: Donzelli.

Bracke, M.A. (2019) *Women and the Reinvention of the Political: Feminism in Italy, 1968–1983*, New York: Routledge.

Care Collective, The (2020) *The Care Manifesto*, London: Verso.

Castelli, F. (2015) *Corpi in rivolta: Spazi urbani, conflitti e nuove forme della politica*, Milan: Mimesis.

Castelli, F. (2019) *Spazio pubblico*, Rome: Ediesse.

Cavallero, L. and Gago, V. (2019) *Una lectura feminista de la deuda: vivas, libres y desendeudadas nos queremos*, Quito: Fundación Rosa Luxemburgo.

Chironi, D. (2019) 'Generations in the feminist and LGBT movements in Italy: the case of *Non Una Di Meno*', *American Behavioral Scientist*, 63(10): 1469–1496.

Cirillo, L. (ed) (2018) *Se il mondo torna uomo: Le donne e la regressione in Europa*, Rome: Alegre.

Cirimele, N. and Panariello, M. (2018) 'Non Una di Meno, un grido globale', *DWF*, 120(4): 8–14.

Custodi G., Olcuire S. and Silvi M. (2020) 'Trois fenêtres pour un panorama. Contributions des réflexions féministes, genrées et queer produites en Italie dans le cadre des disciplines spatiales à partir des années 1990', Hors-série: Multitudes Queer, *Études Francophones* (33).

EIGE (European Institute for Gender Equality) (2015) *Reconciliation Policies: Study on Good Practices on Reconciliation of Work, Family and Private Life in EU Member States*. Available from: https://eige.europa.eu/publications/factsheet-reconciliation-policies [Accessed 25 June 2021].

Fusani, C. (2007) 'Violenza sulle donne, a Roma in centomila "Contro la paura, riprendiamoci i nostri diritti"', *La Repubblica*, 24 November. Available from: https://www.repubblica.it/2007/11/sezioni/cronaca/viole nza-donne/corteo/corteo.html [Accessed 22 March 2021].

Gago V., Malo, M. and Cavallero L. (2020) *La Internacional Feminista: Luchas en los Territorios y Contra el Neoliberalismo*, Madrid: Traficantes de Sueños.

Hanhardt, C.B. (2013) *Safe Space: Gay Neighborhood History and the Politics of Violence*, Durham, NC: Duke University Press.

Haraway, D. (1988) 'Situated knowledges: the science question in feminism and the privilege of partial perspective', *Feminist Studies*, 14(3): 575–599.

hooks, b. (1991) *Yearning: Race, Gender and Cultural Politics*, London: Turnaround.

Irschik, E. and Kail, E. (2016) 'Vienna: progress toward a fair shared city', in I.S. de Madariaga and M. Roberts (eds) *Fair Shared Cities: The Impact of Gender Planning in Europe*, Aldershot: Ashgate, pp 297–324.

Kern, L. (2020) *Feminist City: Claiming Space in a Man-Made World*, London: Verso.

Lorde, A. (1984) *Sister Outsider: Essays and Speeches*, Berkeley, CA: Crossing Press.

Macchi, S. (2006) 'Politiche urbane e movimenti di donne: specificità del caso italiano', in G. Cortesi, F. Cristaldi and J.D. Fortuijn (eds) *La città delle donne: Un approccio di genere alla geografia urbana*, Bologna: Pàtron Editore.

Mastrodonato, L. (2021) 'Il 98% di chi ha perso il lavoro è donna, il Covid è anche una questione di genere', *Wired*, 2 February. Available from: https://www.wired.it/economia/lavoro/2021/02/02/istat-lavoro-donne-pande mia-disoccupazione/ [Accessed 25 June 2021].

NUDM (Non Una di Meno) (2017) *Abbiamo un piano: Piano femminista contro la violenza maschile sulle donne e la violenza di genere* [*We Have a Plan: Feminist Plan Against Male Violence over Women and Gender Violence*]. Available from: https://nonunadimeno.files.wordpress.com/2017/11/abbia mo_un_piano.pdf [Accessed 15 April 2022].

Oddi Baglioni, L. and Zaremba, C. (2003) *La memoria del Governo Vecchio: Storie delle ragazze di ieri*, Rome: Palombi.

Olcuire, S. (2019) 'Città a misura di donne o donne a misura di città? La mappatura come strumento di governo e sovversione del rapporto tra sicurezza e genere', in C. Belingardi, F. Castelli and S. Olcuire (eds) *La libertà è una passeggiata: Donne e spazi urbani tra violenza strutturale e autodeterminazione*, Rome: IAPh Italia, pp 85–100.

Pain, R. (1991) 'Space, sexual violence and social control: integrating geographical and feminist analyses of women's fear of crime', *Progress in Human Geography*, 15(4): 415–431.

Paoletti, R. (2018) 'These must be the places', in Cirillo, L. (ed.) *Se il mondo torna Uomo. Le donne e la regressione in Europa*, Rome: Alegre.

Peroni, C. (2012) 'Violenza di genere e prostituzione nel discorso pubblico: norme, controllo, sessualità', in Simone, A. (ed.) *Sessismo democratico. L'uso strumentale delle donne nel neoliberismo*, Rome: Mimesis.

Pisanello, C. (2017) *In nome del decoro. Dispositivi estetici e politiche securitarie*, Verona: Ombre Corte.

Rich, A. (1984) 'Notes towards a politics of location', in *Blood, Bread, and Poetry: Selected Prose 1979–1985*, London: Little, Brown.

Roberts, M. (2016) 'Gender, fear, and the night-time city', in I.S. de Madariaga and M. Roberts (eds) *Fair Shared Cities: The Impact of Gender Planning in Europe*, Aldershot: Ashgate, pp 67–82.

Roestone Collective, The (2014) 'Safe space: towards a reconceptualization', *Antipode*, 46(5): 1346–1365.

Saraceno, C. (1984) 'Shifts in public and private boundaries: women as mothers and service workers in Italian daycare', *Feminist Studies*, 10(1): 7–29.

Simone, A. (2012) *Sessismo democratico: l'uso strumentale delle donne nel neoliberismo*, Milan: Mimesis.

Spain, D. (2016) *Constructive Feminism: Women's Spaces and Women's Rights in the American City*, Ithaca, NY: Cornell University Press.

Valentine, J. (1989) *Women's Fear of Male Violence in Public Space: A Spatial Expression of Patriarch*, PhD thesis, Reading: University of Reading.

Willson, P. (2010) *Women in Twentieth-Century Italy*, New York: Palgrave Macmillan.

2

'Everywhere' or 'Over There'? Managing and Spatializing the Perceived Risks of Gender–Based Violence on a Girls' Night Out

Emily Nicholls

Introduction

Participating in the late-night leisure opportunities afforded by the night-time economy (NTE) is an important component of many women's lives. However, in research contexts such as the UK, Australia, New Zealand and Singapore, drinking and clubbing can be understood as activities imbued with tensions for female revellers (Lyons and Willott, 2008; Cullen, 2011; Tan, 2014; Fileborn, 2016). On the one hand, these activities can be bound up with female friendship and femininity and be theorized as pleasurable and empowering for women (Hutton, 2006). On the other, the NTE can be understood as a site of risk-management and associated with the policing and control of women's bodies (Buckley and Fawcett, 2002; Tan, 2014). Crucially, the particular, (hetero)sexualized patterns of engagement that are encouraged and even expected in mainstream nightlife venues may serve to normalize interactions that sit on a continuum of gender-based violence (GBV) for women (Kavanaugh, 2013). It is important to consider the ways in which the various pleasures and dangers of the NTE are experienced and negotiated and how this continues to be shaped by various facets of identity including – but not limited to – one's gender and sexuality. In particular, the normalization of (hetero)sexualized behaviours in mainstream bars, pubs and clubs – and the impact that this has on women's understandings and negotiations of risk and safety – demands further attention.

For the purposes of this chapter, gender-based violence (GBV) will be defined as acts of violence, harassment or aggression perpetuated against individuals because of their gender and sexuality (presumed or otherwise) that take place against a wider backdrop of unequal power relations and social structures (Anitha et al, 2021). GBV exists on a spectrum and incorporates a range of practices not limited to: rape, sexual assault, unwanted sexual attention (including verbal comments and non-consensual touching), and homophobic or transphobic violence and abuse. GBV can include behaviours that may not be legally considered an offence but are perceived as unwanted, threatening and non-consensual encounters by those who experience them (Gunby et al, 2020).

Drawing on primary research on the 'girls' night out' in north-east England, this chapter will explore the ways in which a continuum of GBV in and around licensed venues is managed and understood by women through a lens that draws attention to the role of space and place. The chapter will consider the ways in which GBV was positioned by participants as a pervasive and unavoidable aspect of participation in the NTE. At the same time, GBV was also associated with venues or parts of the city centre labelled as problematic, dangerous or risky at night. In this sense, risk was simultaneously understood as embedded throughout *all* mainstream spaces of the NTE yet also regarded as concentrated within particular, 'no-go' areas.

The development of the night-time economy

Public drinking in the UK and other Western contexts has historically been a masculine pastime (Gofton, 1990), with the working-men's club or community pub in industrial villages, towns or cities representing a space where alcohol and masculinity symbolically intersected (Campbell, 2000). By the 1990s, the landscape of UK public drinking had shifted, and cities began to develop dedicated NTEs as an attempt to revive ailing urban areas and extend consumption opportunities in city-centre spaces into the evening and late night. In this way, formerly industrial citites and towns became 'remoulded as spheres of leisure and consumption' (Smith, 2014: 24).

The term 'night-time economy' describes what Shaw terms 'night-time economic activity, specifically, the entertainment and retail provisions of cities at night' (2010: 893). While early ambitions may have been to develop UK urban spaces into '24-hour cities' offering a continental-style and cosmopolitan late-night café culture with a range of different social, cultural and leisure opportunities, in reality, most city centres are characterized by clusters of licensed, mainstream bars, pubs and clubs targeted at cash-rich young consumers and encouraging heavy and rapid consumption. Any ambitions to create diverse, multipurpose social and cultural late-night spaces have been further thwarted by liberalized planning laws that have given rise to a series of what Jayne et al (2011) wittily describe as UK 'blandscapes'. Marketization and deregulation has facilitated the growth of large corporations and chain bars at the expense of local and independent venues (Shaw, 2010), to the point where many UK city centres now display what Smith calls 'an unavoidable element of uniformity that transcends local specificity' (2014: 11).

Alongside the development of the NTE and its associated drinking expectations, women have become more active participants in nightlife and drinking spaces (Atkinson and Sumnall, 2016), at least in urban environments.[1] The urban NTE has been theorized as an increasingly 'feminized' context where broader changes in women's social positions have allowed them to enter this traditionally male space (Jackson and Tinkler, 2007), although a more cynical view might regard this 'feminization' as a move by the alcohol and nightlife industries to target women as a new consumer market (Hollands and Chatterton, 2002). The 1980s and 1990s certainly saw an expansion of alcohol marketing to more explicitly target women (Chatterton and Hollands, 2003), but of course this is not to say that clubbing and drinking are not important for women in the UK and beyond. Research suggests that the 'night on the town' offers important opportunities for young women to relax and escape from the often mundane realities of everyday life (Guise and Gill, 2007). In particular, the under-researched phenomenon of the 'girls' night out' may offer unique opportunities to socialize with female friends and spend time away from work and domestic/caring responsibilities (Nicholls, 2019). The NTE has also been conceptualized as a space where women can experiment with different feminine identities (Hutton, 2006), rewrite gendered and sexual scripts through shared embodied practices such as collective drinking (Waitt et al, 2011) and use alcohol consumption to excuse behaviour that transgresses boundaries of acceptable femininity and sexuality (Peralta, 2008). However, it is important to consider the ways in which this might be more difficult for women who are positioned further from 'respectable femininity' in the first place due to – for example – their sexuality, race or class. Furthermore, the ability of any woman to use the NTE as a space for escape, resistance or transgression is likely to be somewhat constrained by concerns about risk and safety, as this chapter will illustrate.

Femininity, risk and gender-based violence in the night-time economy

Temporal distinctions clearly impact upon urban spaces, and engaging with the NTE marks a distinct way of experiencing the city after dark. The NTE can be understood as a 'liminal' space of possibility and pleasure (Hayward and Hobbs, 2007), where part of the attraction of the night may be navigating uncertainty, pleasure and risk. However, negotiating these tensions may be difficult for women, who have traditionally been denied access to late-night leisure and are expected to engage in safekeeping practices as a 'condition' of their femininity. If we understand gender as performative – in that bodies only become gendered through the continued repetition of behaviours, traits and practices that are associated with masculinity and femininity (Butler, 1990) – then being risk-averse and adopting various 'safekeeping' practices is inextricably bound up with the performance of appropriate femininity (Campbell, 2005). In other words, women are charged with taking responsibility for their own safety and may be subjected to blame if they are seen to have made themselves 'vulnerable' to GBV or other seemingly risky encounters or situations through failing to adhere to standards of appropriate feminine behaviour (Brooks, 2008; Tinkler et al, 2018). This may be even more significant for – for example – women of colour, disabled women, transwomen or women who identify as lesbian, bisexual, gay or queer, who may experience specific forms of GBV that are bound up with racist, ableist, transphobic or homophobic abuse.

The risks that women perceive and navigate are compounded in so-called mainstream nightlife venues where (hetero)sexualized patterns of interaction are normalized and magnified. As Lindsay (2006) suggests, mainstream venues tend to play popular/chart music and target a specific, heterosexual consumer base. Indeed, an important feature of such spaces is their 'heterosexualization'; the mainstream NTE is a site where music and dancing, dress and bodily presentation, atmosphere and alcohol consumption work to create a sexualized and heteronormative environment where certain patterns of interaction are encouraged (Fileborn, 2016). There is a broad expectation that men should 'pursue' women in these spaces and act in sexually assertive ways while women remain passive (Kavanaugh, 2013). While this may of course be a pleasurable part of the night for revellers who may seek out or desire sexual encounters, it can be argued that the line between expected (hetero)sexualized patterns of interaction and unwanted sexual attention or harassment is a thin one, and this may contribute to the normalization of various forms of GBV in these spaces (Tinkler et al, 2018).

Previous research highlights the wide range of 'safekeeping' strategies used by women to manage risk and safety in the spaces of the NTE globally (see Brooks, 2008; Sheard, 2011; Waitt et al, 2011; Fileborn, 2016; Nicholls, 2017), including seeking safety in numbers, moderating alcohol consumption and guarding drinks against 'spiking'. However, research that considers the 'girls' night out' as a specific form of engagement with the NTE remains limited. This is an important omission as these types of night out may come with specific opportunities (for example, to spend time with female friends) yet also with specific challenges (such as attendance at mainstream venues in an all-female group, which may invite specific forms of harassment and unwanted attention). Gunby et al (2020) argue that research into the specificities of the 'unwanted sexual attention' aspect of GBV in the NTE – and its management – remains limited in a UK context (see also Anitha et al, 2021). This chapter will address some of these limitations, drawing on primary research in the UK to illustrate the ways in which the perception and management of GBV is a spatialized process in the context of a girls' night out.

The 'Girls' Night Out' project

Newcastle-upon-Tyne is the largest city in the north-east of England; formerly known for shipbuilding and heavy industry, but with a more recent reputation as a vibrant 'party city' (Buckley and Fawcett, 2002). The NTE is similar to that of a large number of UK city centres with mostly mainstream nightlife but with small alternative or niche scenes. In 2012 and 2013, semi-structured and in-depth interviews were conducted with 26 young women aged 18–25 who went on 'girls' nights out' in Newcastle as part of a PhD project. While it is important to recognize that women engage with the NTE in Newcastle in an array of ways, the interviews sought specifically to explore the ways in which the boundaries of 'appropriate' femininity were defined and negotiated through embodied practices in the specific and under-researched context of the girls' night out.

Participants were recruited through a range of methods including snowball sampling, social media posts and presentations at local college and university classes. There was some diversity in terms of sexuality (two thirds identified as straight, five as bisexual, four as lesbian and one as queer) but less in terms of race (all participants identified as White British). Just under half self-identified as 'working-class', with the remainder saying they were 'middle-class' or 'do not identify with a class'. Half of participants were not local to the city and were studying at one of the two universities, four were local and had A-levels or were attending college and the remaining nine were local and had attended or were attending university in Newcastle or elsewhere. Some of the participants also self-identified as 'Geordie' (a term that can generally be argued to describe working-class people originally from the city).

Rich and in-depth data was collected, with the semi-structured approach providing scope to uncover the 'perceptions, attitudes and experiences' of participants (Sheard, 2011: 623). The young women were invited to talk through all aspects of a typical girls' night out, positioning them as 'authors of valid and reliable accounts of embodied experience' (Howson, 2005: 39). There was widespread agreement among participants that this type of night is characterized by attendance at mainstream nightlife venues with a group of female friends following an extended session of drinking and getting ready at the home of one friend. Further discussion centred on themes such as dress and appearance, drinking practices and risk management. Interviews were recorded, transcribed, manually coded and subjected to thematic analysis. All participants were given pseudonyms to help preserve anonymity.

'Everywhere': the pervasive threat of gender-based violence on a girls' night out

Risk and safekeeping were seen as important considerations for almost all of the young women and many discussed the topic extensively. The ways in which assumptions about the NTE as a risky space came through in women's discussions of drinking, dress and behaviour highlighted how considerations of risk and safety could be threaded throughout every aspect of the night out as young women continue to be expected to engage in active risk management in these contexts (Brooks, 2008). The possibility of rape or sexual assault heavily policed the behaviour of participants; while none talked about directly experiencing this in the NTE (although of course this does not mean none had), the mere threat of it shaped their experiences of a girls' night out. As Campbell (2005) argues, the *fear* of rape and sexual assault produces particular types of vulnerable, feminine bodies, makes GBV seem inevitable and affects women's behaviour and the ways in which they move through and use space.

Participants remarked that 'unwanted attention' from men was the most common form of GBV experienced when they were drinking and clubbing with female friends, suggesting a hesitance to overtly name sexual risks that is mirrored in other research with young women (Griffin et al, 2009). Their understandings of 'unwanted attention' included acts which might be recognized legally as sexual offences or crimes, but also other behaviours that were nonetheless experienced as non-consensual, threatening and uncomfortable. The 'unwanted attention' participants reported they had received from men on a night out included; feeling 'watched' or 'stared at'; drink spiking; unsolicited conversations, catcalling, shouted comments or insults and unwanted touching and groping (see also Brooks, 2008; Sheard, 2011; Fileborn, 2016).

One significant finding across the data was the normalization and – at times – the trivialization of GBV in mainstream nightlife spaces. The participants associated *all* mainstream nightlife spaces with the risks of unwanted sexual attention and harassment and positioned this kind of interaction as inevitable and expected. For example, Nicole described being groped as 'something which happens on a regular basis', and went on to explain:

'Things like that, you kind of let go. Are they acceptable? Probably not. ... But I think it would be *worse* in a supermarket because it's not a social environment, really. ... You can kind of accept someone's had a few drinks … bit cheeky. … If they did it in a supermarket, I'd be like "what the hell are you doing?!" I think that could be perceived as *worse*. I suppose it's just the atmosphere you're in more than anything else. From a serious atmosphere to one where it's a little bit silly, and everyone's a bit drunk.' (Nicole, 24)

Nicole's comments echo findings reported elsewhere suggesting that sexual harassment and GBV are understood as 'just what happens' in the context of a night out (Anitha et al, 2021). Space and context are important, as Nicole suggests that within the specific spatial and temporal contexts of the NTE, the 'rules' about appropriate conduct may be different to the rules in spaces such as supermarkets, echoing findings in previous research about the specific ways in which the context of the NTE excuses or even *encourages* types of heterosexual interaction that would not be permitted elsewhere (Boyd, 2010). Some participants also reported that simply the layout of mainstream venues could make women feel more vulnerable (for example dancefloors in the centre of nightclubs with specific space around the edges for men to 'watch' women). Nicole also suggests that perpetrator drunkenness can, to an extent, excuse certain behaviours that would not be acceptable in other, more 'serious' spaces (although of course, this is not to say that GBV does not routinely occur in those spaces). In this sense, alcohol may function not just as an excuse for women to behave in transgressive ways but as an excuse for the 'cheeky' behaviour of others that is experienced nonetheless as uncomfortable or unpleasant. The belief that some degree of GBV is unavoidable and should be expected in these spaces was also reinforced through appeals to essentialist notions of male sexuality as somehow 'naturally' uncontrollable and uncontainable, as seen in Kate's (20) comment that "men think with their penises" and are likely to be incited or aroused by women in these particular contexts who might be dressed – in her words – "more provocatively" than in other settings. This of course presents a source of tension for women who – as I have discussed elsewhere – are simultaneously expected to dress in particular '(hetero) sexy' ways yet to avoid being seen to 'lead guys on' through their dress and appearance (Nicholls, 2017).

A degree of unwanted attention was further normalized through the expectation that women should respond by simply deciding to 'let it go', as Nicole suggests. While actions like being groped or harassed might be actively and assertively called out in other spaces, the expected response in the NTE might be to downplay or ignore such behaviour, as noted by other participants who claimed that when they experience verbal or physical harassment their strategy is to "keep wur [our] heads down" (Kirsty, 23), avoid a visible reaction or "just ignore it" (Alex, 19). Where such encounters might be more difficult to ignore completely, it was still important to carefully diffuse an uncomfortable situation in a way that would not be confrontational:

'You don't know what to *say*! You know ... you don't wanna say "oh bugger off", so you try and talk, but you try and turn away as well ... so you're tryin' not to give them ... I don't know ... without telling them to "eff off!" [both laugh] ... You have to keep jokin', make it awkward!' (Joanna, 24)

Referring here to situations where men persistently follow her, wolf-whistling and shouting to get her attention, Joanna describes the avoidance of strategies that might be seen as confrontational. The implication is that harassment from men should be managed in a way that doesn't involve swearing or even risking making a situation feel 'awkward' in any way, perhaps through the use of humour or trying to turn away. Other participants, such as Donna (21), also talked about the difficulties her heterosexual friends might experience in extracting themselves from particular scenarios on a night out without seeming 'rude', for example walking away after a man has bought them a drink or started to dance with them. Tinkler et al (2018) report similar findings, suggesting that 'appropriate' reactions to GBV are often limited to responses that are indirect, passive or even polite. Of course, to react otherwise may risk escalating an uncomfortable or risky situation.

'Over there': creating 'risky spaces' on a girls' night out

There was agreement across the interviews that simply to enter the mainstream NTE is to enter a space where women may experience forms of GBV. However, while this was positioned as something pervasive, unavoidable and perhaps expected on a night out, the participants simultaneously worked to 'contain' risk by associating it with particular venues or areas within Newcastle's city centre. As Holt and Griffin (2005) also suggest, risk management in the NTE is likely to be spatialized, for example through the ways women move through public space after dark or make choices about venues to frequent or avoid.

All participants carved the city centre into particular zones or areas which at the time of the research could be broadly demarcated by pricing, branding and clientele. Generally, the so-called Diamond Strip (a street of upmarket cocktail bars with associations of affluence and status) was the most popular part of the mainstream NTE and was frequented by most participants, regardless of class, sexuality, age or their status as students or locals. However, all participants were acutely aware of the Diamond Strip's shared border with what was perceived to be a less desirable and more dangerous part of town, the Bigg Market. Historically, the Bigg Market has been understood as an infamous – perhaps notorious – site of Geordie drinking culture, traditionally serving a local, working-class and male crowd (Hollands and Chatterton, 2002). The Bigg Market was often described by participants as a no-go area, while the venues they preferred to frequent were depicted as familiar and comfortable. In this sense, the subjective and affective experience of *feeling* safer could be created through drawing spatialized distinctions between venues or areas that were felt to be safe and comfortable, and those that were unfamiliar, risky or dangerous.

A number of participants noted that the main advice they had received from others (usually from parents or family, even if they were not local), was to avoid the Bigg Market at all costs, as illustrated by Lydia here, describing advice given to her by her father before she came up to Newcastle to study: "Never, ever go down Bigg Market, ever ... like, avoid it, take the other road. When you go down and left is the Bigg Market, and right is ... go the other way" (Lydia, 21). As suggested here, often even passing through this problematic space was to be avoided, as the participants created mental maps that carved up city centre space and allowed them to chart 'safe' routes through it. Mason's (2001) research with lesbian women indicates that women may draw on 'knowledges' of homophobic violence to construct 'safety maps' that help them to navigate public space. A similar practice is evident here; one where 'knowledges' may be collective ones that are passed on and shared by others. Several participants depicted the Bigg Market as a site of violent altercations (including glassings and stabbings) and also a space where women might be highly likely to experience forms of GBV, particularly in the form of sexually predatory behaviour from heterosexual men. Hollands and Chatterton describe the space as having a 'boisterous and sexually charged atmosphere' (2002: 308), and this certainly seemed to be reflected in the ways in which it was perceived by participants. Lydia goes on to describe the space as "dicey", and to describe an occasion where she did actually walk through the Bigg Market, characterized at the time of the research by a combination of more traditional pubs serving an older, local clientele, 'disco pubs' and tightly packed takeaway venues and taxi ranks. She felt nervous and intimidated as a result of some of the physical features of the space, particularly the crowded cobbled streets and busy takeaways, and the intoxicated people "pouring out" of busy venues and occupying the street.

While characteristics of the physical space and built environment may contribute to feelings of danger, as suggested earlier, concerns about risk, safety and crime often manifest as fears about certain *people*, and it is important to consider the ways in which the participants' anxieties about the Bigg Market were entangled with the types of people they expected to find there. Perhaps unsurprisingly, notions of social class were important in shaping the ways in which participants spoke about the Bigg Market, with terms such as 'rough' and 'cheap' commonly used and with the area described more explicitly as 'chavvy'[2] (Ruth, 21) or frequented by older, visibly intoxicated working-class revellers. Descriptions of the area as a "stereotypical Geordie type area" (Zoe, 23) also functioned as veiled ways to talk about class and equate being local/Geordie with an undesirable working-class identity: "The local *men* especially [pause] are more *chavvy* ... and a bit more ... like, *forward* ... in the way that they ask you stuff. It actually makes me feel uncomfortable" (Lucy, 21). Here, Lucy discursively links local men in the Bigg Market with being 'chavvy' (that is, working-class) and argues that these men are more likely to engage in the types of behaviour that might be seen as "forward" or make women feel harassed and uncomfortable in the NTE. This is also echoed in the work of Wattis et al (2011), who report that the students they spoke to in a similarly working-class, northern town viewed the area and the local residents as risky or dangerous in some way. As they argue, in deindustrialized urban settings, 'local people become a distinct group from students, and are constructed as problematic amidst connections to crime and other social problems' (Wattis et al, 2011: 761). In this sense, participants' associations of older, visibly intoxicated and 'local' men with an increased likelihood of GBV (and with aggression and violence more generally) firms up boundaries between 'us' and 'them', and between the type of people who are perceived to go out in the Bigg Market and the type likely to frequent similar venues to participants. Indeed, a sort of 'territorial' boundary-drawing between students and locals (with locals associated with all forms of violence) is echoed in previous research (see Holt and Griffin, 2005), although the accuracy of such assumptions can of course be challenged.

Interestingly, the participants who were local to Newcastle themselves often worked particularly hard to distance themselves from the Bigg Market and to make it very clear this was not a part of town they would frequent. Very early in the interview, Kirsty (23) made a point of bringing this up and saying "we're not them kinda Bigg Market fans". Similarly, her sister Nicole (24) who identified as proudly 'Geordie' and working class, was careful to distinguish between hard-working locals such as herself and the perceived 'underclass' prone to excessive drinking, rowdy behaviour and violence that she associated with the Bigg Market. In this way, these participants could associate themselves with the 'respectable' rather than the 'rough' wedge of the working class (Nayak, 2003) and could also work, much like their student peers, to tie risk and violence (in all its forms) to a particular dangerous and undesirable space within the city centre and those who frequented it.

Conclusion

This chapter highlights some of the ways in which young women may talk about their experiences of GBV and risk on a girls' night out, and the various ways in which they might seek to manage or to *accept* a degree of gendered and sexualized risk in the bars, pubs and clubs of the mainstream NTE. As this discussion has shown, there was some tension in the ways in which participants talked about GBV on night outs, through positioning risk as pervasive and omnipresent in the NTE *but* at the same time associating it with particular venues, settings and parts of town. Interestingly, risk could be simultaneously perceived to be largely confined to particular 'rough' areas in the city centre, yet at the same time, a degree of GBV (particularly in the form of being groped, stared at or verbally harassed) was regarded as an embedded and normalized part of the entire mainstream nightlife scene.

On the one hand, it is perhaps unsurprising that young women may work to 'contain' risk in particular geographical areas, a strategy noted in other research where regarding certain areas as risky or 'off-limits' is a common safekeeping strategy (Green and Singleton, 2006). Women may work to justify their continued presence in these spaces through positioning the venues they frequent as less risky or problematic than other parts of town. Crucially, the drawing of lines and boundaries around more or less 'risky' spaces is as much about risky *people* as it is about geography; social class (intersecting with age and student/local distinctions) was central to the ways in which the participants positioned the Bigg Market as a site of risk. While the nature of the space itself *was* important – the tightly packed venues, the activity spilling out onto the cobbled streets – anxiety was often centred around who was seen to occupy that space and frequent the venues there. In this way, the findings build upon earlier work suggesting class and student/local distinctions may be important for women in conceptualizing risk (Holt and Griffin, 2005; Wattis et al, 2011).

On the other hand, women struggled to reconcile the notion that risk is confined to certain no-go spaces, as forms of GBV quite obviously affected them in myriad ways, even in the spaces that they depicted as more comfortable, familiar and safe. It was clear from the data that any claims the NTE in the UK has been 'feminized' must be treated with caution, as mainstream nightlife venues 'remain highly masculinised in terms of the male domination of space and the policing of compulsory heterosexuality' (Chatterton and Hollands 2003: 148). In such spaces, particular patterns of (hetero)sexualized behaviour and interaction may be normalized to such an extent that we see 'a blurring of definitional boundaries regarding what constitutes sexual victimisation versus normal heterosexual behaviour' (Kavanaugh 2013: 29). The normalization of harassment and other forms of GBV in such contexts is compounded by the expectation that women should try to downplay it, ignore it or meet it with strategies such as polite dismissal or humour.

It is important to consider the implications this has for women of a range of sexualities as they use, move through and occupy public spaces that are highly (hetero)sexualized and where a degree of unwanted attention or harassment is normalized and expected. While the perceived confinement of risk to particular spaces or venues comes with its own consequences (for example in terms of limiting women's ability to feel that they can move freely through public space), the normalization of GBV across the NTE – and perhaps more widely – is an issue of even greater significance. The labelling of being stared at, groped or harassed as 'everyday' or expected may help to legitimize a broader spectrum of GBV and reinforce the idea that women should both expect and accept GBV in their daily lives.

Notes

1   See, for example, Leyshon (2008) on women's differing experiences in rural pubs in the UK.
2   'Chavvy' derives from the British term 'chav', a pejorative term used to describe or insult the (White) working-class (Tyler, 2008).

References

Anitha, S., Jordan, A., Jameson, J. and Davy, Z. (2021) 'A balancing act: agency and constraints in university students' understanding of and responses to sexual violence in the night-time economy', *Violence Against Women*, 27(11): 2043–2065.

Atkinson, A.M. and Sumnall, H.R. (2016) '"If I don't look good, it just doesn't go up": a qualitative study of young women's drinking cultures and practices on social network sites', *International Journal of Drug Policy*, 38: 50–62.

Boyd, J. (2010) 'Producing Vancouver's (hetero)normative nightscape', *Gender, Place &Culture*, 17(2): 169–189.

Brooks, O. (2008) 'Consuming alcohol in bars, pubs and clubs: a risky freedom for young women?', *Annals of Leisure Research*, 11(3/4): 331–350.

Buckley, C. and Fawcett, H. (2002) *Fashioning the Feminine: Representation and Women's Fashion from the Fin de Siècle to the Present*, New York: I.B. Tauris.

Butler, J. (1990) *Gender Trouble: Feminism and the Subversion of Identity*, London: Routledge.

Campbell, A. (2005) 'Keeping the "lady" safe: the regulation of femininity through crime prevention literature', *Critical Criminology*, 13(2): 119–140.

Campbell, H. (2000) 'The glass phallus: pub(lic) masculinity and drinking in rural New Zealand', *Rural Sociology*, 64(4): 562–581.

Chatterton, P. and Hollands, R. (2003) *Urban Nightscapes: Youth Cultures, Pleasure Spaces and Corporate Power*, London: Routledge.

Cullen, F. (2011) '"The only time I feel girly is when I go out": drinking stories, teenage girls, and respectable femininities', *International Journal of Adolescence and Youth*, 16(2): 119–138.

Fileborn, B. (2016) *Reclaiming the Night-Time Economy: Unwanted Sexual Attention in Pubs and Clubs*, London: Palgrave Macmillan.

Gofton, L. (1990) 'On the town: drink and the "new lawlessness"', *Youth and Policy*, 29: 33–39.

Green, E. and Singleton, C. (2006) 'Risky bodies at leisure: young women negotiating space and place', *Sociology*, 40(5): 853–871.

Griffin, C., Bengry-Howell, A., Hackley, C., Mistral, W. and Szmigin, I. (2009) '"Every time I do it I annihilate myself": loss of (self-)consciousness and loss of memory in young people's drinking narratives', *Sociology*, 43(3): 457–476.

Guise, J.M.F. and Gill, J.S. (2007) '"Binge drinking? It's good, it's harmless fun": a discourse analysis of accounts of female undergraduate drinking in Scotland', *Health Education Research*, 22(6): 895–906.

Gunby, C., Carline, A., Taylor, S. and Gosling, H. (2020) 'Unwanted sexual attention in the night-time economy: behaviors, safety strategies, and conceptualizing "feisty femininity"', *Feminist Criminology*, 15(1): 24–46.

Hayward, K. and Hobbs, D. (2007) 'Beyond the binge in "booze Britain": market-led liminalization and the spectacle of binge drinking', *British Journal of Sociology*, 58(3): 437–456.

Hollands, R. and Chatterton, P. (2002) 'Changing times for an old industrial city: hard times, hedonism and corporate power in Newcastle's nightlife', *City*, 6(3): 291–315.

Holt, M. and Griffin, C. (2005) 'Students versus locals: young adults' constructions of the working class Other', *British Journal of Social Psychology*, 44(2): 241–267.

Howson, A. (2005) *Embodying Gender*, London: Sage.

Hutton, F. (2006) *Risky Pleasures? Club Cultures and Feminine Identities*, Aldershot: Ashgate.

Jackson, C. and Tinkler, P. (2007) '"Ladettes" and "modern girls": "troublesome" young femininities', *Sociological Review*, 55(2): 251–272.

Jayne, M., Valentine, G. and Holloway, S.L. (2011) *Alcohol, Drinking and Drunkenness: (Dis)orderly Spaces*, Aldershot: Ashgate.

Kavanaugh, P.R. (2013) 'The continuum of sexual violence: women's accounts of victimization in urban nightlife', *Feminist Criminology*, 8(1): 20–39.

Leyshon, M. (2008) '"We're stuck in the corner": young women, embodiment and drinking in the countryside', *Drugs: Education, Prevention, and Policy*, 15(3): 267–289.

Lindsay, J. (2006) 'A big night out in Melbourne: drinking as an enactment of class and gender', *Contemporary Drug Problems*, 33(1): 29–61.

Lyons, A.C. and Willott, S.A. (2008) 'Alcohol consumption, gender identities and women's changing social positions', *Sex Roles*, 59(9/10): 694–712.

Mason, G. (2001) 'Body maps: envisaging homophobia, violence and safety', *Social & Legal Studies*, 10(1): 23–44.

Nayak, A. (2003) 'Last of the "real Geordies"? White masculinities and the subcultural response to deindustrialisation', *Environment and Planning D: Society and Space*, 21(1): 7–25.

Nicholls, E. (2017) ' "Dulling it down a bit": managing visibility, sexualities and risk in the night time economy in Newcastle, UK', *Gender, Place & Culture*, 24(2): 260–273.

Nicholls, E. (2019) *Negotiating Femininities in the Neoliberal Night-Time Economy: Too Much of a Girl?*, London: Palgrave Macmillan.

Peralta, R.L. (2008) ' "Alcohol allows you to not be yourself": toward a structured understanding of alcohol use and gender difference among gay, lesbian, and heterosexual youth', *Journal of Drug Issues*, 38(2): 373–399.

Shaw, R. (2010) 'Neoliberal subjectivities and the development of the night-time economy in British cities', *Geography Compass*, 4(7): 893–903.

Sheard, L. (2011) ' "Anything could have happened": women, the night-time economy, alcohol and drink spiking', *Sociology*, 45(4): 619–633.

Smith, O. (2014) *Contemporary Adulthood and the Night-Time Economy*, Basingstoke: Palgrave Macmillan.

Tan, Q.H. (2014) 'Postfeminist possibilities: unpacking the paradoxical performances of heterosexualized femininity in club spaces', *Social & Cultural Geography*, 15(1): 23–48.

Tinkler, J.E., Becker, S. and Clayton, K.A. (2018) ' "Kind of natural, kind of wrong": young people's beliefs about the morality, legality, and normalcy of sexual aggression in public drinking settings', *Law and Social Inquiry*, 43(1): 28–57.

Tyler, I. (2008) 'Chav mum chav scum', *Feminist Media Studies*, 8(1): 17–34.

Waitt, G., Jessop, L. and Gorman-Murray, A. (2011) ' "The guys in there just expect to be laid": embodied and gendered socio-spatial practices of a "night out" in Wollongong, Australia', *Gender, Place & Culture*, 18(2): 255–275.

Wattis, L., Green, E. and Radford, J. (2011) 'Women students' perceptions of crime and safety: negotiating fear and risk in an English post-industrial landscape', *Gender, Place & Culture*, 18(6): 749–767.

3

Internal Homelessness and Hiraeth: Boys' Spatial Journeys Between Childhood Domestic Abuse and On-Road

Jade Levell

Introduction

When children live in homes where domestic violence and abuse (DVA) is occurring they can occupy a precarious position. Home shifts from being a place of safety to a place of fear. To deal with this situation the young people discussed in this chapter instead sought other spaces to dwell; on-road. It is essential to focus on the lives of boys and young men who live at the complex intersection of childhood DVA and on-road or gang involvement because these are so often hidden victims. Due to essentialized stereotypes of young street-based masculinity, boys in this position are often quickly labelled as 'at risk' of youth offending or becoming risks to others, rather than seen as being victimized at home themselves.

In this chapter I will explore some of the ways in which the participants spoke about their childhoods which centred upon being 'on-road' and gang-involved at the same time as they were experiencing DVA at home. I explore this in both a spatial and a gendered way; how do boys cope with being childhood victims of male violence? How does strategic use of space factor into their coping strategies? Drawing on the concept of 'technologies of space', I consider how these men constructed their (masculine) subjectivities in spatially specific ways. The move between the private and public spheres operated as gendered strategies for coping with childhood DVA. When home ceases to be a place in which young people feel safe then this can lead them to seek environments elsewhere that offer them the space, both physically and mentally, to escape the abusive environment and seek to harness more agency and control over their circumstances.

Research into child survivors of DVA and how they cope has been historically limited. Research into gendered experiences of this are even rarer. The participants discussed how they coped with this in varying ways involving the shift to occupying public space in opposition to the unsafe private domestic sphere. Several of the men discussed pursuing violence in public spaces as a way to process the complex emotional responses to the DVA as well as to perform masculinity ('be a man'). If we are to understand how to support children who cope with adversity in their early years, with the aim of diverting them from involvement in youth offending, it is essential to shine a light on how they cope and survive.

Theory
Space, agency, resistance, dwelling

Maria Tamboukou (1999, 2013) theorized technologies of space as a distinct area of focus within Foucault's concept of 'technologies of self'. This concept in a Foucauldian sense was concerned with the ways in which individuals create their selves through a 'number of operations on their own bodies and souls, thoughts, conduct, and way of being, so as to transform themselves in order to attain a certain state of happiness, purity, wisdom, perfection, or immortality' (Nilson 1998: 97). Tamboukou used a feminist lens to analyse the way in which women's personal narratives were 'interwoven' with their experiences of spatial and hierarchical boundaries. These combined to create a 'particular set of technologies in the constitution of the female self' (Tamboukou 2013: 93). Specifically, she looked at the geographical, personal and social spaces of women, traced though their narrative accounts of their lives. She is particularly interested in approaching the analysis from a feminist perspective through focusing on the 'the role of space in the structuring of gender relations and the formation of subjectivities' (1999: 127). Tamboukou noted that by focusing on the ways that both space and place cut through private and public arrangements it reveals the way in which '[s]paces are made meaningful through certain practices which women strategically use to act upon themselves' (1999: 127). Using this analytic frame, which focuses on the interaction between gender, power and space, offers a pertinent insight into the way that individuals construct their identities in relation to the spaces they inhabit.

In Tamboukou's research, she looked at the way in which imagined spaces offered freedom for women from the material reality of other spaces that constrained them (Riessman, 2008). This can also be applied to the notion of the road, which was discussed by all the men that took part in the study. The road is a complex space, which is somewhere between an imagined place, a

51

description of a youth subculture, and a way of being in the world. The term was utilized by men in the study in a variety of ways, as something that you are 'on', as connected with the literal roads and streets, as a mentality and as describing a subculture that includes drug dealing. Definitions from the literature reflect this complexity. It is a phrase that allows for the 'complexity and fluidity of urban street life' (Young, 2016: 11). Gunter (2010: 352) noted that it was on a continuum, from, 'hyper masculine modes of behaviour, incorporating violent and petty crime ... and low-level drug dealing', to 'friendships, routine and the familiar'. The term rests on a gendered and masculine experience which is the antithesis of the domestic and constrained life (Earle, 2011).

The importance of space in the construction of individual identities was discussed by Earle (2011), whose work in young offenders institutions found that men drew on 'spatialized identities', largely described by their home postcodes, to identity as belonging somewhere (2011: 139). The term is reminiscent of 'white American men's romanticization of "the frontier" and "the wilderness"' which rests on 'a highly gendered, masculine, experience of the world' (Earle, 2011: 135). It is the antithesis of the domestic and constrained life that marks a different masculine ideal for 'other' men in society. It provides an alternative mode of being that is accessible to men who are not able to access traditional markers of masculine behaviours and achievements. In this way, it is important not to romanticize the term 'on-road' as referring to, '"authentic sovereignty" and "freedom from constraints"' when the reality may instead be, 'what might otherwise be seen as panicky, chaotic, adrenalin-fuelled edgework experiences' (Earle, 2011: 134). 'On-road' does not only refer to gang membership but serves more as a broader term that has a range of connotations. Young and Hallsworth (2011) developed a definition for 'on-road':

> The 'hood' or the 'ghetto' where young people, worn down by marginalisation and exclusion, struggled to survive in a society they believed did not care or cater for their needs. At its most extreme, the hood – and by extension 'the road' – was a place where young people adopted a 'hood mentality', a fatalistic attitude to life that held 'no dreams, no ambition, no drive; no nothing'. (2011: 3)

Gunter (2010) has focused on youth transitions that occur within adolescence as a way to conceive young people's journeys into gang involvement. He was interested in the range of transitions that were available to young people in an East London locale. Gunter notes that he focused on the 'complex interplay between social class, spatial locality, race/ethnicity, gender ... and their combined impact on the young people's lives' (2010: xvii). To conceptualize the journey that some young people make from home life to involvement in road life, Gunter utilizes both Matza's idea of 'drift' as well as the notion of 'flirtation' as a way to describe the non-committal way that young people enter road life.

Gender regimes and homes of violence

In order to conceptualize the way victims of DVA, both adults and children, experience DVA at home, the term 'gender regimes' is pertinent. This term refers the ways in which patriarchal attitudes, relations and symbols which are founded on gender inequality permeate the boundaries of home when there is ongoing DVA. Morris coined the term 'abusive household gender regime' (AHGR) to refer to the 'perpetrators' imposition of a coercive web-like regime on household members and the interlocking of many forms of abuse, which entrap victims' (Morris 2009: 414). She noted, 'Gendered symbolism is intrinsic to abuse; there is always meaning-making inherent in both the perpetration of violence and the experiences of its victims' (Morris 2009: 420). This can play out in various ways in the home environment, including in the practices and tactics of DVA, which creates the 'fabric' of the AHGR, whereby, 'violence towards women and children is interwoven through time and intimate space into their daily lives, into their bodily and emotional reactions, into their beliefs and into their relationships with themselves and others', what Morris calls the 'web of entrapment' (Morris 2009: 417).

The foundation for the theory of AHGR's was Connell's (2005) theory of masculinities. Connell focused on the ways in which societies are organized around hierarchical gender regimes which are based on the idealization of hegemonic masculinity, against which all other iterations of masculinity are ordered. Connell conceptualized gender regimes as, 'units or specific institutions in which people's lived experiences are configured through gender and gender relations between individuals are shaped. Households can be understood as gender regimes – micro social forms in which gender operates' (Morris 2009: 420). Utilizing Connell's masculinity theory here is pertinent as it was the focus of my analysis of the narratives of men who experienced DVA in childhood and later became involved on-road and with gangs. Connell's framework gives space to understand the ways in which boys and young men come to terms with experience of DVA in childhood.

Internal homelessness: hiraeth

The way in which home can be inverted through painful experiences was articulately worked with by Arthur (2007) in their book subtitled *Home Is Where the Hurt Is*, an inversion of course of the traditional phrase, 'home is where the heart is'. The sense of a loss of the symbolic safety and refuge of home is profoundly articulated in the Welsh language with the concept of 'hiraeth'. It is a term that encapsulates the homesickness that can occur when home, as a heartfelt concept, is a place that is either inaccessible and/ or non-existent. The complex meaning is: '[the] homesickness, longing, nostalgia, and yearning, for a home that you cannot return to, no longer exists, or maybe never was. It can also include grief or sadness for who or what you have lost, losses which make your "home" not the same as the one you remember' (Kielar, 2016). This longing for a lost home and sense of mourning is encapsulated in this term. It has said to have originated in Welsh language as a specific response to the colonization of Wales. This resulted in the feeling that, 'home isn't the place it should have been. It is an unattainable longing for a place, a person, a figure, even a national history that may never have actually existed. To feel hiraeth is to feel a deep incompleteness and recognize it as familiar' (Petro, 2012). The reason why this term is pertinent to the discussion around children's experiences of DVA is that it is encapsulates a sense that was described to me by the men that I spoke to about their experiences. I propose that to experience domestic violence at home in childhood can result in children to experience internal homelessness, or a feeling of hiraeth.

The concept of home is about the social and affective production of a space, as much as the physical location and material structure itself. The whole premise of the term 'home' as opposed to 'house' is to signify an emotional bond with a place, underlined by safety and warmth. When DVA is happening at home, then it could be argued that it ceases to function as this safe refuge, but rather the domestic sphere becomes a place of discomfort or danger. Adverse experiences at home causing an 'internal homelessness' have been previously explored by Passaro (1996) when looking at the situation of homeless men. She found that the men in her research related it to their experiences at home, 'feeling unwanted and abused by their families, "homeless" while still at home' (Passaro, 1996: 53). It is this concept that resonates with the narratives of the men in this study.

Methodology

This chapter draws on the findings of a life-history narrative study, part of a doctoral study, that focused on the lives of men who had experienced DVA in childhood and who were also later on-road and gang-involved. The aim of the study was to look at gender performance in particular masculinities. Eight men took part, accessed through networking and snowball sampling. The project used music elicitation as an interview tool, asking the participants to bring three music tracks which helped them tell their life stories (Levell, 2019). These music-enabled interviews offered a visceral space that aimed to invert the traditional power imbalances of social research interviews and provide for the participants an opportunity to curate the interview space themselves. The participants resided in three large cities in England and were from diverse ethnic backgrounds. I spoke to four Black British men, one Black African refugee, one mixed-race man and two White British men. They shared their life stories retrospectively and at the time of participating ranged from 21 to 50 years old.

Findings

Home as uninhabitable

> 'The longest [sic] I stay out of home the better because I don't wanna be there.'
>
> Eric

A common theme among the narratives of childhood DVA was a desire to be outside of the parental home. This was explored in various ways, from feeling an overwhelming powerlessness to stop the abuse their mother was experiencing, as well as at times coexisting child abuse, which made the men seek spaces to spend time away from home. In addition to home being uninhabitable for the young men, they also discussed the way that home was not a secure space to invite friends to, which only exacerbated their feeling of isolation and inability to make friendships. Home life became something to avoid as much as possible, which suggests that their sense of isolation was (at least in part) being spatially produced and reinforced.

Eric was atypical from the other men I met because he occupied a dual space, having found refuge in participation in school life alongside his involvement in on-road/gang life. He located his engagement in both spheres as coming from a desire to be out of the home environment for as much of the day as possible. In addition, he mentioned that the violence at home was causing him an emotional response that he did not know how to deal with. So, through engagement in the street peer group, he found an outlet for these emotions he had been dealing with.

> 'My home life was just horrible, it was just, I used to do extra curriculum, so I don't come home because you know and coz I was struggling to fit in, my parents were struggling to fit in but they didn't know, they didn't know so then they were exploding into violence of their own. Um, so then you wouldn't wanna be at home, so you find the extra-curricular, I would do basketball, I would do youth parliament, connections, connect youth, everything, just so I can stay the longest. The longest I stay out of home the better because I don't wanna be there. So you get this kid that is doing youth parliament,

connections, I'm doing running, that life on the streets it's not for you, it's never gunna be for you, but eventually because you are gunna, you keep seeing it at home, and you don't know how to deal with those emotions.'

What Eric's case highlights is that involvement on-road and gang-involved is not necessarily incompatible with a productive school life. Linking back to Tamboukou's conceptualization of technologies of space, this can help us to understand how this spatial shift from operating in the mainstream only offered so much as a coping mechanism. According to Eric's testimony here, it seems that participation in school life offered him practical distractions that he needed, but it was the on-road life that offered an outlet for Eric to deal with his emotions. Where school life fell down was in his desire for acceptance, as well as the lack of options to process his emotions around the abuse, which he found through pursuit of the on-road space.

For Dylan, the first space he mentioned was his relationship to his childhood home. The DVA rendered this an unsafe space and he noted that he spent time on the streets because he wanted to escape his "broken home" and went to the streets to escape the DVA at home. Even though this is a common phrase I find it poignant when he uses it to describe his childhood home. Dylan remembered experiencing domestic abuse from a young age. He noted that he used to hear his mum scream and feel he could not do anything about it. At the time he would have been a young boy, who dealt with the DVA at home by engaging on-road.

Despite Dylan's home life being a push factor out to street life, he was clear that he perceived that he still had a choice in how he was responding to his home environment:

'I knew right from wrong I knew what I was doing, and I still done it, and now I choose not to do those things. People can't say I was forced into it or groomed into it, because if anything I groomed myself into it because I went there to escape what was happening in the house.'

Although he recognizes that he was going to the streets to escape the violence at home, he locates that as a decision that he made, rather than being victimized by his circumstances. Dylan is reframing his spatialized mode of coping as one which has choice and agency at the centre. Dylan talked about his decision to go out on to the streets as both being due to the push factor of the DVA at home and as a conscious decision. Throughout his interview, it was clear that Dylan constructed his actions as a choice so as not to undermine the care his mother provided for him. Through outlining his material wealth as a child, that his mother worked hard to provide for him, he is saying that he was adequately provided for.

Lack of control over domestic space

One theme that was featured in Jordan's narrative was the journey from an unsafe home to independence. Underpinning this discussion was almost like a 'coming of age' story, a journey from dependence to independence which revealed messages about masculinity and what it takes to become a man. The first song that Jordan chose was entitled, 'Never Coming Home' (by Westside Gun ft. Tiona D), which opened the space for Jordan to share the story of his home life and the process of him leaving his childhood home. He explored in depth the different relationships to home that he had experienced but spoke about it in the third person, so as to depersonalize it and speak more generally. He noted: "I got kicked out of my house from when I was 15 and I've never been home since. ... I've had to make my own home and as a result you've had to become a man and take care of your responsibilities and you start to build your future." Here Jordan uses the music track to explore the discourse around the notion of 'home'. Jordan really uses the track title, 'Never Coming Home' as stimulus for a full exploration of the meaning of the term, 'home' to him and his peers. Initially he talks about his "broken home", which is an evocative phrase, simple yet tragic. Jordan then talks about his own "transition" from home, a term which sounds gentler and more gradual than his next comment that he got "kicked out", which conveys a more violent and urgent departure. Jordan emphasized that he has not returned home, despite having visited. He clearly distinguishes these visits as still coming from a place of being estranged – the 'kicking out' could not be undone. By making the distinction between seeing his mum, but still not going home, it emphasizes that 'going home' is more significant than simply visiting a place. Rather, 'home' is a symbolic place as well. Jordan then relates this to masculinity, as he has had to make his own home, an integral part of becoming a man for him, signifying an inherent independence and self-reliance that for Jordan is an inherent part of achieving a successful type of masculinity.

Sam conveyed a sense of the lack of control that he had over his spatial contexts as a child. He noted that, "at home with my mum ... and she kept sending me to my dad's and my dad kept beating me and I kept telling my mum not to, but she kept sending me there anyway". Here he is suggesting that as a child he was unable to assert his own wishes but was rather moved according to the wishes of his parents. He conveyed a lack of choice and agency about the conditions on which he inhabited spaces. For instance, he was 'sent' to his father's where he would be beaten and when he got a dog it was not allowed in the house, so he in turn felt rejected.

Eric also experienced a lack of control over his spatial context as a child, as he was a refugee who moved to the UK aged seven years. Eric talked about the inaccessibility of his home in terms of having friends around:

'I would sit down and talk to people and they would invite me to come and see their house. That would be a mistake to me, I shouldn't have, because when you go to their house you know how different you are living. And I think what kills it, you can't invite, you don't want to invite them to your house, never, you'd be scared ... they're definitely gunna jump up this is not normal, yea I know the violence part, you never know what the next day people are going to say, so you don't want them in your house.'

This passage shows the anxiety that Eric felt around socializing with his peers in his parental home. It clearly conveys the way in which the men's childhood homes were places which they were left uncomfortable to occupy, to dwell in, because of the DVA. What these excerpts also outline is the way in which the men were still living in their parental homes at these points; however, the process of homelessness was underway, as their home failed to have the markers of safety and comfort, a place where they liked to dwell. The dynamic had shifted, and they were at the point where the road was offering a more attractive place to dwell and affiliate.

On-road as a space for resistance

Several of the participants talked about the transition between home and on-road. Men constructed this process differently in their narratives according to whether they conceived it as a transition they made due to being pushed or pulled. Some men emphasized grooming that they underwent to join a gang, whereas others were at pains to show their agency. The discursive approach taken tied into the men's wider narratives and how they positioned themselves in their narratives. It is pertinent to explore how the men constructed the relationship between the home and the road. Could it be that the road is actually more predictable or controllable than the domestic environment? That the 'code of the street' is more knowable than a volatile and abusive situation at home? That the benefits for men residing (as a headspace and an actual space) in the public sphere is that it is more like 'home' – despite it being a complete inversion of what 'home' generally means? Perhaps 'domestic violence' as in 'violence in the home' is in itself a paradox – that once it occurs the home has gone. Sam told me: "Abused, hurt, broken, not heard, crying out, crying out, crying out, not heard, not heard not heard, and when someone's not heard they rebel, so wasn't heard and then I rebelled and run to the streets."

As outlined in the previous section, there was a sense among all of the participants that home was no longer a safe place and so they sought opportunities to be outside of their parental home as much as possible. Although as can be seen here, whereas Dylan earlier framed his experiences of going on-road as due to him 'grooming himself', Sam described it more as a rebellion, that he was actively running away from his home. Jordan also talked about being made physically homeless as a young person, although he framed it as a shift to independence.

The connection between domestic violence happening at home and going to the street as a way to avoid it was a connection made by many of the men I spoke to. The most prevalent theme was that going to the streets was a form of escape from a violent, uncomfortable or dangerous home environment. Several expressed that it began as a case of trying to get out of the house as much as possible, which led them to the make initial contact with people who then became the gang. Some participants perceived that they were groomed by an existing gang, whereas others viewed the group of friends evolving into the gang as they grew older together. Creating alternative spaces away from home where there is violence present is a known coping strategy for children living with DVA (Mullender et al, 2002). The group dynamic of the on-road space was heavily implicated in gang-involvement for the men that I spoke to. As outlined earlier, being on-road is a broader physical and mental state than the gang alone, yet the collective attributes of a gang offered the men a supportive group when they were younger. It is important to note here, however, that for many of the participants, when looking at this in retrospect it did not necessarily fill that gap; however, at the time this was the function participants felt that being on-road was providing.

Dylan described his emerging engagement on-road, and with the peer group that would later become his gang peers. They initially sought each other to create an alternative family on the streets, who understood each other's circumstances as many were also experiencing DVA at home: "A lot of my friends was going through the same thing and that's why we congregated and we kinda like a family on the streets, and we pledged allegiances and we, do you know, and that's how it stayed for years and years to come."

A common explanation of a motivator for gang-involvement is the construction of an alternative family. In Glynn's (2014) research on young gang-involved men he found that father-absence was a reoccurring theme that, along with low self-esteem, impacted on their pursuit of gang life. This was a trend I also saw in my own research, with several participants citing the desire to create a supportive family life outside of home as a key driver.

As Sam's power and capital increased on the streets, so did his own sense of agency. Sam tried to invert his feeling of rejection from his parental home by reclaiming the streets and prison as home instead. He created a resistance narrative this way, which links back to Tamboukou's concept of technologies of space used in resistance:

'I created my new home, my road mentality, I was a roadman, I was the biggest roadman you'd ever know in my life, literally I slept on the road, like, the road ... like when she said come home, that showed it, like what? I am home like, get really defensive about it. I couldn't leave it, it's just my life.'

By naming the streets as his home, Sam claimed back a sense of agency and power over public space. He also discussed doing the same when he was incarcerated in prison:

'I was in prison, like the Govs [Prison Governors] they got scared of me because I'm telling them when I argue, or not even argue when I shout or get aggressive I'm telling them this is my home I've been here longer than you, this is where I live, so they don't know what to do with me, most people want to get out and I'm like I'm home, and they are like what are you talking about, I was bad in jail, I was not, I was not right in my head.'

Bringing this back to the notion of technologies of space, here Sam is creating a sense of ownership over the spaces that initially were sources of oppression. In the narratives about his childhood, the street was the place he ran to out of desperation to leave his family home. In the passages quoted here, Sam is conveying ownership of the street. Similarly, he talks of his experience unsettling and scaring the prison staff when he claimed that the prison also constituted a home, as he was reclaiming power and agency within a punitive system designed to discipline him.

Power operated from all angles in Sam's narrative. He had experience of institutional power systems, through prison, experience with corrupt police, and time spent in a mental health institution. Sam's journey through these systems showed experiences of being both subject to the external power but also resisting it, through identifying prison as his home. As his narrative progressed, there was a point where he started to invert the power structures against him by claiming the prison and the road were his homes. These were interesting examples of how the technologies of space played out, as throughout Sam's story there was no real space that he could call his own outside of the public and institutional spaces of prison and the road. In terms of technologies of self at work here, Sam began his narrative strongly referring to himself as a victim of multiple oppressive experiences; of family violence, of drug dealers grooming him, of sexual exploitation. Then at the point at which he became more involved in the gang he changed to tell a story of his own power, articulated through the masculinized concept of being 'the man' in the gang. It was at this point in the story where he constructed his lack of care for himself as an active choice that he had made in response to his circumstances.

Conclusion

The shift from dwelling in the parental home to dwelling on-road is a change that occurred in a subtle way, mainly because the men were often still living in their childhood homes when the transition was taking place. The spatial shift that has been described in this chapter was as much about mentality as it was physicality, in particular the transference of loyalties that took place when the men started to make a sense of home on the road. These two contrasting fields illustrate the challenge with how to conceptualize 'home' at all. Although where the men's family lived seemed like home, as in a four-walled living space, the sense of being *at* home there was lost, along with the loss of safety, when DVA was present. Inherent in this shift is the move between private to public space. The road then, with its risks and lack of security, offered something to the men that they were drawn to. In between these shifts in dwelling, school was an in-between space, which served to contextualize the men's experiences as different from the norm through their comparison with their peers. For some men, their engagement in school as a coping strategy, both through full participation, or as a space to enact violence, framed as a method of conveying and releasing anger.

Through this process, discourses of masculinity also changed through space. The participants suggested they were emasculated at home, and in some cases being abused themselves. They conveyed a sense of how all-encompassing the environment of living with abuse was, so much so they changed their lives to stay out of home as long as possible. The notion of disaffiliation, as part of the 'process of homelessness', is useful here, as it provides a conceptual understanding of the ways in which the men changed their loyalties from their family within the domestic space, to their peers in the public space.

Ultimately, the men shifted between different spatial contexts both through their natural progression through the life-course, moving from private family space to wider public space, but also as a way to enact resistance from their circumstances. The road was a localized, viable option that afforded them opportunities to use their own agency in a way that was not available in the abusive household. Men conceptualized this shift in varying ways, often looking back on it in a belittling way, but at the time it offered them the chance to affiliate with an alternative community as a way to satisfy their need for support and for a type of love. Through a gendered spatial lens, the changes in dwelling are more understandable and nuanced than has been seen in previous research on this topic. Focusing on the way that young men who are abused cope and use the opportunities of the road to survive is important in understanding how to support men who are on the trajectory to youth offending through this risky form of locale.

References

Arthur, R. (2007) *Family Life and Youth Offending: Home Is Where the Hurt Is*, Abingdon: Routledge.

Connell, R.W. (2005) *Masculinities* (2nd edn), Cambridge: Polity Press.

Earle, R. (2011) 'Boys' zone stories: perspectives from a young men's prison', *Criminology & Criminal Justice*, 11(2): 129–143.

Glynn, M. (2014) *Black Men, Invisibility and Crime*, Abingdon: Routledge.

Gunter, A. (2010) *Growing Up Bad? Black Youth, 'Road' Culture and Badness in an East London Neighbourhood*, London: Tufnell Press.

Kielar, S. (2016) 'Hiraeth', Penn State Word of the Week, 2 April. Available from: https://sites.psu.edu/kielarpassionblog2/2016/04/02/hiraeth/ [Accessed 8 December 2020].

Levell, J. (2019) '"Those songs were the ones that made me, nobody asked me this question before": music elicitation with ex-gang involved men about their experiences of childhood domestic violence and abuse', *International Journal of Qualitative Methods*, 18. Available from: https://doi.org/10.1177/1609406919852010 [Accessed 16 April 2022].

Morris, A. (2009) 'Gendered dynamics of abuse and violence in families: considering the abusive household gender regime', *Child Abuse Review*, 18(6): 414–427.

Mullender, A., Hague, G., Imam, U., Kelly, L., Malos, E. and Regan, L. (2002) *Children's Perspectives on Domestic Violence*, London: Sage.

Nilson, H. (1998) *Michel Foucault and the Games of Truth*, Basingstoke: Macmillan.

Passaro, J. (1996) *The Unequal Homeless: Men on the Streets, Women in Their Place*, Abingdon: Routledge.

Petro, P. (2012) 'Dreaming in Welsh', *The Paris Review*, 18 September. Available from: https://www.theparisreview.org/blog/2012/09/18/dreaming-in-welsh/ [Accessed 8 December 2020].

Riessman, C.K. (2008) *Narrative Methods for the Human Sciences*, Thousand Oaks, CA: Sage.

Tamboukou, M. (1999) 'Spacing herself: women in education', *Gender and Education*, 11(2): 125–139.

Tamboukou, M. (2013) 'A Foucauldian approach to narratives', in M. Andrews, C. Squire and M. Tamboukou (eds) *Doing Narrative Research* (2nd edn), London: Sage, pp 88–107.

Young, T. (2016) *Risky Youth or Gang Members? A Contextual Critique of the (Re)discovery of Gangs in Britain*, London: London Metropolitan University.

Young, T. and Hallsworth, S. (2011) 'Young People, gangs and street-based violence', in C. Barter and D. Berridge (eds), *Children Behaving Badly? Peer Violence Between Children and Young People*, Chichester: Wiley-Blackwell.

4

Using Community Asset Mapping to Understand Neighbourhood-Level Variation in the Predictors of Domestic Abuse

Ruth Weir

Introduction

Understanding and reducing domestic abuse has become an issue of priority for both local and national governments in the UK, with its substantial human, social and economic costs. To date the focus of research in the UK has been on individual-level risk factors of abuse, where variables such as age, gender, ethnicity and repeat victimization have been considered. There have been substantially fewer studies that have considered the geographic variation of abuse and predictors at the neighbourhood level. A recent systemic review of neighbourhood studies of interpersonal violence found that most research was carried out in urban areas in the US, with no research from the UK (Beyer et al, 2015), and the only study from Europe focused on Spain (Gracia et al, 2014).

Although other agencies, such as the National Health Service (NHS), may record some information on domestic abuse, the data is often collected for other purposes, and sharing of data between agencies is an exception, rather than common practice. In the absence of a multi-agency approach the commissioning of services is often therefore reliant on the fifth of incidents that we do know about through police reporting (ONS, 2016). Assumptions have to be made that the victims who do not report their abuse to police are the same in profile as those who do report and that their service needs are the same, which is a significant limitation given the extent of under-reporting.

This chapter explores the variation in reported domestic abuse at the neighbourhood level, drawing upon data from a wider research study that used a mixed method interdisciplinary approach, combining quantitative and qualitative geographic methods with social theory (Weir, 2019). The first stage of the research used spatial statistics to model the predictors of domestic abuse at the lower super output area (LSOA), which have a population of approximately 1,500 people. It was found that police reported that domestic abuse can be predicted accurately at the neighbourhood level using structural and cultural variables from Sampson and Groves's (1989) revised social disorganization theory, which found that community disadvantage, heterogeneity and the turnover of the population affect the ties and social networks that are necessary for effective social control, an idea that drew on the work of Kasarda and Janowitz (1974). The explanatory variables; antisocial behaviour rate; proportion of Black, Asian and minoritized communities;[1] population density and the income scores from the Index of Multiple Deprivation were found to explain 82 per cent of the variation in the data (Weir, 2019).

While exogenous variables, such as income, were good predictors of a social gradient (Gibson and Asthana, 2000), the causal link to other variables, such as the level of antisocial behaviour in an area, could not be confirmed by the model. It has been argued that crime and disorder manifest themselves when neighbourhoods lack colletive efficacy (Sampson and Raudenbush, 1999). Rather than focusing on the individual, where strong personal ties and relationships are needed for self-efficacy, the theory of collective efficacy finds that the local community acts as an essential ingredient to achieving social good and control that will benefit everyone, with neighbours demonstrating trust and a willingness to intervene (Bandara, 1997; Sampson et al, 1997; Sampson, 2003). There has, however, also been research that has found that high levels of collective efficacy in rural areas may produce behaviour that ignores or even encourages domestic abuse (DeKeseredy, Chapter 6, this volume; DeKeseredy and Schwartz, 2009).

Another related concept that the model was unable to measure was social capital. Putnam (2000) explored the multiple dimensions of social capital, but argued that perhaps the most important element is the distinction between bridging and bonding social capital. Bonding social capital reinforces the exclusive identity of homegenous groups (such as church-based women's reading groups), whereas bridging social capital is outward looking, fostering inclusive identities across social groups (such as youth service groups) (Putnam, 2000). It is therefore possible that endogenous or neighbourhood effects could be at work and this needs to be explored further in order to formulate appropriate policy responses (Dietz, 2002; Mohan, 2003). As such, there is a need to work out how to distinguish between neighbourhoods that have higher or lower levels of domestic abuse despite their circumstances and those that have higher or lower level of abuse because of their circumstances.

Without survey data (which is not available at this level of geography) the concepts of collective efficacy and social capital are very difficult to measure using quantitative methods. What is needed is a methodology to explore collective efficacy within the neighbourhoods of interest. One potential way to capture all of this information is through an assessment of community assets within and that serve the neighbourhood. Before discussing the method it is useful to explain how community asset mapping (CAM), a relatively recent development, has come about and what it might offer in addition to existing methodologies.

Community asset mapping

Much of the focus in social work and related disciplines for the last century has been in the labelling and treatment of social problems (Langer and Lietz, 2015). While it was argued that organizations need to know what they are doing wrong in order to change their practices, criticism of the overly negative and problem-oriented approach led to the development of Asset Based Community Developed (ABCD) in the 1990s (Kretzmann and McKnight, 1993; Altschuld, 2015). ABCD is a strengths-based approach to community development that looks at postitive elements in communities by documenting both the tangible and intangible assets (Mathie et al, 2017). It aims to link micro-level assets to the macro-level environment (Rowland, 2008) to ascertain the positive impact that they have on a group of people (Altschuld, 2015). The approach was pioneered by Kretzmann and McKnight (1993) who set out three groups of assets: individuals, associations and institutions. Figure 4.1 shows the types of assets in each of these groups. Rowland (2008) also extended Kretzmann and McKnight's groups to include phyical assets and connections, identifying the importance of treating relationships as being a particulary valuable asset in measuring the concept of social capital.

While the ABCD approach was successful in harnessing the strengths of a community, it was argued that needs should still be assessed (Hansen, 1991). A potential solution came in 2000, when a hybrid approach combining the needs assessment with asset-based approaches was introduced (Altschuld, 2015). However, in times of austerity many government agencies in the UK, such as the NHS and local government, have adopted a commissioning-based approach to service delivery, and the commissioning cycle is still based on assessing need rather than strengths, and translating risk into policy (Walklate and Mythen, 2011).

The needs assessment has tradionally used more quantitative methods to assess the problems in communities through 'hard' data and surveys, whereas the asset-based approaches have drawn on qualitative measures, such as

Figure 4.1: Types of assets within the community

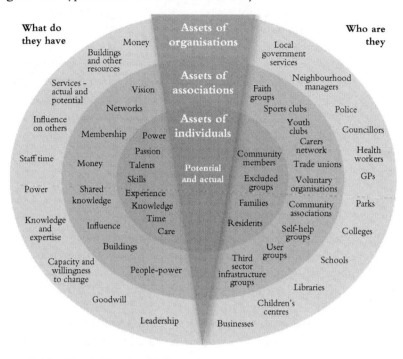

Source: Brighter Futures Together, 2017

interviews and focus groups. One of the methodologies to come out of ABCD has been CAM.

CAM is a process where 'participants make a map or inventory of resources, skills and talents of individuals, associations and organisations' (Brighter Futures Together, 2017). As a methodology CAM has been used by local communities and local agencies, but it has only rarely been employed in academic research or taught as a research method (Goldman and Schmalz, 2005; Lightfoot et al, 2014; Green et al, 2017; South et al, 2017). The methodology has been used most widely in the US, but there has been recent evidence of its use by local government and intiatives in the UK (Glasgow City Council, 2013; Preston City Council, 2016; Brighter Futures Together, 2017; Waverley Borough Council, 2017).

Existing research that uses CAM to understand neighbourhood-level domestic abuse has not been identified, but Altschuld (2015) discussed the importance of the metholodogy in assessing existing assets to measure what a community already has and to leverage this to reduce crime. Ennis and West (2010) articulated concern that a strengths-based approach is only internal looking, and to really understand the structure of society an approach is needed that looks externally as well. Giddens' (1984) theory of structuration states that structure and action are related to one another, with societies, communitnies and groups only having structure because people behave in a fairly predictable way. Converserly, action or 'agency' only exists because individually we have a large amount of socially structured knowledge. Therefore to consider both structure and agency analysis needs to also look externally to the role of assets at the macro level. To overcome some of these concerns this research therefore adopted a hybrid approach by using the existing assessment of community need, the quantitative predictive model, to identify areas that either fit the model, or over- or under-predict the amount of abuse in an area. A CAM exercise has then been conducted in a sample of these areas. Due to the exploratory nature of the CAM exercise there were no set research questions, but a broader aim to identify the assets and strengths in the neighbourhoods and to investigate whether collective efficacy plays a part in the amount of abuse that is reported to the police.

Methodology

The study area

Essex is a large police force in the East of England made up of the county of Essex and the unitary authorities of Southend and Thurrock. The force area has a population of 1.725 million. It is one of the largest non-metropolitan forces in the UK. The location has a mixture of rural, urban and coastal areas with concentrated deprivation but also some very affluent areas. In 2016, it had a total crime rate of 66.0 per 1,000 population (compared to an average of 71.9 across England and Wales), and ranked 23rd out of the 43 police forces in England and Wales (Flatley, 2017).

Neighbourhood definition

Using LSOAs to define neighbourhoods is not ideal and the areas rarely reflect the true way in which residents would visualize their community. The areas were designed for a different purpose, administering the census, so boundaries cut through neighbourhoods and can be quite large in rural areas (Dietz, 2002). However, for the purposes of this research (and in other published studies) they are the lowest level of geography that is available for modelling the other data sets that act as important predictors. The method was useful for identifying areas to visit, but flexibility was built in by looking at assets outside the LSOA boundary but focusing on those that the residents who lived in the neighbourhood would use.

Table 4.1 lists the ten areas that were selected, four were LSOAs where the neighbourhood model accurately predicted the amount of police recorded domestic abuse, three where it under predicted, and three where it over predicted. LSOAs were selected using the standardized residuals,[2] with those

Table 4.1: Lower super output areas selected for community asset mapping with summary statistics, 2011–2014

Prediction	LSOA code	Town	Standardized residual	Number of incidents
Under	E01021277	Laindon	1.98	125
	E01022093	Thaxted	2.26	71
	E01021708	Colchester	2.60	74
Accurate	E01021596	Chelmsford	−0.30	181
	E01021592	Chelmsford	−0.008	191
	E01022082	Saffron Walden	−0.016	37
	E01033722	Colchester	−0.023	140
Over	E01015896	Southend	−1.73	198
	E01022025	Clacton	−1.88	536
	E01021995	Frinton	−2.91	11

Source: Statistics from Essex Police domestic abuse incidents dated November 2011 to December 2014

with high and low values and those close to zero stratified by the volume of incidents (between November 2011 and December 2014), with areas with a range of volumes selected. Figure 4.2 shows the geographical distribution of the CAM areas.

Local gatekeepers were identified by drawing on existing contacts and searching for suitable members of the community, such as those who ran community centres or local agencies. The criteria were someone who had a good knowledge of the particular neighbourhood and who was willing to spend at least two hours walking (or driving in more dispersed areas) around the neighbourhood. If no response was received or there was difficulty in finding someone, another neighbourhood with a similar standardized residual and volume of domestic abuse was found. Interviewees included community centre chairs, a social work student, a council employee and a housing manager. Before each visit a map of the area was sent to the interviewee with a copy of Figure 4.1. They were asked to think about assets that residents who lived in the LSOA would use. The assets did not have to be within the LSOA, but ones that residents might use. For the purposes of this research, assets were defined as associations or organizations that local residents might use or engage with.

Defining the information to be collected

A survey was designed in Survey123 for ArcGIS and completed in an iPhone app, which recorded information about the asset and its location.

Figure 4.2: Map of locations for community asset mapping visits

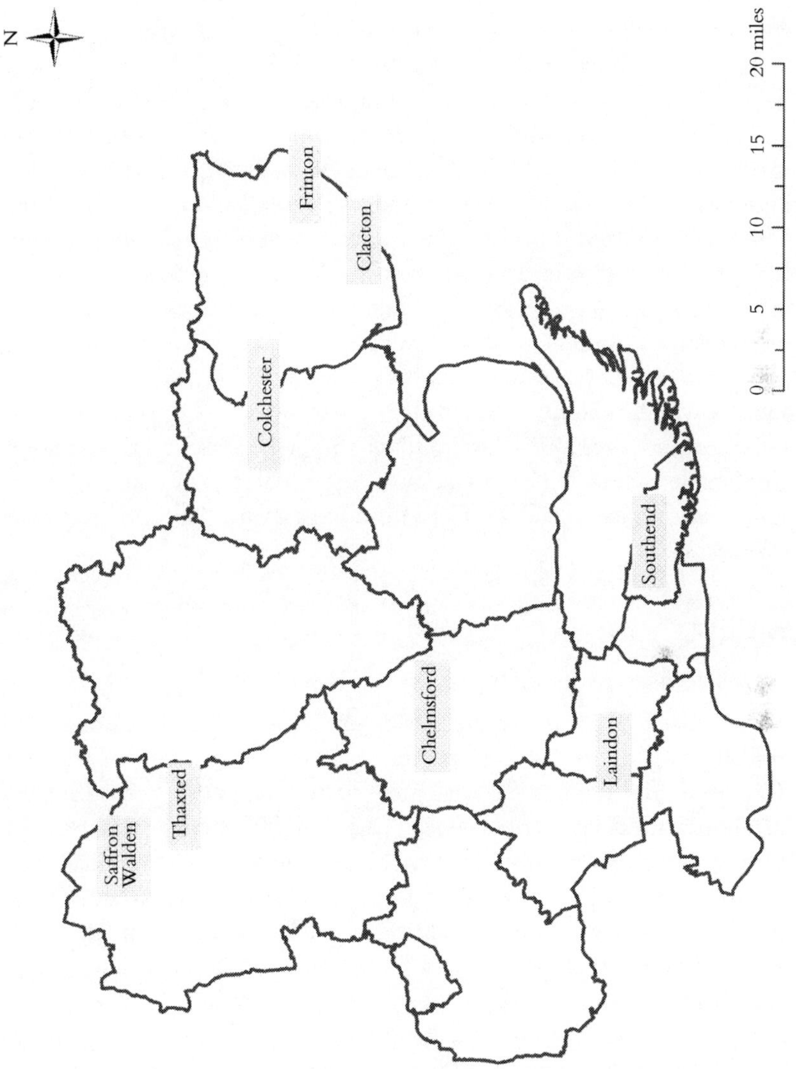

A photograph could also be taken at each location. Each asset mapping exercise started with an interview, where the purpose of the research and visit was explained to the interviewee. The interviewee was asked about their role in the community, how long they had known the area for, whether they worked or lived in the area and any other relevant connections that they had. The interviewee was then asked to guide me around the area and, if necessary, I prompted them to speak about particular assets that might be relevant, such as churches, community centres, third-sector agencies and informal groups. If the asset was open and it was appropriate, we went inside and tried to speak to a member of staff to gain more information about the service that the asset provided. I explained that while my research was on unreported domestic abuse, I was keen to learn about the positive assets in the community, rather than just focusing on need. If the situation arose and it was appropriate (not if clients were present) I asked where they would refer victims who disclosed abuse. Any leaflet or material available about the assets was also collected and details of any additional materials, such as websites were recorded. If the asset was closed, then any available information was recorded and follow up internet searches or telephone calls were made to find out more about the asset. After each visit I uploaded the survey information to ArcGIS to produce a map of all the assets from the selected areas.

Results

Neighbourhood composition

The size and structure of the settlement did seem to influence both the availability of assets and the amount of collective efficacy that was evident. To explore this further, the visit areas were categorized according to Lee's neighbourhood typology (1968). Lee stated that neighbourhoods with clear, well-defined boundaries have higher levels of social participation. His research found that regardless of density most people regarded their home area as one that was approximately 100 acres. This finding was attributed to the distance that people would be prepared to walk. Three types of neighbourhoods were included in Lee's typology, these were the unit, acquaintance and homogenous neighbourhood. The unit neighbourhood has the largest area, with residents having a number of friends scattered over a wide area meaning they are less dependent on those in the nearest streets. These neighbourhoods are heterogeneous in both the make-up of the population and the type of housing. On the other hand, the social acquaintance neighbourhoods are smaller in physical area, with around six streets and, with the exception of a few corner shops and pubs, comprised only houses. People living in these neighbourhoods form acquaintances with their neighbours, rather than friendships. Their sources of security and social control come from their families. The final type of area is the homogenous neighbourhood. These areas are largely made up of lower-middle-class and upper-working-class families. The people in these areas are similar in their outlook and in the type of housing and the area is defined by the size of the similar population. The type of social control exerted by these neighbours is mutual awareness, which is largely cognitive without overt interaction taking place (Lee, 1968).

Unit neighbourhoods

One of the best examples of a unit neighbourhood was Saffron Walden (Box 4.1), with a heterogeneous population and a balanced range of amenities. Most of the assets were found in the town centre and only a few were in the study area LSOA, so the town comes together to share these assets. As shown in Table 4.2 the level of reported domestic abuse in the LSOA I visited was accurately predicted by the model.

Box 4.1: Saffron Walden

Saffron Walden, an affluent town in Uttlesford, has a population of 15,000 and the former town planner who showed me around the area had been involved in the Market Town Health Check. She suggested that this was an optimal size for a settlement, with one secondary school and a feeling of community created by multiple interlocking social circles. She believed that generally people would know a lot of other people in the town. There were a wide range of assets within the town centre, but very few in the LSOA that I was focusing on. The interviewee thought that the town size would make it easy for residents to travel into the town centre to access assets and shops, so it was logical for the assets to be located there. There were a wide range of support services with the Citizen's Advice Bureau, churches, voluntary organizations and associations. She said that many of the voluntary services have a waiting list of people willing to help.

Thaxted also fits the unit neighbourhood typology, but is much smaller than Saffron Walden, with only two LSOAs and a population of under 3,000. The smaller population size and rural nature meant that the range of amenities available within the town are more limited. The lack of suitable services for victims is an issue also raised in research commissioned by the National Federation of Women's Institutes finding that while women in rural and urban areas are equally as likely to experience abuse, those in rural areas identified a lack of relevant services for those experiencing domestic abuse, particularly non-violent coercive control. They also expressed concern

Table 4.2: Lower super output areas categorized by neighbourhood type and model fit

Model fit	Unit neighbourhood	Acquaintance neighbourhood	Homogenous neighbourhood
Over-predicted	Frinton	Southend Clacton	—
Accurately predicted	Saffron Walden	—	Melbourne, Chelmsford Greenstead, Colchester
Under-predicted	Thaxted	Laindon Welshwood, Colchester	—

Source: Author

over being able to confidentially disclose and GPs were found to play a particularly important support role (McCarry and Williamson, 2009), which unfortunately was not a source of data available to analyse in this research.

The amount of domestic abuse reported to the police was higher than predicted by the model in Thaxted, a finding inconsistent with other research (Chakraborti and Garland, 2003; Squire and Gill, 2011), who proposed that under-reporting could be higher and an invisible problem in rural areas. One explanation could be that under-reporting is still high, but whereas areas with multiple services have more options for victims to choose to disclose to, rural victims have nowhere else to report apart from the police and GPs, which could increase the proportion that are disclosing to these agencies.

Another issue of being a small rural unit neighbourhood is that an ecological fallacy (Robinson, 1950) is created by aggregating people into census areas. Weir (2019) found that those with lower incomes are more likely to report domestic abuse to the police. The CAM exercise has generally found that there are a wide range of services in more deprived areas. However, aggregating people into census areas means that those with lower incomes living in generally affluent areas may not have access to the same services as they would if they lived in a homogenously deprived area. Thaxted is generally affluent with an average house price of £415,749 (Rightmove, 2017), which is considerably higher that the UK average house prices, which was £227,000 in 2017 (ONS, 2017). This has led to a big divide between those who can and cannot afford to buy a house in the area. Figure 4.3 illustrates the difference in housing types within the town and the issues created by trying to provide services to a diverse population in a small rural area.

Homogenous neighbourhoods

Chelmsford is the only city in Essex and Melbourne, a neighbourhood within the city, demonstrated strong social capital. Melbourne also fitted closely

Figure 4.3: Thaxted

Source: Author

with Gans's (1962) idea of an urban village, a concept still used in planning today that advocates sustainable, well-designed urban areas, with a sense of place and community (Aldous,1992; Franklin and Tait, 2002; Zarei et al, 2018). The area is long established and the housing manager who showed me around described it as an area where you either stay all your life or you leave (usually after finishing school), therefore demonstrating personal, occupational and residential immobility (for those who stayed), a factor Gans said increased both kinship (through vertical bonds) and friendship (through horizontal bonds). The interviewee said that people did not tend to travel into the area from outside and residents did not travel far out either. The area fits the homogenous neighbourhood typology. With a lot of ex-local authority housing stock, not only are people from similar backgrounds but they also live in similar types of housing (Lee, 1968; Blowers, 1973).

Acquaintance neighbourhoods

Interestingly, the acquaintance neighbourhoods were found in both affluent and deprived areas. An example of this was the LSOA area to the north of Greenstead, which is divided into a small affluent estate and a more deprived estate, neither with many of their own assets, and the interviewee doubted whether the residents of the affluent estate would visit assets in Greenstead. The areas did not demonstrate the community spirit that was visible in the unit and homogenous neighbourhoods. Higher levels of domestic abuse were reported to the police in this area than were predicted by the model, perhaps indicating that residents had fewer places to disclose, increasing the proportion of police reporting.

Collective efficacy and social capital

There were two areas where collective efficacy was visibly lacking. One was Laindon, a 1960s new town and the other the coastal town of Clacton. The town centre in Laindon was quiet and deserted. There is a community hub, but it was shut on the day of the visit. The shopping precinct was suffering from concrete cancer, which is the deterioration of the concrete from exposure to air and water. While there were a number of assets, such as churches, they were closed on the day of the CAM exercise.

In Clacton the interviewee, a local resident, described how the area suffers from multiple issues:

'The town suffers from a lack of facilities to occupy younger residents, with its coastal location and distant proximity to other towns, meaning that young people become disengaged, leading to antisocial behaviour and drug and alcohol issues. The town centre does not have shops that would attract people into the area. I have lived in Clacton for five years, having previously lived in East London. I have tried to engage with the council and CVS to organize events, such as a beach party, but my enthusiasm had not been appreciated and I get the impression that they don't want to do more than they have to. The area lacks the community spirit of my previous neighbourhood, and a lot of people feel isolated, particularly those who were new to the area.'

While both Laindon and Clacton had reduced collective efficacy, the levels of reported domestic abuse compared to predicted abuse showed different patterns. In Laindon more abuse than predicted was reported to the police, whereas Clacton had less abuse reported than predicted. An explanation for higher reporting in Laindon could be that the lack of identifiable and accessible assets led to a smaller number of disclosure options, which would mean a higher proportion of abuse is reported to the police. Clacton, however, had a number of different options for reporting, although the interviewee felt that the awareness of the services was not high. The interviewee described how the population suffers from isolation, mistrust and multiple social issues, which may have prevented people from strong place attachment, with strong place attachment a factor that can prevent people from moving (Lyons and Lowery, 1989). Livingston et al (2010), however, found that improved material or environmental circumstances had a more significant influence on residents moving than attachment. This residential sorting and selective mobility may lead to the creation of areas of concentrated disadvantage, which suffer from multiple social issues (Galster, 2011; Permentier et al, 2011). It may be that the higher level of residential mobility in Clacton and the resultant reduction in collective efficacy has reduced the amount of help that is sought from the range of agencies that are available. This would concur with previous studies (Kasarda and Janowitz, 1974; Sampson et al, 1997; Browning, 2002). Strong social capital, collective action, strong support services, mixed tenure and neighbourhood management have been found to act as protective factors (Lupton and Power, 2002), which would offer an explanation for why the other deprived areas in this study are not all faced with the same level of issues that Clacton has.

In other areas collective efficacy was evident in certain parts of the population, such as older affluent residents in Thaxted, but whether the impact is felt across the population and the life course of individuals was difficult to ascertain. There were particular groups that had higher levels of residential mobility and low engagement. It could be that Putnam's idea of bonding social values, that are built around group homogeneity, are more evident in the affluent population, but less so in those living in the deprived parts of the town (Putnam, 1993). However, there was evidence of bridging social values, an example of which is a recently published book, *Thaxted's People*, which gives a biography of a cross-section of the population though photographs and captions (Griffen, 2017). The book demonstrates a community spirit across social classes. However, they were all members of the community who had lived in Thaxted for several years. Perhaps again the residential mobility component of collective efficacy offers a better explanation, with more transient members of the population failing to integrate into the community and feeling the effects of poverty more than those who have been established for many years (Sampson and Lauritson, 1994). In order to examine the impact of these factors further, it would be helpful to stratify the population by age and other variables, such as their stage in the life course (Völker et al, 2013).

An area that demonstrated the highest levels of collective efficacy and social capital was Saffron Walden. The town has a large number of organizations and agencies and had waiting lists for people wanting to volunteer at organizations such as the foodbank. After the film *I, Daniel Blake* was shown at a local screening in the town over £1,000 was donated to the foodbank. Putnam (2000) described how the areas that gain the most social capital tend to be the areas that are not the most in need, and Saffron Walden is a good example of this. The area already has economic and human capital, whereas areas like Clacton, which have neither, would particularly benefit from increased social capital. Putnam's work has been critiqued on the basis that while he describes the symptoms of low social capital, he does not provide a plan of treatment (Crothers, 2002). In policy terms this is an issue that needs to be addressed and research conducted into what conditions cause social capital to change. It is clear that residential mobility is one factor that needs to be considered.

Discussion

Overall, using CAM as part of a hybrid approach to understanding variations in police reporting has been extremely insightful and has identified a number of agencies that would never had been considered using a needs-based approach. Visiting areas and looking to a community's strengths has enabled a fuller understanding of the dynamics that impact where people will seek help, the importance of social capital and collective efficacy, spatial variation, neighbourhood composition and the varying needs of different populations. The CAM exercise has highlighted that using only police data to resource and commission services will lead to insufficient funding in areas where referral to other agencies is actively encouraged. This does not mean that victims should be encouraged to report to the police instead, but rather that a multi-agency approach to data collection is needed.

Visiting ten different areas identified a lot of variation in types of neighbourhoods, levels of cohesion and multiple issues that may potentially contribute towards the level of abuse. In turn, this has highlighted that it can be productive to concentrate on the neighbourhood level in tackling the many different facets that influence abuse. Future research and policy should consider different spatial scales, and the features of spaces, in developing responses to domestic abuse.

There was only a limited amount of time to visit each neighbourhood, so not all of the assets were open, and a different impression may have been created had the visit taken place on another day. There was only one interviewee in each area, and they may have had their own bias. Everyone had a different role in the community, with differing levels of exposure to the assets in the area. In some areas, more information was collected by looking at leaflets and promotional material, making it difficult to assess how influential the asset might be to different members of the community, whereas in other areas there was direct contact with those providing services and support. A CAM exercise in a true ABCD definition would involve a group of community members and would be conducted by people who knew the area well. The methodology has been adapted for a sole researcher, but nonetheless offers a new and unique understanding of domestic abuse.

Conclusion

The biggest challenge now is for policy makers. Identifying areas where social capital is lacking is more straightforward than attempting to generate it. There is also the issue of accountability: who is responsible for taking this forward? Is it the local community, local organizations or statutory agencies? Mathie and Cunningham (2003) question whether communities need to learn to survive rather than challenging the economic system. This leads to the challenging point of how communities can protect themselves from the external factors, such as the 'Westminster effects', which research has found to disproportionately affect poorer communities (Beatty and Fothergill, 2016; Crossley, 2017: 54), and have been argued to have the strongest effect, both symbolically and materially (Crossley, 2017).

Notes

[1] It should be noted that the proportion of Black, Asian and minoritized communities in the population was included in the model as it was one of the original variables in social disorganization theory. Black, Asian and minoritized communities are explanatory in relation to the extent of abuse due to systematic discrimination and oppression rather than being viewed as being problematic.

[2] The standardized residual is the measure of strength of the difference between an observed value and a predicted value in a regression model.

References

Aldous, T. (1992) *Urban Villages: A Concept for Creating Mixed-use Urban Developments on a Sustainable Scale*, Sutton Coldfield: Urban Villages Group.

Altschuld, J.W. (2015) *Bridging the Gap Between Asset/Capacity Building and Needs Assessments*, London: Sage.

Bandara, A. (1997) *Self-Efficacy: The Exercise of Control*, New York: W.H. Freeman.

Beatty, C. and Fothergill, S. (2016) *The Uneven Impact of Welfare Reform: The Financial Losses to Places and People*, Project Report, Sheffield: Sheffield Hallam University Centre for Regional Economic and Social Research.

Beyer, K., Wallis, A.B. and Hamberger, L.K. (2015) 'Neighborhood environment and intimate partner violence: a systematic review', *Trauma, Violence, and Abuse*, 16(1): 16–47.

Blowers, A. (1973) 'The neighbourhood: exploration of a concept', in H. Brown, A. Blowers, C. Hamnett and D. Boswell (eds) *The City as a Social System*, Milton Keynes: Open University Press, pp 49–90.

Brighter Futures Together (2017) *Map Assets in Your Community*. Available from: http://www.brighterfuturestogether.co.uk/wp-content/uploads/2012/03/fact-sheet-map-assets-in-your-community.pdf [Accessed 25 January 2017].

Browning, C.R. (2002) 'The span of collective efficacy: extending social disorganization to theory to partner violence', *Journal of Marriage and Family*, 64(4): 833–850.

Chakraborti, N. and Garland, J. (2003) 'An "invisible" problem? Uncovering the nature of racial victimisation in rural Suffolk', *International Review of Victimology*, 10(1): 1–17.

Crossley, S. (2017) *In Their Place: The Imagined Geographies of Poverty*, London: Pluto Press.

Crothers, L. (2002) 'Building social capital on the street', in S.L. McLean, D.A. Schultz and M.B. Steger (eds) *Social Capital: Critical Perspectives on Community and 'Bowling Alone'*, New York: New York University Press, pp 218–237.

DeKeseredy, W.S. and Schwartz, M.D. (2009) *Dangerous Exits: Escaping Abusive Relationships in Rural America*, New Brunswick, NJ: Rutgers University Press.

Dietz, R.D. (2002) 'The estimation of neighborhood effects in the social sciences: an interdisciplinary approach', *Social Science Research*, 31(4): 539–575.

Ennis, G. and West, D. (2010) 'Exploring the potential of social network analysis in asset-based community development practice and research', *Australian Social Work*, 63(4): 404–417.

Flatley, J. (2017) *Crime in England and Wales: Police Force Area Data Tables*. Available from: https://www.ons.gov.uk/peoplepopulationandcommunity/crimeandjustice/datasets/policeforceareadatatables [Accessed 4 May 2022].

Franklin, B. and Tait, M. (2002) 'Constructing an image: the urban village concept in the UK', *Planning Theory*, 1(3): 250–272.

Galster, G.C. (2012) 'The mechanism (s) of neighbourhood effects: theory, evidence, and policy implications', in M. van Ham, D. Manley, N. Bailey, L. Simpson and D. Maclennan (eds) *Neighbourhood Effects Research: New Perspectives*, Dordrecht: Springer, pp. 23–56.

Gans, H.J. (1962) *The Urban Villagers: Group and Class in the Life of Italian-Americans*, New York: Free Press of Glencoe.

Gibson, A. and Asthana, S. (2000) 'Estimating the socioeconomic characteristics of school populations with the aid of pupil postcodes and small-area census data', *Environment and Planning A: Economy and Space*, 32(7): 1267–1285.

Giddens, A. (1984) *The Constitution of Society: Outline of the Theory of Structuration*, Berkeley: University of California Press.

Glasgow City Council (2013) *Asset Mapping in Targeted Neighbourhoods*, October. Available from: http://www.glasgow.gov.uk/Councillorsandcommittees/viewSelectedDocument.asp?c=P62AFQNTDX0G2UDN [Accessed 22 August 2017].

Goldman, K.D. and Schmalz, K.J. (2005) ' "Accentuate the positive!" Using an asset-mapping tool as part of a community-health needs assessment', *Health Promotion Practice*, 6(2): 125–128.

Gracia, E., López-Quílez, A., Marco, M., Lladosa, S. and Lila, M. (2014) 'Exploring neighborhood influences on small-area variations in intimate partner violence risk: a Bayesian random-effects modeling approach', *International Journal of Environmental Research and Public Health*, 11(1): 866–882.

Green, A., Luckett, T., Abbott, P. et al (2017) 'A framework for an asset-informed approach to service mapping', *Nurse Researcher*, 25(3): 19–25.

Griffen, A. (2017) *Thaxted's People: Portraits*, Essex: Andy Griffin Photography.

Hansen, D.J. (1991) *An Empirical Study of the Structure of Needs Assessment*, PhD diss., Columbus: Ohio State University.

Kasarda, J.D. and Janowitz, M. (1974) 'Community attachment in mass society', *American Sociological Review*, 39(3): 328–339.

Kretzmann, J.P. and McKnight, J.L. (1993) *Building Communities from the Inside Out: A Path toward Finding and Mobilizing a Community's Assets*, Chicago: Acta.

Langer, C.L. and Lietz, C.A. (2015) *Applying Theory to Generalist Social Work Practice: A Case Study Approach*, Hoboken, NJ: Wiley.

Lee, T. (1968) 'Urban neighbourhood as a socio-spatial schema', *Human Relations*, 21(3): 241–267.

Lightfoot, E., McCleary, J.S. and Lum, T. (2014) 'Asset mapping as a research tool for community-based participatory research in social work', *Social Work Research*, 38(1): 59–64.

Livingston, M., Bailey, N. and Kearns, A. (2010) 'Neighbourhood attachment in deprived areas: evidence from the north of England', *Journal of Housing and the Built Environment*, 25(4): 409–427.

Lupton, R. and Power, A. (2002) 'Social exclusion and neighbourhoods', in J. Hills, J. Le Grand and D. Piachaud (eds) *Understanding Social Exclusion*, Oxford: Oxford University Press, pp 118–140.

Lyons, W.E. and Lowery, D. (1989) 'Citizen responses to dissatisfaction in urban communities: a partial test of a general model', *Journal of Politics*, 51(4): 841–868.

Mathie, A. and Cunningham, G. (2003) 'From clients to citizens: asset-based community development as a strategy for community-driven development', *Development in Practice*, 13(5): 474–486.

Mathie, A., Cameron, J. and Gibson, K. (2017) 'Asset-based and citizen-led development: using a diffracted power lens to analyze the possibilities and challenges', *Progress in Development Studies*, 17(1): 54–66.

McCarry, M. and Williamson, E. (2009) *Violence Against Women in Rural and Urban Areas*, Bristol: University of Bristol.

Mohan, J. (2003) 'Geography and social policy: spatial divisions of welfare', *Progress in Human Geography*, 27(3): 363–374.

ONS (Office for National Statistics) (2016) 'Intimate personal violence and partner abuse'. Available from: https://www.ons.gov.uk/peoplepop ulationandcommunity/crimeandjustice/compendium/focusonviolentcri meandsexualoffences/yearendingmarch2015/chapter4intimatepersonal violenceandpartnerabuse#sources-of-support-for-partner-abuse-victims [Accessed 24 March 2018].

ONS (Office for National Statistics) (2017) 'UK House Price Index: December 2017'. Available from: https://www.ons.gov.uk/economy/inflationandp riceindices/bulletins/housepriceindex/december2017#:~:text=The%20 average%20UK%20house%20price,1%2C000%20higher%20than%20l ast%20month [Accessed 24 April 2021].

Permentier, M., Bolt, G. and van Ham, M. (2011) 'Determinants of neighbourhood satisfaction and perception of neighbourhood reputation', *Urban Studies*, 48(5): 977–996.

Putnam, R.D. (1993) 'The prosperous community: social capital and public life', *The American Prospect*, 4(13): 35–42.

Putnam, R.D. (2000) *Bowling Alone: The Collapse and Revival of American Community*, New York: Simon & Schuster.

Preston City Council (2016) *The Community Mapping Toolkit*. Available from: https://www.scie-socialcareonline.org.uk/the-community-mapp ing-toolkit-a-guide-to-community-asset-mapping-for-community-gro ups-and-local-organisations/r/a11G000000OO8gWIAT [Accessed 21 August 2017].

Rightmove (2017) 'House prices in Thaxted', 30 August. Available from: http://www.rightmove.co.uk/house-prices/Thaxted.html [Accessed 30 August 2017].

Robinson, W.S. (1950) 'Ecological correlations and the behaviour of individuals', *American Sociological Review*, 15(3): 351–357.

Rowland, S. (2008) 'What is asset based community development (ABCD)?' Available from: https://www.neighborhoodtransformation.net/pdfs/ What_%20is_Asset_Based_Community_Development.pdf [Accessed 24 August 2017].

Sampson, R.J. (2003) 'Collective efficacy', in K. Christensen and D. Levinson (eds) *Encyclopedia of Community: From the Village to the Virtual World*, Thousand Oaks, CA: Sage, pp 205–206.

Sampson, R.J. and Groves, W.B. (1989) 'Community structure and crime: testing social-disorganization theory', *American Journal of Sociology*, 94(4): 774–802.

Sampson, R.J. and Lauritsen, J.L. (1994) 'Violent victimization and offending: individual-, situational-, and community-level risk factors', in A.J. Reiss, Jr, J.A. Roth and National Research Council (eds) *Understanding and Preventing Violence, Vol 3: Social Influences*, Washington, DC: National Academy Press, pp 1–114.

Sampson, R.J. and Raudenbush, S.W. (1999) 'Systematic social observation of public spaces: a new look at disorder in urban neighborhoods', *American Journal of Sociology*, 105(3): 603–651.

Sampson, R.J., Raudenbush, S. and Earls, F. (1997) 'Neighborhoods and violent crime: a multilevel study of collective efficacy', *Science*, 227(5328): 918–924.

South, J., Giuntoli, G. and Kinsella, K. (2017) 'Getting past the dual logic: findings from a pilot asset mapping exercise in Sheffield, UK', *Health & Social Care in the Community*, 25(1): 105–113.

Squire, G. and Gill, A. (2011) '"It's not all heartbeat you know": policing domestic violence in rural areas', in R.I. Mawby and R. Yarwood (eds) *Rural Policing and Policing the Rural: A Constable Countryside?* Farnham: Ashgate, pp 159–167.

Völker, B., Mollenhorst, G. and Schutjens, V. (2013) 'Neighbourhood social capital and residential mobility', in M. van Ham, D. Manley, N. Bailey, L. Simpson and D. Maclennan (eds) *Understanding Neighbourhood Dynamics: New Insights for Neighbourhood Effects Research*, Dordrecht: Springer, pp 139–160.

Walklate, S. and Mythen, G. (2011) 'Beyond risk theory: experiential knowledge and "knowing otherwise"', *Criminology & Criminal Justice*, 11(2): 99–113.

Waverley Borough Council (2017) *Community Asset Mapping Guide*. Available from: https://web.archive.org/web/20140920055008/http://www.waverley.gov.uk/downloads/download/1696/community_asset_mapping_guide [Accessed 15 August 2017].

Weir, R. (2019) 'Using geographically weighted regression to explore neighborhood-level predictors of domestic abuse in the UK', *Transactions in GIS*, 23: 1232–1250.

Zarei, M., Fathi, M.S. and Heidari, F. (2018) 'Designing a hypothetical neighbourhood to promote the localism; convergence of urban village approach and democratic urban design patterns: the link between theory and practice', *International Journal of Architecture, Engineering and Urban Planning*, 28(1): 71–81.

PART II

Gender–Based Violence in 'Local–Level' and Transitionary Spaces, from Public Transport to Rural and Digital Spaces

5

Sexual Violence on Public Transport: Applying the Whole-Journey Approach to Assess Women Students' Victimization in Paris and the Île-de-France Region

Hugo d'Arbois de Jubainville

Introduction

In many countries, public transport is conducive to sexual violence against women and girls (Gekoski et al, 2017; Loukaitou-Sideris and Ceccato, 2020). In France, this issue was identified in the early 2000s (Pottier et al, 2002; Jaspard et al, 2003), but not given prominent attention until the High Council for Gender Equality stated in 2015 that '100 per cent of women using public transport have been victims at least once in their lifetime of sexist harassment or sexual assault' (HCEfh, 2015: 5).

Although this result was obtained thanks to a non-representative sample and generalized to the whole population without precaution, this contributed to increased public awareness and scientific interest. Consequently, several studies were conducted on this phenomenon (Debrincat et al, 2016, 2017; Destais, 2017; Scherr, 2017). Recently, Lebugle et al (2020) confirmed that a significant share of sexual offences in the public space occurs on public transport.

However, most French studies remain limited. On the one hand, they do not necessarily take into account the diversity of sexual offences, focusing on the most serious but less frequent ones (for instance, rape), to the detriment of less serious yet more common ones (for instance, sexual harassment). On the other hand, they rarely acknowledge the complexity of

85

the transit environment, not distinguishing means of transport (for example, buses, subways, trains) or places (for example, vehicles, stops, stations).

This chapter is based on the French component of the international project Transit Safety Among College Students (Ceccato and Loukaitou-Sideris, 2020). This project relied on the whole-journey approach to determine at which step of their journey students are victimized, and to identify victimization patterns. The objective of the chapter is to provide a detailed assessment of sexual offences against women students on public transport in Paris and the Île-de-France region.

First, the chapter provides a short literature review on sexual violence in the transit environment. Second, methodology is presented, including data, the whole-journey approach, and subsamples. Third, results are described for rail transport and buses. These results suggest sexual offences occur more frequently on the former than on the latter. Similar victimization patterns appear for both systems, although other patterns are specific to each of them. Eventually, the chapter concludes with implications for researchers and practitioners, as well as limitations.

Literature review
Sexual violence in the transit environment

It is difficult to accurately measure sexual violence on public transport. Administrative data are considered unreliable because offences are under-reported to authorities (Alessandrin et al, 2016; Debrincat et al, 2016; Destais, 2017; Gekoski et al, 2017; Natarajan et al, 2017; Loukaitou-Sideris and Ceccato, 2020). In France, Plantevignes (2020) used police data and identified approximately 5,300 victims of sexual offences on public transport from 2017 to 2019; whereas Scherr (2017) used survey data and estimated that at least 267,000 individuals had been victims of such offences in this environment during the last two years. However, survey data may also be limited because the place of commission is usually recorded for the most recent offence only. This results in loss of information and underestimation of victims and offences (Noble et al, 2017; Scherr, 2017).

Sexual violence in this environment is 'polymorphic', including sexist and sexual harassment, sexual exhibition, sexual assault, rape, as well as other offences with a sexist or sexual dimension (for instance, insults, threats) (HCEfh, 2015: 5). Unwanted attempts at flirting, sexual harassment, and sexual assault such as unwanted touching or groping are common on public transport, whereas rape is much less frequent (Besson, 2008; Lieber, 2008; Jaspard, 2011; HCEfh, 2015; Alessandrin et al, 2016; Debrincat et al, 2016, 2017; Destais, 2017; Guedj, 2017; Gekoski et al, 2017; Natarajan et al, 2017; Noble et al, 2017). Furthermore, physical violence may occur before, during, or after sexual victimization (Scherr, 2017).

The majority of victims are women (Destais, 2017; Natarajan et al, 2017; Scherr, 2017; Loukaitou-Sideris and Ceccato, 2020; Plantevignes, 2020). Victimization rates are particularly high for young women living in large urban areas (HCEfh, 2015; Alessandrin et al, 2016; Gekoski et al, 2017), such as Paris and the Île-de-France region (Scherr, 2017; Plantevignes, 2020). This may be due to the fact young women are the main victims of sexual violence in public space and use public transport very frequently (Jaspard et al, 2003; Jaspard, 2011; Alessandrin et al, 2016; de Berny and Davy, 2016; Lebugle et al, 2020).

Conversely, the majority of offenders are men who are unknown to the victims (HCEfh, 2015; Alessandrin et al, 2016; Debrincat et al, 2016; Destais, 2017; Plantevignes, 2020). They are generally other users who act alone or in a group, and more rarely transport personnel (for example, drivers, inspectors) (Alessandrin et al, 2016; Debrincat, 2016, 2017; Destais, 2017). Younger men tend to commit specific offences (for instance, unwanted touching), whereas older men tend to perpetrate other ones (for instance, sexual exhibition) (Jaspard, 2011).

Sexual violence, especially offences involving physical contact, usually takes place in vehicles such as subways, trains and buses (Alessandrin et al, 2016; Debrincat et al, 2016; Destais, 2017; Gekoski et al, 2017; Natarajan et al, 2017; Scherr, 2017). The way these vehicles are designed (for example, enclosed spaces, narrowness, seating arrangement, blind spots, limited exits, underground) and used (for example, overcrowded, deserted) may increase victimization risk (Jaspard, 2011; Natarajan et al, 2017; Scherr, 2017; Lebugle et al, 2020). For instance, in overcrowded vehicles, offenders take advantage of the physical proximity between users to act, sitting in front or besides them to touch their groin, or standing behind them to touch their buttocks (Scherr, 2017).

Victimization also takes place in transportation nodes and in their vicinity (Alessandrin et al, 2016; Debrincat et al, 2016, 2017; Destais, 2017; Natarajan et al, 2017; Scherr, 2017). This includes stops, platforms, hallways, corridors, stairways, escalators, lifts, car parks and access paths. For example, offenders also take advantage of the way subway and train platforms are designed, standing behind other users to touch their buttocks and flee easily (Scherr, 2017).

Sexual violence occurs throughout the day (Condon et al, 2005; Jaspard, 2011; Debrincat et al, 2016; Destais, 2017; Lebugle et al, 2020). Nevertheless, users are likely to be victimized during rush hours, when going to (or coming back from) their place or work or study (Alessandrin et al, 2016; Debrincat et al, 2016; Ceccato and Paz, 2017; Gekoski et al, 2017; Noble et al, 2017). In this situation, the transit environment may be overcrowded, which may increase physical proximity and victimization risk. Users are also likely to be victimized during the evening and at night, when going to (or coming back from) leisure activities (Alessandrin et al, 2016; Debrincat et al, 2017; Ceccato et al, 2017; Gekoski et al, 2017; Noble et al, 2017). In this situation, the transit environment may be deserted and poorly lit, which may decrease surveillance and increase victimization risk.

Sexual violence can have negative consequences on mobility and well-being. On the one hand, the anticipated risk and actual experience of victimization lead users, notably women, to take precautions which ultimately reduce their mobility (for instance, avoiding public transport at night) (Condon et al, 2005; Lieber, 2008; HCEfh, 2015; Alessandrin et al, 2016; Debrincat et al, 2016; d'Arbois de Jubainville and Vanier, 2017; Destais, 2017; Gekoski et al, 2017; Loukaitou-Sideris and Ceccato, 2020; Noble, 2020). On the other hand, this phenomenon also decreases perceived safety when using public transport (Lieber, 2008; HCEfh, 2015; Alessandrin et al, 2016; Debrincat et al, 2016; Gekoski et al, 2017; Noble et al, 2017; Loukaitou-Sideris and Ceccato, 2020; Noble, 2020).

Limitations of French studies

Most French studies have limitations. The majority of them focus on sexual violence in public space (Pottier et al, 2002; Jaspard et al, 2003; Condon et al, 2005; Besson, 2008; Lieber, 2008; Jaspard, 2011; Alessandrin et al, 2016; Guedj, 2017; Lebugle et al, 2020), but do not assess the dynamics of public transport. On the contrary, other studies focus on transit safety (Noble et al, 2017; Noble, 2020; Plantevignes, 2020), yet do not cover the diversity of sexual offences.

Since the recommendation of the HCEfh (2015), several studies have been conducted specifically on sexual violence on public transport (Debrincat et al, 2016, 2017; Destais, 2017; Scherr, 2017). Yet, these are also limited. Scherr (2017) relied on a survey measuring only sexual exhibition, sexual assault and rape, thus excluding sexual harassment and other offences that are common in this environment. Debrincat et al (2016, 2017), as well as Destais (2017), analysed where violence *in general* takes place, but not where offences *in particular* occur. For instance, they noted violence usually takes place in vehicles, but they did not specify which offences.

Studies usually distinguish women and men, whereas some of them focus on women and girls (Jaspard et al, 2003; Condon et al, 2005; Lieber, 2008; Jaspard, 2011; HCEfh, 2015; Alessandrin et al, 2016; Debrincat et al, 2016, 2017; Scherr, 2017). A few studies suggest transgender individuals are more likely to be victims of sexual violence in public space than cisgender individuals (Alessandrin et al, 2016; Trachman and Lejbowicz, 2020), but do not provide results concerning the transit environment.

Thus, French studies have shown that public transport is conducive to sexual violence against women and girls, but have not yet provided a detailed assessment that takes into account the diversity of these offences and the dynamics of this environment. Further research is required to improve the understanding of this phenomenon and develop adequate measures against it.

Methodology

Transit Safety Among College Students project

This chapter is based on the international project Transit Safety Among College Students, which was conducted in 2018 (Ceccato and Loukaitou-Sideris, 2020). The main objective was to use the whole-journey approach to analyse students' sexual victimization and perceived safety in the transit environment.

The French component of this project was conducted on the Parisian campus of the Institut d'Études Politiques de Paris (Sciences Po). Paris was selected for several reasons: the transportation system of the capital city and the Île-de-France region is vast, including 39 rail lines and more than 1,500 bus lines (OMNIL, 2018); students rely heavily on public transport in this area (de Berny and Davy, 2016); and sexual violence in the public space and the transit environment is more common in this area (Scherr, 2017; Lebugle et al, 2020; Plantevignes, 2020). Sciences Po was selected because its campus hosts more than 10,000 students and is located in the city centre, which means students can use various types of public transport to move around.

After being approved by the university, students were contacted by mass mailing and invited to complete an online self-administered survey. Participation was restricted to students aged 18 and over. Respondents remained anonymous, and were not reimbursed for their time. They had the right to access, consult, modify and delete their answers. They were also provided with the contact details of Sciences Po sexual harassment monitoring unit and helplines in case they felt distressed while participating.

Applying the whole-journey approach

The Transit Safety Among College Students project relied on a survey applying the whole-journey approach. This method has been discussed theoretically (Newton, 2004; Smith, 2008) and implemented to analyse sexual violence on public transport (Natarajan et al, 2017; Ceccato and Loukaitou-Sideris, 2020). According to this approach, victimization can occur during the three main steps of a journey:

- when heading to or from transportation nodes (for example, bus stop, subway station);
- when waiting at transportation nodes (for example, bus stop, subway platform); and
- when riding in vehicles (for example, bus, subway).

This approach allows for an assessment of victimization throughout users' journeys, from their origin to their destination, not only when they ride public transport. It also allows for identification of victimization patterns. For instance, sexual harassment and stalking are more frequent when walking to or from nodes, whereas sexual exhibition and assault are more common when waiting at nodes and riding in vehicles (Natarajan et al, 2017). However, the whole of journey approach has not been formally applied in France yet.

The survey determined if respondents had been victims of sexual offences on public transport during the last three years. It distinguished three general categories including 16 specific offences:

- verbal offences: abusive or obscene language; being called *bébé* (babe) *beauté* (beauty), *chérie* (honey) when called out to; intrusive questions; kissing sounds; sexual advances; unwanted sexual comments on clothing or appearance; unwanted sexual teasing or provocations; and whistling;
- non-verbal offences: masturbation; sexual exhibition; showing pornographic material; stalking or shadowing; and unwanted sexual looks or gestures; and
- physical offences: playing with or pulling hair; sexual assault such as unwanted touching or groping; and sexual assault such as unwanted kissing.

For each offence, the survey determined if victimization occurred when walking to or from nodes, waiting at nodes or riding in vehicles. It was therefore possible to identify nine general cases (for instance, verbal offences when walking) and 48 specific ones (for instance, whistling when walking).

Variables were duplicated for buses and rail transport, which includes subways, tramways, suburban trains and trains. This allowed to analyse these systems separately and ensure comparisons.

Objective

The objective of this chapter is to assess the extent, nature and patterns of sexual violence against women students in the transit environment. Studies suggest sexual harassment and unwanted touching are common on public transport, whereas more serious offences are less frequent (Besson, 2008; Lieber, 2008; Jaspard, 2011; HCEfh, 2015; Alessandrin et al, 2016; Debrincat et al, 2016, 2017; Destais, 2017; Guedj, 2017; Natarajan et al, 2017; Noble et al, 2017; Lebugle et al, 2020). Consequently, it is likely that respondents would mostly report verbal and non-verbal offences, and to a lesser extent physical offences such as unwanted touching or groping.

Victimization rates vary depending on the type of public transport (Alessandrin et al, 2016; Destais, 2017; Plantevignes, 2020). In the Île-de-France region, sexual offences occur more frequently on rail transport than buses (Plantevignes, 2020). Thus, it is likely that respondents would declare having been victims more often on the former than on the latter.

Concerning victimization patterns, sexual harassment and stalking occur more frequently during the walking stage, whereas sexual exhibition and sexual assault are more common during the waiting and riding stages (Natarajan et al, 2017). Consequently, it is likely that such patterns would appear. It is also likely that similar and specific patterns appear for rail transport and buses, as these two systems are different in terms of their design and use.

Subsamples

The French sample was composed of 740 students aged 18 and over, including 574 women (77.6 per cent), 156 men (21.1 per cent), and 10 respondents who did not answer (1.3 per cent). This sample is not representative of Sciences Po student population as participants were not randomly selected.

The present chapter relies on two subsamples: the first is composed of 573 women students using rail transport, and the second of 431 women students using buses. As displayed in Table 5.1, the majority of respondents are French and aged 18–29. The majority of them use rail transport very regularly, as more than 80 per cent declared using it 5–6 days a week or every day. However, they use buses much less frequently, since more than 60 per cent declared using them 1–2 days a week or less often.

Results

Sexual violence on rail transport

The majority of respondents declared having been victims of sexual violence on rail transport. As shown in Figure 5.1, more than half of them reported verbal and non-verbal offences when walking to or from nodes, waiting at nodes, and riding in vehicles. Less than 10 per cent mentioned physical offences when walking or waiting, and more than of third of them when riding.

Table 5.2 displays the detailed results for rail transport. When walking to or from nodes, 46.1 per cent of respondents declared they were called *bébé* (babe), *beauté* (beauty) or *chérie* (honey) by offenders who called out to them. They also reported whistles (44.7 per cent) and unwanted sexual comments on their clothing or appearance (41.7 per cent). To a lesser extent, they mentioned unwanted sexual looks or gestures (34.7 per cent), stalking (34.4 per cent), unwanted sexual teasing or provocations (30.9 per cent) and abusive or obscene language (24.6 per cent). During this stage, victimization rates are highest for whistling and stalking, but lowest for sexual assault such as unwanted touching or groping (7.0 per cent), sexual exhibition (4.5 per cent) and masturbation (2.1 per cent).

Table 5.1: Subsamples description

	Women students using rail transport		Women students using buses	
	N = 573	%	N = 431	%
Nationality				
French	467	81.5	359	83.3
Foreign	55	9.6	36	8.4
Dual	23	4.0	15	3.5
n/a	28	4.9	21	4.9
Age				
18–29	564	98.4	425	98.6
30 and over	9	1.6	6	1.4
n/a	0	0.0	0	0.0
Frequency of use				
Everyday	355	62.0	36	8.4
5–6 days a week	122	21.3	40	9.3
3–4 days a week	54	9.4	70	16.2
1–2 days a week	31	5.4	101	23.4
Less often	11	1.9	184	42.7

Source: Author

Figure 5.1: Sexual violence on rail transport (general categories)

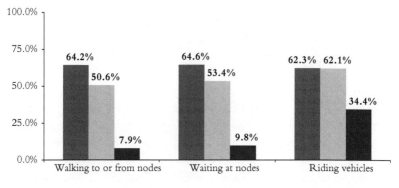

Note: N = 573
Source: Author

Table 5.2: Sexual violence on rail transport (specific offences)

	Walking to or from nodes	Waiting at nodes	Riding in vehicles
	%	%	%
Verbal offences			
Abusive or obscene language	24.6	27.9	30.0
Being called *bébé, beauté, chérie*	46.1	45.7	43.6
Intrusive questions	8.2	9.2	9.9
Kissing sounds	19.9	19.4	16.1
Sexual advances	11.9	12.7	15.0
Unwanted sexual comments on clothing or appearance	41.7	43.8	42.1
Unwanted sexual teasing or provocations	30.9	33.0	32.1
Whistling	44.7	39.6	27.6
Non-verbal offences			
Masturbation	2.1	3.8	13.6
Sexual exhibition	4.5	7.7	11.7
Showing pornographic material	0.3	1.0	1.4
Stalking or shadowing	34.4	29.1	24.1
Unwanted sexual looks or gestures	34.7	42.9	54.6
Physical offences			
Playing with or pulling hair	1.2	1.2	3.1
Sexual assault such as unwanted kissing	0.9	1.0	2.1
Sexual assault such as unwanted touching or groping	7.0	9.1	33.2

Note: N = 573

Source: Author

When waiting at nodes, respondents also reported being called *bébé, beauté, chérie* (45.7 per cent), unwanted sexual comments (43.8 per cent), unwanted sexual looks or gestures (42.9 per cent) and whistles (39.6 per cent). To a lesser extent, they experienced unwanted sexual teasing (33.0 per cent), stalking (29.1 per cent) and abusive language (27.9 per cent). During this stage, victimization rates are lower for whistling and stalking, but slightly higher for unwanted touching (9.1 per cent), sexual exhibition (7.7 per cent) and masturbation (3.8 per cent).

Eventually, when riding in vehicles, respondents also reported unwanted sexual looks or gestures (54.6 per cent), being called *bébé, beauté, chérie*

(43.6 per cent) and unwanted sexual comments (42.1 per cent). To a lesser extent, they mentioned unwanted touching (33.2 per cent), unwanted sexual teasing (32.1 per cent), abusive language (30.0 per cent), whistling (27.6 per cent) and stalking (24.1 per cent). During this stage, victimization rates are highest for sexual assault such as unwanted touching, as well as sexual exhibition (11.7 per cent) and masturbation (13.6 per cent).

Sexual violence on buses

A lower but not negligible share of respondents declared having been victims of sexual violence on buses. As shown in Figure 5.2, more than half of them reported verbal offences when walking to or from and waiting at bus stops, and more than 40 per cent when riding on buses. To a lesser extent, more than 40 per cent mentioned non-verbal offences when walking, and more than 30 per cent when waiting and riding. Around 5 per cent experienced physical offences when walking and waiting, and around 15 per cent when riding.

Table 5.3 displays the detailed results for buses. When walking to or from bus stops, 41.3 per cent of respondents declared they were called *bébé, beauté* or *chérie* by offenders who called out to them. They also reported whistles (41.1 per cent), unwanted sexual comments (35.7 per cent) and stalking (31.3 per cent). To a lesser extent, they mentioned unwanted sexual looks or gestures (24.1 per cent), unwanted sexual teasing (22.0 per cent), abusive language (17.4 per cent) and kissing sounds (16.0 per cent). During this stage, victimization rates are highest for most verbal offences and stalking, but lowest for unwanted touching (2.8 per cent).

When waiting at bus stops, respondents also reported being called *bébé, beauté* or *chérie* (37.4 per cent), unwanted sexual comments (31.6 per cent),

Figure 5.2: Sexual violence on buses (general categories)

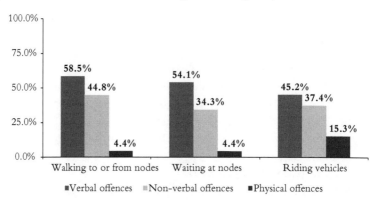

Note: N = 431

Source: Author

Table 5.3: Sexual violence on buses (specific offences)

	Walking to or from nodes	Waiting at nodes	Riding in vehicles
	%	%	%
Verbal offences			
Abusive or obscene language	17.4	15.3	17.2
Being called *bébé, beauté, chérie*	41.3	37.4	30.4
Intrusive questions	6.0	7.7	7.4
Kissing sounds	16.0	12.8	9.7
Sexual advances	9.3	11.8	7.9
Unwanted sexual comments on clothing or appearance	35.7	31.6	27.4
Unwanted sexual teasing or provocations	22.0	19.0	17.2
Whistling	41.1	29.7	15.3
Non-verbal offences			
Masturbation	2.6	2.3	4.6
Sexual exhibition	3.0	4.4	4.2
Showing pornographic material	0.5	0.2	0.9
Stalking or shadowing	31.3	13.9	11.1
Unwanted sexual looks or gestures	24.1	27.4	33.6
Physical offences			
Playing with or pulling hair	0.7	0.9	1.9
Sexual assault such as unwanted kissing	0.9	0.5	1.2
Sexual assault such as unwanted touching or groping	2.8	3.5	14.2

Note: N = 431

Source: Author

whistling (29.7 per cent) and unwanted sexual looks or gestures (27.4 per cent). To a lesser extent, they experienced unwanted sexual teasing (19.0 per cent), abusive language (15.3 per cent) and stalking (13.9 per cent). During this stage, victimization rates are lower for most verbal offences and stalking, whereas the rate for unwanted touching remains low (3.5 per cent).

Finally, when riding buses, respondents mostly reported unwanted sexual looks or gestures (33.6 per cent), being called *bébé, beauté* or *chérie* (30.4 per cent) and unwanted sexual comments (27.4 per cent). They also mentioned unwanted sexual teasing (17.2 per cent), abusive language (17.2 per cent)

95

and whistling (15.3 per cent). During this stage, victimization rates for most verbal offences and stalking are lowest, whereas the rate for unwanted touching is highest (14.2 per cent).

Discussion: assessing the extent, nature and patterns of sexual violence

Confirming earlier research in this field, sexual violence occurs more frequently on rail transport than on buses. Victimization rates for verbal, non-verbal and physical offences are higher when women students use this type of public transport. This is notably the case for sexual assault such as unwanted touching or groping. First, this may be due to frequency of use. Women students use rail transport more often, and this is probably the case for offenders too, which may increase victimization risk. Second, this may be due to vehicle design, as seating arrangement and blind spots may decrease the chance of detection and make it easier for offenders to commit sexual violence. Reduced mobility within narrow vehicles may also make it harder for victims to move away from perpetrators. This is aggravated when vehicles are overcrowded, for instance during rush hours, which increases physical proximity between users (Jaspard, 2011; Natarajan et al, 2017; Scherr, 2017; Lebugle et al, 2020). Third, this may be due to the fact subway and train drivers are not accessible, unlike bus drivers who are closer to users and may act as guardians by deterring offenders (Lieber, 2008; Alessandrin et al, 2016).

Regarding the nature of sexual violence, women students are mostly victims of verbal and non-verbal offences. They mentioned being called *bébé* (babe), *beauté* (beauty) or *chérie* (honey) by offenders who called out to them, unwanted sexual comments on their clothing or appearance, and whistles. They also reported unwanted sexual looks and gestures, as well as stalking. A third of them declared having been victims of unwanted touching when riding on rail transport. These results are consistent with previous studies, according to which unwanted attempts at flirting, sexual harassment and sexual assault are common in the transit environment (Besson, 2008; Lieber, 2008; Jaspard, 2011; HCEfh, 2015; Alessandrin et al, 2016; Debrincat et al, 2016, 2017; Destais, 2017; Guedj, 2017; Natarajan et al, 2017; Noble et al, 2017; Lebugle et al, 2020).

Regarding victimization patterns, some of them are similar for both systems. Specific verbal offences (that are, being called *bébé, beauté* or *chérie*, kissing sounds, whistles) and stalking occur more frequently when walking to or from transportation nodes. This is in line with Natarajan et al (2017) who noted that this stage is conducive to sexual harassment and being followed. Unwanted sexual looks or gestures, as well as unwanted touching, are more frequent when riding in vehicles. This is also consistent with studies suggesting that physical proximity between users within vehicles may increase victimization risk (Jaspard, 2011; Natarajan et al, 2017; Scherr, 2017; Lebugle et al, 2020).

Other patterns are specific to each system. Concerning rail transport, sexual exhibition and masturbation occur more frequently when riding in vehicles. This may be due to reasons discussed earlier, such as frequency of use, vehicles design and use, or inaccessibility of drivers. Concerning buses, unwanted sexual comments occur more often when walking to or from and waiting at nodes. This may be due to the open environment of bus stops. Women who are waiting are exposed to offences committed not only by other users, but also by pedestrians, cyclists and drivers (Alessandrin et al, 2016).

More generally, the fact that women students are exposed to various sexual offences throughout their journeys may reflect the sexist atmosphere of the transit environment and the public space. These offences, ranging from whistles to sexual assault, are committed by men against young women who are usually not accompanied (but in front of witnesses), and occur during victims' daily activities and use of the public space (Condon et al, 2005; Lieber, 2008; Jaspard, 2011; Lebugle et al, 2020). They constantly remind victims they are women navigating hostile public places, in which they are considered sexually available, and at risk of greater sexual violence (Lieber, 2008). Lebugle et al (2020: 348) highlighted that 'the sexualised dimension of interpersonal relations is much more significant for women than for men, and more disturbing', as men are less often victims of such offences and consider them less serious.

Conclusion

Implications for researchers and practitioners

This study has implications for researchers. Relying on the whole-journey approach allows for a detailed assessment of sexual violence on public transport, covering the diversity of these offences as well as the complexity of this environment. The results obtained thanks to this method expand those from previous French studies (HCEfh, 2015; Debrincat et al, 2016, 2017; Destais, 2017; Scherr, 2017) and overcome some of their limitations.

Consequently, future studies on this topic should disaggregate results by offence type and journey stage. The whole-journey approach should be formally implemented in France and other countries facing similar difficulties in assessing this phenomenon. This method could also be applied to analyse other offences occurring on public transport (for instance, physical violence, thefts).

This study also has implications for practitioners. Transit operators and police services should apply the whole-journey approach and combine it with administrative data to map out sexual violence against women, and to develop measures accordingly. For example, focusing on vehicles may prevent victimization during the riding stage, but not necessarily during the walking and waiting stages. It is therefore important to develop measures that could be implemented in vehicles, nodes and their vicinity, or that are specific to each setting.

Women users value the increased presence of human guardians (for instance, police officers, transport personnel) to improve transit safety (Debrincat et al, 2016, 2017; Natarajan et al, 2017; Noble, 2020). The visibility and accessibility of guardians may prevent victimization and increase perceived safety (Lieber, 2008; Alessandrin et al, 2016; Debrincat et al, 2016, 2017). This could be done by increasing the presence of formal guardians in vehicles, nodes and their vicinity. Guardians must be adequately trained, as many victims of sexual violence declared they were not taken seriously by transport personnel and police officers (Debrincat et al, 2016, 2017; Natarajan et al, 2017). Alternatively, this could be done by raising awareness and teaching users how to act as informal guardians when others are victims of sexual violence. This is particularly important because users rarely intervene when they witness such offences (Alessandrin et al, 2016; Debrincat et al, 2016, 2017; Loukaitou-Sideris and Ceccato, 2020).

Women users also value emergency devices (for example, emergency telephones) to improve transit safety, although these are less popular than human guardians (Debrincat et al, 2016, 2017; Natarajan et al, 2017; Noble, 2020). This could be done by increasing the number of devices in vehicles, nodes and their vicinity. Devices should be accessible and easy to use, as victims do not necessarily know they can use them in case of sexual violence, or how to use them (Debrincat et al, 2016, 2017).

Concerning buses, women users appreciate on-demand stops at night (Debrincat et al, 2016, 2017; Noble, 2020). They may ask the driver to stop the bus between two formal stops, in order to reduce the walking distance to their destination. This is relevant as the walking stage is conducive to sexual harassment and stalking (Natarajan et al, 2017). However, this does not address sexual violence during other stages of the journey or moments of the day.

Limitations

This study is not without limitations. First, the sample was not representative of the student population of Paris and the Île-de-France region. It was indeed composed of students who were not randomly selected, but who opened the email from their university and accessed the survey. This may have increased the share of respondents who were motivated or concerned, for instance because they had experienced victimization (Noble, 2020).

Second, the survey did not include all sexual offences, such as 'upskirting' and taking pictures without consent (Gekoski et al, 2017; Natarajan et al, 2017). It did not include rape either, although this offence rarely occurs in the transit environment (Besson, 2008; Lieber, 2008; Jaspard, 2011; HCEfh, 2015; Alessandrin et al, 2016; Debrincat et al, 2016, 2017; Destais, 2017; Guedj, 2017; Natarajan et al, 2017; Noble et al, 2017; Lebugle et al, 2020).

Third, the survey did not distinguish the various types of rail transport, because this would have increased the number of questions, and may have deterred respondents from completing it. Yet, it is likely that victimization rates and patterns would vary depending on these types. For instance, in the Île-de-France region, sexual offences occur more frequently on subways and suburban trains than on tramways (Plantevignes, 2020).

Hopefully, these limitations are not insurmountable. Using a sample of randomly selected participants and weighting data should produce more robust results (Noble, 2020). Including other sexual offences should provide a more detailed picture of this phenomenon. Eventually, adapting the survey to local contexts and distinguishing the types of rail transport should help to identify similarities and differences between these means of transport.

References

Alessandrin, A., César-Franquet, L. and Dagorn, J. (2016) *Femmes et déplacements*, November, Bordeaux: Ville de Bordeaux.

Besson, J.-L. (2008) 'Origines, destinations, relations spatiales des mis en cause et des victimes de violences sexuelles à Paris en 2005', *Focus*, 3, Paris: OND.

Ceccato, V. and Loukaitou-Sideris, A. (2020) 'Studying sexual harassment in transit environments: research design and basic concepts', in V. Ceccato and A. Loukaitou-Sideris (eds) *Transit Crime and Sexual Violence in Cities: International Evidence and Prevention*, New York: Routledge, pp 32–41.

Ceccato, V. and Paz, Y. (2017) 'Crime in São Paulo's metro system: sexual crimes against women', *Crime Prevention and Community Safety*, 19(3/4): 211–226.

Ceccato, V., Wiebe, D.J., Eshraghi, B. and Vrotsou, K. (2017) 'Women's mobility and the situational conditions of rape: cases reported to hospitals', *Journal of Interpersonal Violence*, 35(15/16): 2917–2946.

Condon, S., Lieber, M. and Maillochon, F. (2005) 'Insécurité dans les espaces publics: comprendre les peurs féminines', *Revue française de sociologie*, 46(2): 265–294.

d'Arbois de Jubainville, H. and Vanier, C. (2017) 'Women's avoidance behaviours in public transport in the Ile-de-France region', *Crime Prevention and Community Safety*, 19(3/4): 183–198.

de Berny, C. and Davy, A.-C. (2016) *Territoires de la vie étudiante en Île-de-France*, October, Paris: IAU-ÎdF.

Debrincat, M., Dupart, C. and Laurent, C. (2016) *Étude sur le harcèlement sexiste et les violences sexuelles faites aux femmes dans les transports publics*, 14 June, Paris: FNAUT.

Debrincat, M., Dupart, C. and Moggio, C. (2017) *Harcèlement sexiste dans les transports collectifs routiers et les pôles d'échange multimodaux: l'analyse de la FNAUT*, 26 July, Paris: FNAUT.

Destais, A. (2017) *Le harcèlement sexiste dans les transports en commun et à leurs abords au sein de l'agglomération caennaise*, Caen: Préfet du Calvados.

Gekoski, A., Gray, J.M., Adler, J.R. and Horvath, A.H. (2017) 'The prevalence and nature of sexual harassment and assault against women and girls on public transport: an international review', *Journal of Criminological Research, Policy and Practice*, 3(1): 3–16.

Guedj, H. (2017) 'Viols, tentatives de viol et attouchements sexuels', *Interstats Analyse*, 18, Paris: SSMSI.

HCEfh (2015) *Avis sur le harcèlement sexiste et les violences sexuelles dans les transports en commun: se mobiliser pour dire stop sur toute la ligne au harcèlement sexiste et aux violences sexuelles dans les transports*, Paris: HCEfh.

Jaspard, M. (2011) *Les violences contre les femmes*, Paris: La Découverte.

Jaspard, M., Brown, E., Condon, S. et al (2003) *Les violences envers les femmes en France: une enquête nationale*, Paris: La Documentation Française.

Lebugle, A., Debauche, A. and Lieber, M. (2020) 'Les violences dans les espaces publics', in E. Brown, A. Debauche, C. Hamel and M. Mazuy (eds) *Violences et rapports de genre: enquête sur les violences de genre en France*, Paris: INED, pp 327–352.

Lieber, M. (2008) *Genre, violences et espaces publics: la vulnérabilité des femmes en question*, Paris: Les Presses de Sciences Po.

Loukaitou-Sideris, A. and Ceccato, V. (2020) 'Sexual crime on transit: a global, comparative look', in V. Ceccato and A. Loukaitou-Sideris (eds) *Transit Crime and Sexual Violence in Cities: International Evidence and Prevention*, New York: Routledge, pp 297–304.

Natarajan, M., Schmuhl, M., Sudula, S. and Mandala, M. (2017) 'Sexual victimization of college students in public transport environments: a whole journey approach', *Crime Prevention and Community Safety*, 19(3/4): 168–182.

Newton, A.D. (2004) 'Crime on public transport: "static" and "non-static" (moving) crime events', *Western Criminology Review*, 5(3): 25–42.

Noble, J. (2020) *Sentiment d'insécurité dans les transports franciliens: enquête 2019*, Paris: Institut Paris Région.

Noble, J., Jardin, A., Robert, P. and Zauberman, R. (2017) *Insécurité et victimations dans les transports en commun franciliens: exploitation des données de 8 enquêtes Victimation et sentiment d'insécurité en Île-de-France (1998–2014) de l'Institut d'Aménagement et d'Urbanisme de la Région*, Guyancourt: CESDIP.

OMNIL (2018) 'Caractéristiques du réseau, accessibilité et intermodalité 2009–2017', *OMNIL*. Available from: http://www.omnil.fr/spip.php?art icle117 [Accessed 21 April 2022].

Plantevignes, S. (2020) 'Les vols et violences dans les réseaux de transports en commun en 2019', *Interstats Analyse*, 31, Paris: SSMSI.

Pottier, M.-L., Robert, P. and Zauberman, R. (2002) *Victimation et insécurité en Île-de-France: les résultats de la première enquête (2001): rapport final*, Guyancourt: CESDIP.

Scherr, M. (2017) 'Les atteintes sexuelles dans les transports en commun', *Repères*, 34, Paris: ONDRP.

Smith, M. (2008) 'Addressing the security needs of women passengers on public transport', *Security Journal*, 21(1/2): 117–133.

Trachman, M. and Lejbowicz, T. (2020) 'Lesbiennes, gays, bisexuelles et trans (LGBT): une catégorie hétérogène, des violences spécifiques', in E. Brown, A. Debauche, C. Hamel and M. Mazuy (eds) *Violences et rapports de genre: enquête sur les violences de genre en France*, Paris: INED, pp 355–388.

6

Woman Abuse in Rural Places: Towards a Spatial Understanding

Walter DeKeseredy

Introduction

The interdisciplinary field of criminology includes a broad range of analyses, but its primary focus is on individuals as offenders and victims (Weisburd et al, 2012; Hart et al, 2020). This focus is especially the case in the study of woman abuse, regardless of where it takes place. Why this is so is a question that can only be answered empirically, and it is beyond the scope of this chapter to do so. Rather, heavily influenced by the work of Australian feminist criminologists Kate Farhall (2020) and Bridget Harris (2016), the main objective of this chapter is twofold: (1) to examine what the extant social scientific literature reveals about how the social and contextual characteristics of rurality contribute to high rates of male-to-female abuse in private places and (2) to suggest new directions in empirical work. It is first necessary, though, to define the concepts *rural* and *woman abuse*.

What is rural?

Donnermeyer (2020: 19) is one of numerous rural criminologists to note that 'the concept of rural is indeed a problem'. On the same page, he also reminds us that:

> it is a headache without an aspirin potent enough to take away the intellectual pain. ... The reality is that there is no such thing as a single rural sector within a country anywhere in the world, but rather a wide and varied collection of localities with smaller populations and population densities. No single word in the English language, or any other language for that matter, possesses enough linguistic power to

encapsulate the multiplicities of rural realities; a diversity that likewise offers 'interesting social laboratories' and marvellous opportunities for 'new pathways in criminology'!

So, there is no best or uniform definition of rural, and Harris and Harkness (2016) correctly point out that 'manufacturing one' is not a useful way to understand any type of crime and method of social control in Australia and elsewhere. They also sensitize us to the fact that rural criminologists approach crime in non-metropolitan places in a variety of ways, depending on their disciplinary backgrounds, the data sets available to them, and other reasons. Though I agree with Harris and Harkness's (2016: 8) notion that 'the absence of a uniform interpretation' of rural 'is not perceived as a failing but as a necessary freedom which enhances understandings of non-urban locations', I also concur with Saunders's (2015: 3) call for a 'clear and functional working definition of "rural" to move away from' what Woods (2011: 1) sees as the rural being a 'messy and slippery idea'.

Following Scott et al (2007: 3), for the purpose of this chapter, 'a line must be drawn somewhere'. Guided by my previous work with Donnermeyer (see DeKeseredy et al, 2007; Donnermeyer and DeKeseredy, 2014), a nominal definition of 'rural' is offered here. Rural areas, then, are places that have four things in common. First, they have smaller population sizes and/or densities. Second, rural residents are more likely to 'know each other's business, come into contact with each other, and share a larger core of values than is true of people in urban areas' (Websdale, 1995: 102). Third, in this period of late modernity, rural communities are much less autonomous than ever before. The standardization of education, along with other factors, such as new means of electronic communication, have removed some of the unique features of rural culture and narrowed the difference between rural and urban lifestyles. Finally, cultural, social and economic divides are much more obvious in rural places than ever before, especially in North America. Transportation systems linking rural and urban areas, the spread of suburbs into formerly rural areas, the presence of industries with absentee ownership, tourism, retirement income constituting the economic base for many rural areas, and the development policies of nation states – all of these broader structural factors have changed the social and cultural landscapes of rural locales (Smith, 2017; DeKeseredy, 2021b; Donnermeyer, 2019a).

Definition of woman abuse

Unlike liberal feminists who now dominate the study of violence against women (Pease, 2019; DeKeseredy, 2021a),[1] I am among a dwindling group of progressive criminologists who are heavily influenced by radical feminist thought[2] and who (1) sharply reject terms like *intimate partner violence* and

(2) continue to offer gender-specific conceptualizations of the harms covered in this chapter for the following reasons. First, decades ago, feminist critics (for example, Breines and Gordon, 1983) remarked that terms like 'intimate partner violence', 'domestic violence', and 'marital violence' provide an inaccurate 'mutual combat' image of violence in heterosexual relationships (Berk et al, 1983). Put differently, these terms assume that men and women are equally violent. What critics also pointed out is that gender-neutral definitions do not address who initiates the violence, variance in physical strength and fighting competence between men and women, the extent of willingness to use this violence, and whether violence is in self-defence (DeKeseredy and Hinch, 1991).

It is essential to clearly name what one is talking about. It may be perfectly legitimate in certain contexts to discuss both male-on-female and female-on-male violence, but this is not one of those contexts. The violence examined here is primarily committed by men, and the persons who are the objects of such violence are primarily women (Pease, 2019; DeKeseredy, 2021b). Hence, the term *woman abuse* is used throughout this chapter, and it is defined as the misuse of power by a male intimate partner or ex-partner against a woman, resulting in a loss of dignity, control and safety as well as a feeling of powerlessness and entrapment experienced by the woman who is the direct victim of ongoing or repeated physical, psychological, economic, sexual, verbal and/or spiritual abuse. Woman abuse also includes persistent threats or forcing women to witness violence against their children, other relatives, friends, pets and/or cherished possessions by their partner or ex-partners. Woman abuse is integrally linked to the social/economic/political structures, values and policies that create and perpetuate inequality (DeKeseredy and MacLeod, 1997).

Of course, there are other harms women experience that are not included in this definition. However, following Kelly (1987, 1988), all types of woman abuse exist on a continuum ranging from non-physical acts, such as obscene text messages, to physical ones, like rape. Although the idea of the continuum is often used to portray movement from the least serious to the most serious, to scholars like Kelly (1988: 76) and to many adult female survivors, all these behaviours have a 'basic common character'. They are all means of 'abuse intimidation, coercion, intrusion, threat and force' used primarily to control women. No behaviour on the continuum is automatically considered more harmful than another, and, as Kelly (1988: 48) states, women's experiences 'shade into and out of a given category such as sexual harassment which includes looks, gestures and remarks as well as acts which may be defined as assault or rape'.

The continuum enables researchers to document and name a broad array of painful, interrelated behaviours that thousands of women experience daily, many of which are exempt from the purview of the criminal justice system and that are trivialized or minimized by the law, the general public and the mainstream media (McGlynn et al, 2017; DeKeseredy, 2021b). Researchers may analyse sexual harassment, sexual contact, forced intercourse, beatings and other harms separately, but for countless numbers of women, these variants of abuse 'seep into one another' (Ptacek, 2016: 128). The intertwining of different forms of victimization is also defined as *poly-victimization*. This concept refers to 'the experiences of multiple victimizations of *different kinds*, such as sexual victimization, witnessing family violence, and exposure to community violence, not just multiple episodes of the same kind of victimization' (Mitchell et al, 2018: 762).

Saunders (2018: 69) provides an Australian rural example of workplace sexual harassment seeping into rape. A 21-year-old female miner told her:

> I had to ask for access to a bathroom once a month because I had my period! So eventually instead of access to a bathroom, they got me access to a Toyota so that I could drive away to a toilet. So the entire crew knew exactly when I was cycling every single month. And ... they used to piss in the connecting pipes for me to discover when I got back from the drive. And looking back on it now, I also realize that the blokes were also pissing on my boots when I was gone. ... And then during all of this there was this guy who was being really lovely and helpful and friendly at work. And then on my last night as we walked back to our rooms from dinner at the camp, he grabbed me and pulled me into a storeroom and raped me. So [pauses for tears] And after, he just said that didn't want his wife and children to know.

There are also safety-related reasons for using the continuum. A common worry is that narrow legalistic definitions of violence discourage women from seeking social support. If an abused woman's perpetrator's conduct does not coincide with what researchers, criminal justice officials, politicians or the public refer to as violence or abuse, she may be left in a 'twilight zone' where she knows that she has been assaulted, but others do not define it or categorize it in a way that would encourage her to seek help (Momirov with Duffy, 1997; DeKeseredy and Schwartz, 2013). As revealed by a rural Ohio sexual assault survivor interviewed by DeKeseredy and Schwartz (2009: 49), "I don't sit around and share. I keep it to myself. ... I'm not one to sit around and talk about what happened."

What do place and space have to do with it?

Harris's (2016: 70) conceptualizations of space and place guides the literature review provided here.[3] Places are 'fixed geographic locations', while spaces are 'practiced place[s]' that are (de Certeau, 1984: 117), as Harris states: 'created and shaped by the actors that occupy places and actions that occur there at any given moment. Spaces are fora where philosophies, identities, power and control are expressed and resisted, and so any study of space involves a study of the practical and ideological components of an area' (de Certau, 1984: 70).

Issues of place and space are implicitly covered throughout much of the extant social scientific literature on woman abuse in rural and remote areas (Farhall, 2020). For example, two recent reviews of international bodies of knowledge (see DeKeseredy, 2019, 2021b) show that geographic and social isolation is a key theme. So is inadequate (if any) public transportation and the fact that rural women, by comparison, have fewer social support services than their urban and suburban counterparts. If truth be told, one would be hard pressed not to find these three themes addressed throughout all types of academic work on the abuse of rural women. This supports Farhall's (2020: 100) claim that 'despite the heterogeneity of non-metropolitan areas, broad commonalities can be identified across these locales, which may impact on the occurrence, and complicate the experience of' woman abuse.

Male peer support

Farhall (2020: 100) also contends that there are 'traditional, gendered cultural norms that drive or exacerbate violence' which 'can be understood as manifestations of place'. Feminist sociological research supports her assertion. For instance, in rural communities around the world (as well as in many metropolitan places), there are community norms prohibiting abused women from seeking social support (DeKeseredy, 2019). What is more, *male peer support* is endemic to rural places. This concept is defined as the attachments to male peers and the resources that these men provide that encourage and legitimate woman abuse (DeKeseredy, 1988). Until Saunders (2015) published her study of the workplace harassment of women in rural Australia, most of the rural male peer support research focused on male-to-female physical and sexual assaults in private places (for example, households). Additionally, the term 'male peer support' is not used in the Australian literature. Rather, it is referred to as *mateship*, which as Saunders (2015: 49) says:

> provides men with an opportunity to transcend the natural competitiveness that is attributable to male dynamics in the interest of working together for a common purpose (quite often to remedy a threat of some nature). Frequently, the 'threat' takes the form of the unwanted presence of females in a predominantly male environment (such as a traditionally male workplace), giving men the opportunity to 'band together' to 'put the woman back in her place'.

Male peer support can also lead to gang rape, such as what happened to this rural Ohio woman interviewed by DeKeseredy and Schwartz (2009: 69):

> Well, him and his friend got me so wasted. They took turns with me and I remembered most of it, but, um, there were also drugs involved. Not as much on my behalf as theirs. I was just drunk. And I did not remember most of it, and the next morning I woke up feeling so dirty and degraded and then it ended up getting around that I was the slut. ... And in my eyes that was rape, due to the fact that I was drunk. And I definitely didn't deserve that. And I was hurting. I was hurting the next day.

Some 67 per cent of the 43 women interviewed by DeKeseredy and Schwartz reported on a variety of ways in which their ex-partners' male peers perpetuated and legitimated separation/divorce sexual assault. To make matters worse, some of their friends were part of a 'good ol' boys network' consisting of criminal justice officials (Websdale, 1998). Consider what this woman told DeKeseredy and Schwartz (2009: 93):

> Cops are number-one bad for unwanted sex, for forcing unwanted sex on their mates and violence. They've got to change the whole structure of the protective system with more women on the force. They're all men – how's a man gonna relate to what a woman went through? It's a good ol' boys network. And it's terrible that our police have come to that. They're not protection.

Patriarchal social organization

The good ol' boys network and male peer support contribute to high levels of *collective efficacy* that promote woman abuse and discourage women from seeking help. Collective efficacy is commonly defined as 'mutual trust among neighbors combined with a willingness to act on behalf of the common good, specifically to supervise children and to maintain order' (Sampson et al, 1998: 1). Jakobsen's (2016, 2018) Tanzanian research supports scholarly reminders that criminologists should reconceptualize collective efficacy as a form of social organization that enables crimes like violence against women. She (2018: 47) also challenges the 'long-assumed association of violent crime with disorder, disruption, and deviance from social norms'. Instead, she found that violence against women in Tanzania is 'socially legitimate'. Jakobsen's (2016: 415) study shows that with 'violence against women there can in itself be a form of community law enforcement, in that it enforces community norms with the permission of the state to maintain a specific social order'. Likewise, in another part of the Global South – Australia – Saunders (2015: 2) found that sexual harassment in rural workplaces is a 'cultural norm' and 'a debilitating condition that has grown and spread to the point of excessive prevalence within particular communities'.

The empirical work on woman abuse done by Jakobsen, DeKeseredy and Schwartz, and Saunders confirms that what may appear to outsiders as *social disorganization* is often 'simply a different form of social organization if one takes the trouble to look closely' (Wacquant, 1997: 346). Social disorganization is 'the inability of a community structure to realize the common values of its residents and maintain effective controls' (Sampson and Groves, 1989: 777). However, the common values of many rural communities are male dominance and female subservience, and these places are structured in such a way as to promote and legitimate woman abuse.

Male patriarchal attitudes and beliefs

Spaces and places are gendered (Farhall, 2020), and rural communities and the households that exist within them are no exception. In point of fact, rural communities in general are more conservative and patriarchal than urban and suburban places (Harris, 2016; DeKeseredy, 2019). As Pruitt (2008: 441) observes, 'rural women appear even more burdened than their urban counterparts, due in large part to the more rigid and traditional gender-role expectations of their communities'. It is not surprising, then, that rural men's patriarchal attitudes and beliefs are strongly connected to the abuse of women (Wendt, 2016; DeKeseredy and Schwartz, 2009; DeKeseredy, 2021b). Thus, what Websdale (1998: 194) argued 24 years ago still holds true today. When developing strategies aimed at preventing rural woman abuse, 'any social policy initiatives must use the structure of rural patriarchy, in all its intricate manifestations, as an essential frame of reference'.

DeKeseredy and Schwartz's (2009) rural Ohio project provides salient examples of the association between patriarchal control and separation/ divorce violence. Of the 43 women in their study, 69 per cent said that their partners believed that men should be in charge and control of domestic household settings. As well, most of their respondents said they were raped because their partners wanted to show them 'who was in charge'. Tanya was one of many interviewees who had a partner fiercely determined not to let her go:

> He did it because I was his and he felt he could. And it was his way of letting me know that, ah, first of all, of letting me know I was his. And secondly, letting me know that um, that I wasn't safe anywhere. And I, when we were together ... when he forced me to go back together with him, ah, he, ah ... raped me as another form of, of possession. And I think also as a reminder of what could happen. And ultimately,

at one point, I believed he raped me as part of his means of killing my unborn child. (DeKeseredy and Schwartz, 2009: 72)

Hall-Sanchez's (2014: 505) qualitative study done in roughly the same geographic area uncovered similar results. Debbie, for instance, told her:

I remember one time … I did try to get away from him and it was rough, and it was 'you're gonna do this because you're my wife!' and 'you said that we were back together again!' Because I didn't want to get hurt. Because I knew if I started a fight with him then, it would've gotten ugly. I felt terrible. … I just wish this was over, you know. … I just don't want this. And it went on and on and finally he just, it was over. And I remember going outside on the deck and cryin' and cryin'. … I felt filthy and it was my husband. … And I threw up and I got sick and screamed and … I felt horrible, just dirty.

There is global feminist resistance to patriarchy (Enloe, 2017), but it is still very much alive. 'In most societies around the world', irrespective of whether they are urban, suburban, or rural, 'the gender structure is patriarchal' (Renzetti, 2013: 8). Consider rural Montenegro. Despotovic et al (2019: 95) found that: 'The remains of the classic Montenegrin patriarchal family still exist in the Montenegrin village today. The woman is still sought after somewhere as a workforce, as an economic unit, and as a reproductive unit for the production of children, especially sons'.

Male pornography consumption

Male pornography consumption is a highly destructive symptom of patriarchy and a behaviour that is strongly associated with male peer support (DeKeseredy and Corsianos, 2016; DeKeseredy, 2020). Like urban and suburban places, rural communities are riddled with pornography (DeKeseredy, 2021b), and thousands of internet porn videos feature violent, degrading images of rural people (DeKeseredy et al, 2014). Also, the US male porn consumption rate is the world's highest and this problem, together with other factors discussed in this chapter, puts rural US women at greater risk of experiencing non-lethal woman abuse than US women living in more densely populated areas (DeKeseredy, 2019).

A mushrooming social scientific literature demonstrates that male porn use is a significant determinant of a wide range of abusive experiences in the lives of many adult and young women and it is strongly associated with sexual behaviour in general (DeKeseredy, 2020; Tarzia and Tyler, 2021; Wright, 2020). For example, based on interviews with 55 rural Ohio survivors of separation/divorce sexual assault, DeKeseredy and

Hall-Sanchez (2017) found that 41 had male partners who viewed porn, and imitation is a major theme that emerged from talking to them. One of their respondents, for instance, knew her ex-partner viewed violent porn and describes the familiar language and demeaning behaviours often featured in violent porn videos:[4]

> I remember him making me give him oral sex and holding me by the hair and I don't remember if it was after a fight or what. He's done that I don't know how many times. He used to urinate on me and then want sex. I mean after getting hit and stuff. ... He would talk the whole time he was doing that and saying things like uh, 'you're my bitch' or 'you like it bitch, don't you?' And stuff like that. Um, 'this is my ass, you know. I'll kill for my ass.' Stuff like that and it would be just as violent as the beatings and basically you just lay there and let it happen. (DeKeseredy and Hall-Sanchez, 2017: 839)

DeKeseredy and Hall-Sanchez (2017) uncovered four other key themes: learning about sex through pornography; introducing other sexual partners; filming sexual acts without consent; and the broader culture of pornography (for example, sex work and fetishes). Regardless of what motivates abusive men to consume porn, DeKeseredy and Hall-Sanchez's rural data bring to the fore some cases of women whose abusive experiences are directly linked to their ex-partners' use of porn. Was, however, porn the direct *cause* of these women's victimization? This question certainly cannot be answered using DeKeseredy and Hall-Sanchez's (2017) qualitative data or quantitative correlational data. The problem is that it might very well be that the same factors that cause a man to abuse women might also cause him to consume porn (DeKeseredy and Corsianos, 2016). Still, DeKeseredy and Hall-Sanchez's data show a positive relationship between porn use and sexual and physical assaults on rural women.

There are, to be sure, other characteristics of rural places that contribute to woman abuse, including mining as documented by Australian and North American research (for example, Carrington et al, 2011). So do high rates of gun ownership (DeKeseredy, 2021b), the emergence of resource-based booms (Ruddell and Britto, 2020), male hunting subcultures (Hall-Sanchez, 2014, 2019), men's heavy alcohol consumption (Hogg and Carrington, 2016), and environmental disasters like fires, droughts and floods (Alston, 2013; Parkinson and Zara, 2013; Wendt, 2016). Additionally, there is mounting evidence that many rural women are now at higher risk of being abused because of isolation caused by the COVID-19 pandemic (Bouillon-Minois et al, 2020; DeKeseredy, 2021b). The continued use of spatial analyses will surely uncover other major risk factors and unquestionably, more research is necessary.

New avenues of empirical inquiry

Much has been learned about woman abuse in rural and remote places since the publication of Gagné's (1992) path-breaking ethnographic study of the plight of women in rural Appalachia.[5] In fact, Gagné's work played an important role in sparking the research reviewed here, and again, more empirical work is required. The following recommendations constitute just the tip of the iceberg, and it is likely that many readers could suggest more topics to examine and the use of additional research techniques. One method that is sorely needed is a cross-cultural survey, one that is crafted specifically to test hypotheses from theories. The bulk of quantitative studies of rural woman abuse done so far have not tested theories and focus heavily on rural, urban and suburban variations (Edwards, 2015; DeKeseredy and Rennison, 2020).

Also essential are prospective and longitudinal studies because most of the surveys conducted to date are cross-sectional, which makes it difficult to identify risk and prospective factors related to perpetration (Edwards, 2015; DeKeseredy, 2021b). One noticeable exception to this rule is the national, population-based longitudinal study of Australian women conducted by Dillon et al (2016).

There is a shortage of quantitative studies of male-to-female psychological abuse in rural places. The few that have been done (Zakar et al, 2016, for instance) demonstrate that it is the most common type of abuse that rural women experience. This is not to say, though, that qualitative studies of psychological and other types of non-physical abuse are plentiful. Definitely, more are needed because the few that have been conducted (for example, DeKeseredy and Schwartz, 2009) reveal that woman abuse is multidimensional in nature and many survivors report that non-physical assaults are their worst experiences. For example, a small-scale study of woman abuse in two rural parts of Southwest Ontario, Canada (Perth and Huron Counties) reveal what the researchers define as *emotional abuse* played a key role in women's traumatic experiences (Center for Community Based Research, 2013: 17). One participant confirms that abuse is multifaceted: "Many of those types of violence are intertwined ... physical abuse, sexual, emotional abuse – I mean I don't know that you can separate them out." Additionally, emotional abuse was reported to be the most prevalent in the research sites.

There is, especially in Australia, a rapidly growing body of research on what Harris (2016) defines as *spaceless violence*. Major examples are technology-facilitated stalking and image-based sexual abuse[6] that can target women anywhere they use electronic devices like smartphones or tablets. Harris (2016: 83) postulates that 'those who experience technology-facilitated stalking are in greater danger of being seriously or fatally harmed, and survivors who are geographically isolated are exposed to even greater risk when living significant distances from police and health services'. She may be right, but as of now, we know little about the extent, nature, distribution, causes and consequences of the online victimization of women living in rural and remote areas (DeKeseredy and Hall-Sanchez, 2018; DeKeseredy, 2021b).

Conclusion

Perhaps it is most fitting to begin this conclusion by returning to Harris (2016: 84) who argues that:

> To truly understand context, it is crucial to examine [woman abuse] through, not only historical or geographical lenses, but also through a spatial lens. A framework of place, space, and spacelessness offers insight into the incidence, experiences and responses to violence as well as how violence could be more effectively prevented and survivors protected and empowered.

Spatial studies help many abused rural women come 'out of the shadows' (Fong, 2010). More research, including comparative work, is on the horizon. The connections between Australian and US feminist scholars are especially strong and contribute to the development of new global perspectives on woman abuse in rural contexts. Even so, the field will not advance as much as it should unless it makes a point of doing spatial analyses outside of the Global North and in non-English-speaking countries, and the results should be featured in widely read and cited journals. Such work will often require translators and, hopefully, leading publishers of journals like Sage and Taylor and Francis will recognize the importance of covering the costs of translational work.

This chapter is but one chronicle of 'travels through crime and place'[7] and the journey taken by feminists who study the abuse of women in rural places and spaces is just beginning. Certainly, woman abuse in rural and remote areas is a social issue that is constantly evolving and never-ending (Ledwitz-Rigby, 1993). Hopefully, some colleagues will do the types of research suggested here and supply new progressive answers to the question 'What is to be done about woman abuse in non-metropolitan areas?' In the words of True (2012: 183), 'Researching violence against women – the point is to end it'.

Notes

[1] Liberal feminists contend that women are discriminated against based on their sex, as they are denied access to the same political, financial, career and personal opportunities as men (Brubaker, 2019). For them, the problem of gender inequality can be solved by clearing the way for 'women's rapid integration into what has been the world of men' (Ehrenreich and English, 1978: 19).

2   Radical feminists argue that the most important set of social relations is found in patriarchy. All other social relations, such as class, are secondary and originate from male–female relations (Beirne and Messerschmidt, 2014).

3   The heading for this section is a modified version of the title of Donnermeyer's (2019b) contribution to DeKeseredy et al's (2019) anthology.

4   This current era features the degradation, abuse and humiliation of women never seen before in the mass media. I am not referring to erotica, which is 'sexually suggestive or arousing material that is free of sexism, racism, and homophobia and is respectful of all human beings and animals portrayed' (Russell, 1993: 3). Rather, my conceptualization of porn focuses squarely on what Etheredge and Lemon (2015: 4) refer to as sexual media that are 'violent and regularly depict participants (mainly young women) in distressed situations or scenarios where they are being violently and inhumanely treated'.

5   Like the concept 'rural', the term 'Appalachia' is defined in many ways. However, it generally refers to a US geographic region associated with the Appalachian Mountains and the people who work there (DeKeseredy and Schwartz, 2009).

6   Prime examples of such abuse are videos made by men with the consent of the women they were intimately involved with, but then distributed online without their consent following women's termination of a relationship (Henry et al, 2021; Salter and Crofts, 2015).

7   This quotation is the title of DeLeon-Granados's (1999) scholarly monograph.

References

Alston, M. (2013) 'Environmental social work: accounting for gender in climate disasters', *Australian Social Work*, 66(2): 218–233.

Beirne, P. and Messerschmidt, J.W. (2014) *Criminology: A Sociological Approach* (6th edn), New York: Oxford University Press.

Berk, R.A., Berk, S.F., Loseke, D.R. and Rauma, D. (1983) 'Mutual combat and other family violence myths', in D. Finkelhor, R.J. Gelles, G.T. Hotaling and M.A. Straus (eds) *The Dark Side of Families: Current Family Violence Research*, Thousand Oaks, CA: Sage, pp 197–212.

Bouillon-Minois, J., Clinchamps, M. and Dutheil, F. (2020) 'Coronavirus and quarantine: catalysts of domestic violence', *Violence Against Women*, ahead of print. Available from: https://doi.org/10.1177/1077801220935 194 [Accessed 22 April 2022].

Breines, W. and Gordon, L. (1983) 'The new scholarship on family violence', *Signs*, 8(3): 490–531.

Brubaker, S.J. (2019) *Theorizing Gender Violence*, San Diego, CA: Cognella.

Carrington, K., Hogg, R. and McIntosh, A. (2011) 'The resource boom's underbelly: the criminological impact of mining development', *Australian and New Zealand Journal of Criminology*, 44(3): 335–354.

Center for Community Based Research (2013) *A Study of Violence Against Women in Perth and Huron Counties*, Kitchener, ON: Social Research & Planning Council Perth and Huron.

de Certeau, M. (1984) *The Practice of Everyday Life*, Berkeley: University of California Press.

DeKeseredy, W.S. (1988) 'Woman abuse in dating relationships: the relevance of social support theory', *Journal of Family Violence*, 3(1): 1–13.

DeKeseredy, W.S. (2019) 'Intimate violence against rural women: the current state of sociological knowledge', *International Journal of Rural Criminology*, 4(2): 312–331.

DeKeseredy, W.S. (2020) *Understanding the Harms of Pornography: The Contribution of Social Scientific Knowledge*, report prepared for Culture Reframed. Available from: https://www.culturereframed.org/wp-cont ent/uploads/2020/02/CR_Harms_of_Porn_Report_2020.pdf [Accessed 8 June 2021].

DeKeseredy, W.S. (2021a) 'Bringing feminist sociological analyses of patriarchy back to the forefront of the study of woman abuse', *Violence Against Women*, 27(5): 621–638.

DeKeseredy, W.S. (2021b) *Woman Abuse in Rural Places*, Abingdon: Routledge.

DeKeseredy, W.S. and Corsianos, M. (2016) *Violence Against Women in Pornography*, Abingdon: Routledge.

DeKeseredy, W.S. and Hall-Sanchez, A.K. (2017) 'Adult pornography and violence against women in the heartland: results from a rural southeast Ohio study', *Violence Against Women*, 23(7): 830–849.

DeKeseredy, W.S. and Hall-Sanchez, A.K. (2018) 'Male violence against women in the Global South: what we know and what we don't know', in K. Carrington, R. Hogg, J. Scott and M. Sozzo (eds) *The Palgrave Handbook of Criminology and the Global South*, Cham: Palgrave Macmillan, pp 883–900.

DeKeseredy, W.S. and Hinch, R. (1991) *Woman Abuse: Sociological Perspectives*, Toronto: Thompson Educational.

DeKeseredy, W.S. and MacLeod, L. (1997) *Woman Abuse: A Sociological Story*, Toronto: Harcourt Brace.

DeKeseredy, W.S. and Rennison, C.M. (2020) 'Thinking theoretically about male violence against women in rural places: a review of the extant sociological literature and suggestions for future theorizing', *International Journal of Rural Criminology*, 5(2): 162–180.

DeKeseredy, W.S. and Schwartz, M.D. (2009) *Dangerous Exits: Escaping Abusive Relationships in Rural America*, New Brunswick, NJ: Rutgers University Press.

DeKeseredy, W.S. and Schwartz, M.D. (2013) *Male Peer Support and Violence Against Women: The History and Verification of a Theory*, Boston, MA: Northeastern University Press.

DeKeseredy, W.S., Muzzatti, S.L. and Donnermeyer, J.F. (2014) 'Mad men in bib overalls: media's horrification and pornification of rural culture', *Critical Criminology*, 22(2): 179–197.

DeKeseredy, W.S., Rennison, C.M. and Hall-Sanchez, A.K. (eds) (2019) *The Routledge International Handbook of Violence Studies*, Abingdon: Routledge.

DeKeseredy, W.S., Donnermeyer, J.F., Schwartz, M.D., Tunnell, K.D. and Hall, M. (2007) 'Thinking critically about rural gender relations: toward a rural masculinity crisis/male peer support model of separation/divorce sexual assault', *Critical Criminology*, 15(4): 295–311.

DeLeon-Granados, W. (1999) *Travels Through Crime and Place: Community Building as Crime Control*, Boston, MA: Northeastern University Press.

Despotovic, A., Joksimovic, M. and Jovanovic, M. (2019) 'Contemporary and traditional in the life of a rural woman', *Agriculture and Forestry*, 65(3): 93–104.

Dillon, G., Hussain, R., Kibele, E., Rahman, S. and Loxton, D. (2016) 'Influence of intimate partner violence on domestic relocation in metropolitan and non-metropolitan young Australian women', *Violence Against Women*, 22(13): 1597–1620.

Donnermeyer, J.F. (2019a) 'The international emergence of rural criminology: implications for the development and revision of criminological theory for rural contexts', *International Journal of Rural Criminology*, 5(1): 1–18.

Donnermeyer, J.F. (2019b) 'What's place got to do with it? Explaining violence in a rural context', in W.S. DeKeseredy, C.M. Rennison and A.K. Hall-Sanchez (eds) *The Routledge International Handbook of Violence Studies*, Abingdon: Routledge, pp 95–120.

Donnermeyer, J.F. (2020) 'Social justice and problematizing the concept of "rural"', in A. Harkness (ed) *Rural Crime Prevention: Theory, Tactics and Techniques*, Abingdon: Routledge, pp 19–29.

Donnermeyer, J.F. and DeKeseredy, W.S. (2014) *Rural Criminology*, Abingdon: Routledge.

Edwards, K.M. (2015) 'Intimate partner violence and the rural–urban–suburban divide: myth or reality?', *Trauma, Violence, & Abuse*, 16(3): 359–373.

Ehrenreich, B. and English, D. (1978) *For Her Own Good: 150 Years of the Experts' Advice to Women*, Garden City, NJ: Anchor.

Enloe, C. (2017) *The Big Push: Exposing and Challenging the Persistence of Patriarchy*, Oakland, CA: University of California Press.

Etheredge, L. and Lemon, J. (2015) *Submission to the Royal Commission into Family Violence, Victoria 2015: Pornography, Problem Sexual Behaviour and Sibling on Sibling Sexual Violence*, Victoria, AU: Royal Commission into Family Violence. Available from: www.rcfv.com.au/getattachment/B8A61 74A-6C6F-495F-BF7B-9CA9BF902840/Etheredge,-Linette [Accessed 22 April 2022].

Farhall, K. (2020) 'Towards an integrated theoretical framework for understanding women, work and violence in non-metropolitan contexts', *Journal of Rural Studies*, 76: 96–110.

Fong, J. (ed) (2010) *Out of the Shadows: Woman Abuse in Ethnic, Immigrant, and Aboriginal Communities*, Toronto: Women's Press.

Gagné, P.L. (1992) 'Appalachian women: violence and social control', *Journal of Contemporary Ethnography*, 20(4): 387–415.

Hall-Sanchez, A.K. (2014) 'Male peer support, hunting, and separation/divorce sexual assault in rural Ohio', *Critical Criminology*, 22(4): 495–510.

Hall-Sanchez, A.K. (2019) 'Male hunting subcultures and violence against women', in W.S. DeKeseredy, C.M. Rennison and A.K. Hall-Sanchez (eds) *The Routledge International Handbook of Violence Studies*, Abingdon: Routledge, pp 329–338.

Harris, B. (2016) 'Violent landscapes: a spatial study of family violence', in A. Harkness, B. Harris and D. Baker (eds) *Locating Crime in Context and Place: Perspectives on Regional, Rural and Remote Australia*, Sydney: Federation Press, pp 70–84.

Harris, B. and Harkness, A. (2016) 'Introduction: locating regional, rural and remote crime in theoretical and contemporary context', in A. Harkness, B. Harris and D. Baker (eds) *Locating Crime in Context and Place: Perspectives on Regional, Rural and Remote Australia*, Sydney: Federation Press, pp 1–12.

Hart, T.C., Lersch, K.M. and Chataway, M. (2020) *Space, Time, and Crime* (5th edn), Durham, NC: Carolina Academic Press.

Henry, N. McGlynn, C., Flynn, A., Johnson, K., Powell, A. and Scott, A.J. (2021) *Image-Based Sexual Abuse: A Study on the Causes and Consequences of Non-Consensual Nude or Sexual Imagery*, London: Routledge.

Hogg, K. and Carrington, K. (2016) 'Crime and violence outside the metropole: an Australian case study', in J.F. Donnermeyer (ed) *The Routledge International Handbook of Rural Criminology*, Abingdon, Routledge, pp 181–189.

Jakobsen, H. (2016) 'Community law enforcement in rural Tanzania', in J.F. Donnermeyer (ed) *The Routledge International Handbook of Rural Criminology*, Abingdon: Routledge, pp 409–417.

Jakobsen, H. (2018) 'How violence constitutes order: consent, coercion, and censure in Tanzania', *Violence Against Women*, 24(1): 45–65.

Kelly, L. (1987) 'The continuum of sexual violence', in J. Hanmer and M. Maynard (eds) *Women, Violence and Social Control*, Atlantic Highlands, NJ: Humanities Press International, pp 46–60.

Kelly, L. (1988) *Surviving Sexual Violence*, Minneapolis: University of Minnesota Press.

Ledwitz-Rigby, E. (1993) 'An administrative approach to personal safety on campus: the role of a president's advisory Committee on Women's Safety on Campus', *Journal of Human Justice*, 4(2): 85–94.

McGlynn, C., Rackley, E. and Houghton, R. (2017) 'Beyond "revenge porn": the continuum of image-based sexual abuse', *Feminist Legal Studies*, 25(1): 25–46.

Mitchell, K.J., Segura, A., Jones, L.M. and Turner, H.A. (2018) 'Poly-victimization and peer harassment involvement in a technological world', *Journal of Interpersonal Violence*, 33(5): 762–788.

Momirov, J. with Duffy, A. (1997) *Family Violence: A Canadian Introduction* (2nd edn), Toronto: Lorimer.

Parkinson, D. and Zara, C. (2013) 'The hidden disaster: domestic violence in the aftermath of natural disaster', *Australian Journal of Emergency Management*, 28(2): 28–35.

Pease, B. (2019) *Facing Patriarchy: From a Violent Gender Order to a Culture of Peace*, London: Zed Books.

Pruitt, L.R. (2008) 'Place matters: domestic violence and rural difference', *Wisconsin Journal of Law, Gender and Society*, 23(2): 347–416.

Ptacek, J. (2016) 'Rape and the continuum of sexual abuse in intimate relationships: interviews with US women from different classes', in K. Yllö and M.G. Torres (eds) *Marital Rape: Consent, Marriage, and Social Change in Global Context*, New York: Oxford University Press, pp 123–138.

Renzetti, C.M. (2013) *Feminist Criminology*, Abingdon: Routledge.

Ruddell, R. and Britto, S. (2020) 'A perfect storm: violence toward women in the Bakken oil patch', *International Journal of Rural Criminology*, 5(2): 204–227.

Russell, D.E.H. (1993) *Against Pornography: The Evidence of Harm*, Berkeley, CA: Russell Publications.

Salter, M. and Crofts, T. (2015) 'Responding to revenge porn: challenging online legal impunity', in L. Comella and S. Tarrant (eds) *New Views on Pornography: Sexuality, Politics and the Law*, Santa Barbara, CA: Praeger, pp 233–253.

Sampson, R.J. and Groves, W.B. (1989) 'Community structure and crime: testing social disorganization theory', *American Journal of Sociology*, 94(4): 774–802.

Sampson, R.J., Raudenbush, S.W. and Earls, F. (1998) *Neighborhood Collective Efficacy: Does It Work?*, Washington, DC: United States Department of Justice.

Saunders, S. (2015) *Whispers from the Bush: The Workplace Sexual Harassment of Australian Rural Women*, Sydney: Federation Press.

Saunders, S. (2018) 'Blurred lines: the intersection of gendered harm in rural Australia', *Domestic Violence Report*, 23(5): 69–72.

Scott, J., Hogg, R., Barclay, E. and Donnermeyer, J.F. (2007) 'Introduction: there's crime out there, but not as we know it: rural criminology – the last frontier', in E. Barclay, J.F. Donnermeyer, J. Scott and R. Hogg (eds) *Crime in Rural Australia*, Sydney: Federation Press, pp 1–12.

Smith, K. (2017) 'Changing gender roles and rural poverty', in A.R. Tickamyer, J. Sherman and J. Warlick (eds) *Rural Poverty in the United States*, New York: Columbia University Press, pp 117–140.

Tarzia, L. and Tyler, M. (2021) 'Recognizing connections between intimate partner sexual violence and pornography', *Violence Against Women*, 27(14): 2687–2708.

True, J. (2012) *The Political Economy of Violence Against Women*, New York: Oxford University Press.

Wacquant, L.J.D. (1997) 'Three pernicious premises in the study of the American ghetto', *International Journal of Urban and Regional Research*, 21(2): 341–353.

Websdale, N. (1995) 'An ethnographic assessment of the policing of domestic violence in rural eastern Kentucky', *Social Justice*, 22(1): 102–122.

Websdale, N. (1998) *Rural Women Battering and the Justice System: An Ethnography*, Thousand Oaks, CA: Sage.

Weisburd, D., Groff, E.R. and Yang, S.M. (2012) *The Criminology of Place: Street Segments and Our Understanding of the Crime Problem*, New York: Oxford University Press.

Wendt, S. (2016) 'Intimate violence and abuse in Australian rural contexts', in J.F. Donnermeyer (ed) *The Routledge International Handbook of Rural Criminology*, Abingdon, Routledge, pp 191–199.

Woods, M. (2011) *Rural*, Abingdon: Routledge.

Wright, P.J. (2020) 'Pornography and sexual behavior: do sexual attitudes mediate or confound?', *Communication Research*, 47(3): 451–475.

Zakar, R., Zakar, M.Z. and Abbas, S. (2016) 'Domestic violence against rural women in Pakistan: an issue of health and human rights', *Journal of Family Violence*, 31(1): 15–25.

7

Algorithmic Bias in Digital Space: Twitter's Complicity in Gender-Based Violence

Cat Morgan and Sarah Hewitt

Introduction

On Twitter, when a woman is attacked for expressing a view or opinion, other people are often 'called in' or 'called over' from other virtual spaces to engage in a 'pile-on' (an orchestrated attempt to silence others by getting as many people as possible to criticize, question and threaten). Her voice is lost, and the effort of fighting to be heard no doubt becomes too much for some. In this chapter we examine how Twitter can be used to promote violence against women (VAW) to silence them. We do this by exploring computer-mediated communication briefly before drawing on more contemporary research to highlight the ongoing issue.

We engage with literature from two disciplines, web science and sociology, drawing them together (Repko and Szostak, 2020) to address our focus. Web science is a relatively new discipline in computer science, which ascertains how people and the Web co-create each other (Halford et al, 2010). Using an interdisciplinary approach enables us to understand Twitter as a digital space: how human and machine processes interact and why reporting processes do not work for everyone. Sociology is a broad discipline that allows us to investigate how digital spaces develop and the social rules that guide them. Given that a corpus of literature has focused on VAW online, we investigate – as far as is possible – Twitter's use of automated machine learning to detect instances of abuse.

Throughout this chapter, we identify how and why we consider Twitter a virtual geographic space that can be measured and analysed. We contend that the rules, algorithms and corporate policies that govern digital spaces shape women's experiences. We contextualize the proliferation of online misogyny and gendered cyberhate, which targets women. We assess the use of automated machine learning processes in managing reports of abusive behaviours and argue that they reinforce gender inequalities (Noble, 2018). We conclude by summing up the main points of this chapter and sharing our suggestion for ways that VAW may be tackled by Twitter and improve everyone's platform.

Twitter as a virtual geographic space

We access social media sites like Twitter via our mobile phones, laptops, tablets and so forth. Twitter exists 'out there' in the virtual world; a disembodied space that anyone can enter and leave at any time. It is a 'virtual space' that exists as a concept, provided by physical machines (servers) and lines of code. 'Users' exist in the real, physical world, and provided they have revealed their geographical location honestly, we can identify their position on a map. They may be thousands of miles away from us physically yet occupy the same space and time as us virtually when we interact online. In fact, we do not even need to be 'present' in the online space simultaneously, as discussions can take place over hours, days, weeks or even months.

Cyberspace is constructed in metaphors to reflect the real physical world; for example, video conferencing platforms Zoom has 'conference rooms', and Microsoft Teams has a 'lobby'. Our point is that we use these cyberspace metaphors to describe physical space, which makes platforms such as Twitter an extension of the real world; Harris and Vitis refer to this as 'spacelessness' (2020: 325). While we may think of cyberspace in metaphors that anchor it in the physical world, there are many differences. Cartography maps our planet's surface, whereas cybermaps are thematic (such as we see in electronic games) or become site maps represented as a topological structure (Jiang and Ormeling, 2000). Here, the nodes have no meaning or function except to describe their connections (see Figures 7.1 and 7.2). In a social network, connections link people with others precisely like a traditional map records places where people are now or have been.

How we measure distance on social media must be thought about differently from how we measure it in the physical world: it is not miles or kilometres but is relational. Social networks must be considered otherwise, as they do not represent distance so much as connections between people. One method for conceptualizing and measuring online space is network theory. Network theory allows us to conceptualize and measure social networks to show the connections between people or objects. 'Objects' can be thought of as actors or users of the (social media) network and are referred to as 'vertices'. 'Edges' are the links or actors. A social network can be 'undirected',

Figure 7.1: Undirected network

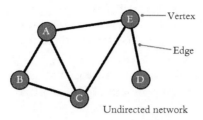

Undirected network

Figure 7.2: Directed network

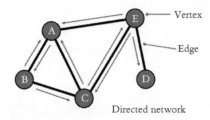

Directed network

like Facebook, where 'friendships' are mutual, whereas 'follows' on Twitter are not. An individual is free to follow whomever they choose (unless they are blocked), but a follow back is not automatic.

Software exists that will use Twitter data to map the network ties between individuals and carry out a series of calculations to establish the distance between individuals, identify individuals with the most ties, or individuals that act as a 'bridge' between clusters. So, what does a network look like? Figure 7.1 shows a small, undirected network. Here, we can see that vertex D is only connected to vertex E, whereas vertex A is connected to B, C and E directly, and through E to D. Facebook is an undirected network.

Figure 7.2 represents a directed network. Here, we can see that vertex D is not connected to any other node, whereas node A is connected to nodes B and E only. Twitter is a directed network.

From a geospatial perspective, the length of the edges in either network is arbitrary. Distance is calculated using the number of journeys (typically referred to as 'hops') it would take to get from, say, node A to node D. In Figure 7.1, it is two. In Figure 7.2, it is four (A to B to C to E to D). These are highly simplified examples, but the concept should be clear. Facebook, an undirected network, initially connected *everyone*, but privacy concerns meant that the platform had to allow people to remain invisible or 'unfriend'. Twitter enables people to 'block' or to make your account 'protected'. These options disrupt the network in terms of distance, but for individuals or, for example, hashtags, distances are still valid.

While social networks require a separate way of measuring them as a space, focused on connections rather than distances, we should not think of them as different from the physical world. Instead, Malpas argued, the virtual is embedded: 'the virtual is a *product* or *artefact* of the everyday' (2009: 135 original emphasis). Social networks such as Twitter are built and used according to our 'everyday actions' and social rules in the real world so that our social engagements are (or should be) conducted on the same terms as we use in our everyday lives. We say 'should be' because, since Malpas, there has been much research into behaviours on social media, particularly how behaviour may change when communicating in an environment where we are not familiar with the person we are conversing with and where we are afforded a sense of anonymity.

Defining and describing gendered cyberhate

Scholarly investigations of misogyny online have led to a range of terms, including: 'cybersexism' (Penny, 2013); 'e-bile' (Jane, 2014a); 'gendertrolling' (Mantilla, 2015); 'online misogyny' (Jane, 2016; Banet-Weiser, 2018) and 'technology-facilitated sexual violence' (Henry and Powell, 2018). We use Jane's (2017, 2020) term 'gendered cyberhate' to refer to a range of discourse and behaviours that target women, including trolling, rape threats, pile-ons, racism and doxing. The Women's Media Center Speech Project designed the Online Abuse Wheel, which outlines more behaviours and demonstrates the connection between technology, violence and gender – more so, that gendered cyberhate is part of a continuum of male violence that aims to keep women in their proper place in the hierarchy: inferior to men.

By 2013, digital misogyny – gendered cyberhate, as we will now refer to it – had garnered much attention in mainstream media following the abuse of several high-profile women. For example, Caroline Criado Perez was targeted with thousands of tweets, some containing death and rape threats, having campaigned with Labour MP Stella Creasy for a woman to be on the back of a banknote (Blunden, 2015). In the same year, the classicist Mary Beard received abuse via Twitter following her appearance on the television programme *Question Time*. She later delivered a lecture at the British Museum entitled *Oh Do Shut Up Dear!* exploring how women's voices had been silenced through history (Mead, 2014). There are, no doubt, many other examples of misogynist comments on other social networking sites, blogs and the comments sections of newspaper articles. Other websites such as Reddit have whole sections of the online space devoted to examples of, for instance, pornography, all posted anonymously. Many more examples across the Web are documented in Citron's (2014) *Hate Crimes in Cyberspace*.

Flaming

Many different labels that describe the expression of extreme conflict on social media have emerged over the years. One of the earliest was 'flaming'. Not everyone agreed that 'flaming' took place. Still, it was often a result of a misunderstanding that computer-mediated communication must be understood within the framework of the interplay between sender, receiver and interpreter (O'Sullivan and Flanagin, 2003). O'Sullivan and Flanagin's (2003) study was centred on emails sent and received within the work environment. In contrast, a later study by Alonzo and Aitken (2004) applied the uses and gratifications theory (which focuses on motivation) to determine that 'assertiveness and sensation seeking predicted flaming' (Alonzo and Aitken, 2004: 205). Significantly, their findings show that the primary motivation was disinhibition; 68 per cent of men wrote flames for the purposes of entertainment, compared with 32 per cent of women.

Trolling

If we agree that *motivation* is the critical factor for flaming, 'trolling' is this form of behaviour taken to the extreme. In *This is Why We Can't Have Nice Things*, Phillips (2015) examines trolling and describes it as a 'spectrum of behaviours' (2015: 23) ranging from 'rickrolling' where a user posts a misleading link (Heffernan, 2018), to that which is particularly aggressive and can meet the legal definition of harassment. One of the most prolific examples of trolling is Gamergate in 2014, targeting women in the gaming industry. Designers Zoe Quinn and Brianna Wu, and game critic Anita Sarkeesian, were the target of sustained and targeted trolling (Salter, 2018). The hashtag #GamerGate became the focal point of a concerted effort to threaten women's participation in a technological sphere (Banet-Weiser, 2018). Hashtags were introduced by users to make content searchable (Gannes, 2010), which were then built into the design of Twitter to enable users to converse with many users on the same subject (Murthy, 2018). Trolling tactics used were death and rape threats, doxing (sharing personal information that could be used to locate someone in the real world), and shared memes using #GamerGate to create a hate and abuse campaign. Gamergate was motivated by the desire to protect gaming and tech culture from women, who sought equity in representation and themes (Salter, 2018). After Gamergate, Wu highlighted the lack of support from the industry: 'We need the male professionals in our field to understand the unconscious bias that they consistently show against women' (2015).

Toxic misogyny

The level of gendered cyberhate that existed on Twitter (and other social networking sites) also became the focus of some scholarly research. One of the first was Jane's paper '"Back to the kitchen, cunt"' (2014b). Read against a background of stories like those previously mentioned, Jane (2014b) suggested that misogynist language was becoming a lingua franca. While this chapter does not discuss the use of language as a pointer to social and cultural attitudes and traditions, it is reasonable to state that how we communicate with each other encodes various meanings, including our social status and perceived gender hierarchy. If misogynist language is becoming commonplace, it is also reasonable to suppose that the language may be re-enforcing that hierarchy, even if (and, arguably, especially if) the bias is unconscious.

In the same year, McLean and Maalsen discussed a 'geography of revitalised feminism in social media' (2013). They described Twitter as a 'paradoxical space', existing as it does in a place where we might expose some personal details about ourselves in return for conversation and connection. Their paper discussed the social media campaign 'destroy the joint', which was orchestrated following a comment by the then prime minister of Australia's challenge to a radio presenter that women were 'ruining the country'. The campaign and various sub-campaigns analysed in the paper were generally successful. The authors are optimistic about the impact the use of social media can have on platform gender inequality. This may be true, but a campaign can be hard to attack on social media. The easier targets are the women behind the campaigns, although it should be remembered that the #GamerGate campaign already referred to was used to attack *individual* women.

Contemporary social, cultural and political conditions have facilitated the proliferation of toxic misogyny: this has been strengthened by Brexit in the UK and Trump's rise to the US presidency in 2016 (Ging and Siapera, 2019). An Amnesty International UK report surveyed women across eight countries, and found that 23 per cent had been digitally abused or harassed at least once; 27 per cent were threatened with physical or sexual violence; 47 per cent experienced sexist or misogynistic abuse, and 36 per cent felt their physical safety was threatened (Amnesty International UK, 2017). In 2014, the UK think tank Demos published a report *Misogyny on Twitter* (Bartlett et al, 2014). One of the key findings was that between 26 December 2013 and 9 February 2014, the word 'rape' was used more than 100,000 times, with approximately 12 per cent of those uses being threatening. That is 1,250 examples of VAW in just over a month (Bartlett et al, 2014). An investigation by Hardaker and McGlashan (2016) used the case study of abuse that Criado Perez received in 2013, explicitly focused on using the word 'rape' and sexual aggression on Twitter. They recorded 92 days' worth of activity on Twitter involving Criado Perez and found that the *n*-gram 'rape threats' occurred 1,419 times, 43.69 per cent of the collected corpus of tweets. Hardaker and McGlashan identified 'high-risk users' as those who tweeted threats (and used hate speech) to give rise to legal action.

Although Twitter does not require users to disclose their gender, it is, in fact, a male-centric digital space, where 70 per cent of users worldwide are male (Statista, 2020). The use of Twitter by Men's Rights activist groups forms part of the 'manosphere' alongside YouTube, 4chan and the r/MensRights subreddit. Typically, how the media frames digital misogyny minimizes the abuse and scrutinizes women's behaviours (Lumsden and Morgan, 2017). Significantly, the Criado Perez incident led to calls for tighter regulation of online spaces, for processes for reporting abuse to be improved, and a request for both the platform and law enforcement to take online abuse seriously. Media reporting shapes public perceptions of digital misogyny, and reinforces and reproduces inequalities that frame women as asking for abuse. These inequities exist in offline and digital spaces, where they proliferate. Women who use digital spaces to express an opinion increase their visibility. If the subject is political, indeed controversial, there is an increased likelihood that they will be targeted.

Can machine learning (a division of artificial intelligence) help?

Computer science has brought various tools and techniques to bear on identifying misogynist language on Twitter. There are two main approaches – the first is based on natural language processing. Language, any language, has both semantic structure and an expansive lexicon. Computational linguistics tends to use natural language processing tools that focus on language; the second method disregards semantics and vocabulary completely and converts words to numbers before applying one or more probability-based functions. An example of this is a machine classifier that does not require human input other than a small amount of pre-labelled data to use as a training set.

Hardaker and McGlashen (2016) used word counts and collocation to analyse the collection of tweets generated for analysing the violent threats aimed at Criado Perez. These algorithms represent the most straightforward application of statistical analysis; a broadly similar approach is used by Waseem and Hovy (2016). These techniques are referred to by Schmidt and Wiegand (2017) as 'surface features', which gives an overview of hate speech detection. They discuss methods that include metadata (such as the writer's location or gender) and multimodal information such as images, gifs, videos and so on. They use examples of word *n*-gram and *n*-character counts, more complex machine learning techniques such as topic modelling and classifiers and, more recently, the application of neural networks (NNs). NNs sound sophisticated, and although developed some years ago, it is only recently that advances in technology have meant that they can be utilized. NNs still use pattern recognition (the essence of most machine learning), but they take several 'looks' at the data before passing the most likely outcome to the next layer, which repeats the process. The number of layers and 'looks' (or analysis) in each layer is set by the researcher. Convoluted NNs (CNNs) add more complex layers of decision making, including a final 'loss layer' (the data that has been ignored or 'lost' in the process). If the algorithm decides incorrectly, the data is fed back, providing additional feedback and self-training. Zhang et al (2018) used a CNN and found that the accuracy of classifying hate speech in tweets could be improved using pre-labelled data sets and comparing the results with previous attempts. In some cases, the improvement was slight (less than 1 per cent), but given the volume of tweets containing hate speech generated, every bit helps.

We do not know, of course, which approaches Twitter uses to detect cyberhate. This kind of information is commercially sensitive and remains a secret (we will return to this in the Conclusion). However, as well as using machine learning to detect cyberhate, Twitter also relies on users to report tweets that break the rules. The process for doing this has been made more manageable, but as we will see in the next section, it still does not resolve the issue of VAW.

Rules enforcement and the problem with machine learning: is Twitter facilitating VAW?

In 2018, an Amnesty International report found that 'Twitter's inconsistency and inaction on its own rules creates a level of mistrust and lack of confidence in the company's reporting process' (Amnesty International, 2018: 33). Since then, Twitter has 'proactively reduce[d] abuse' on the platform (Twitter Investor Relations, 2019). Twitter frequently updates rules, most recently (as at the time of writing) in September 2020, when all users were notified of this change. The rules define abusive behaviours: a user 'may not engage in the targeted harassment of someone or incite other people to do so. We consider abusive behaviour an attempt to harass, intimidate, or *silence someone else's voice*' (Twitter, 2020a, our emphasis). Twitter had been reliant on the users submitting a report of potentially abusive tweets; it now uses automated machine learning models to identify and remove them.

Twitter has stated that they remove more than 50 per cent of tweets with abusive content before being notified by a user (Twitter Investor Relations, 2019). It is unclear how Twitter defines what constitutes abusive language, and there is no information about how a report of abusive language was not in breach of the rules. While these uncertainties remain, it appears that Twitter is inconsistent in enforcing its own rules and that the culture of trust, safety and respect is not for everyone. Furthermore, it evidences how misogyny is built into the digital space through architecture and corporate policies. Bourdieu would have recognized this as the exercise of cultural capital. It is clear from the ongoing debate that Twitter is not a separate cultural space but one that is, in fact, embedded *within* wider popular culture. Further still, since COVID-19, this process has been taking 'longer than usual', and machine learning and automation processes have been increased (Twitter, 2020b).

A report by the Web Foundation (2020) argued that social media platforms define abuse differently. However, most of them do not openly explain this, and different understandings of what abuse *is* may not be fully considered. Moderators may not understand that a particular word or phrase is abusive in a specific country or dialect. Twitter has teams of moderators that review tweets and, based on predetermined conditions, decide whether they are abusive or not. These decisions should be made using guidelines written by others who could have biases or blind spots, supported by a corporate policy that may be similarly flawed or reinforce bias (Noble, 2018). Twitter rules identify what could be construed as abusive. Still, the policy can be both subjective and expansive enough to show that they are acting without overly policing a global communication platform. If guidelines are not specific enough, then moderators could decide based on their subjective knowledge and experience.

The potential for bias is the same for a non-automated moderation process, with less human oversight and less chance that a problem will be recognized and action taken. Automated processes are increasingly used; therefore, substantial efforts should be made to ensure their models and guidelines are not biased. Ultimately, Twitter is culpable for the failures of its automated systems and human moderators. If Twitter can censor far-right political tweets and misinformation, they can, and should, act to limit the gendered cyberhate levelled at women and other marginalized groups.

Conclusion

We have argued that Twitter is a legitimate extension of the physical space in which we live. It has rules both in terms of use and expected user behaviour, users naturally group into communities, and the space can be mapped using network science. The speech that people use on Twitter is regulated by Twitter itself but is also regulated in the wider sense by the law operating in the country where the originator of hate speech resides. However, the cover of anonymity provided by the platform has clearly led to many individuals feeling as if they can make the threats of sexual VAW.

Computer scientists have suggested ways to detect gendered cyberhate. While not 100 per cent accurate, one has to ask whether temporarily removing some tweets that are not offensive or illegal is a price worth paying. It should also be remembered that not all people will agree on whether a tweet contains gendered cyberhate or not – cultural and social context are key in shaping this. Furthermore, the way language itself is used changes, and words or phrases can take on new meanings. Keeping track of these is not easy. We should also not forget to consider the human moderator's demographics, which may impact how they view a reported tweet's content and context.

At the heart of this tension, Twitter is trying to walk the line between making the platform safer for women *while at the same time* increasing traffic through users clicking on external links and adverts. The click-through rate is what drives Twitter's success or failure. Twitter and Facebook have become the behemoths of social networking. There are conflicts when we look at how the law operates, as well. In the US, any attempt at censorship – even if legitimate – is met with considerable protest. While the law is more explicit in England and Wales, law enforcement officials lack the technical skill and resources to investigate all but the most high-profile cases. If the originator of the illegal tweet is in the US, there is almost nothing they can do.

Cyberhate is nothing new; it has long been a feature of cyberspace used to marginalize and drive women (and others) from the platform. Cyberhate is a tool used by misogyny, which is 'not only widespread and deeply entrenched in Western culture, it is naturalised' (Banet-Weiser and Miltner, 2016: 171). Dale Spender (1996) viewed cyberspace as instrumental for women to connect and share their experiences with each other but noted that men had more influence over that space. Women are still not the 'full participants' in digital spaces that they imagined. It is mostly men who shape the system and the rules, determining how women are treated and how full their membership of digital space. If cyberspace is constructed using language and language is inherently patriarchal (Cameron, 1985), power is inherently directed towards men. Moreover, how we communicate with each other encodes various meanings, including our social status and perceived gender hierarchy.

We have argued that Twitter must transparently outline what they constitute to be abusive language and behaviours. This might improve user understanding. It is doubtful that this will occur. Recently, Twitter stated that they already remove 50 per cent of abusive tweets following improvements made to their machine learning model (Kastrenakes, 2019). There is little evidence to support this other than the blogs and media platforms that continue to quote them as fact.

The existing procedures do not work for *everyone*, and they should. Our suggestions are that Twitter educates moderators and engineers in ethics to minimize privilege and bias. Furthermore, Twitter should actively employ women, ethnic minorities and diverse communities to broaden their developer knowledge base. Algorithms should be rewritten to include language analysis that actively targets and removes abusive language and user accounts. Reporting procedures should consist of specific examples of inappropriate and abusive language so that both the context and the content is made more transparent. Twitter should provide an open consultation of their reporting procedures via @TwitterSafety, a process performed recently about civic integrity (Twitter Safety, 2020), which would allow users to contribute to the platform's usability.

People built Twitter, people use it, people have made it successful, and people are suffering due to what is almost certainly a small minority of men trying to drive women away from yet another sphere of public life. Opening up the process by which hate is identified and removed will benefit not only women but also all social media users.

References

Alonzo, M. and Aitken, M. (2004) 'Flaming in electronic communication', *Decision Support Systems*, 36(3): 205–213.

Amnesty International (2018) *#ToxicTwitter: Violence and Abuse Against Women Online*, Report No ACT 30/8070/2018, 21 March, London: Amnesty International. Available from: https://www.amnesty.org/en/documents/act30/8070/2018/en/ [Accessed 13 January 2019].

Amnesty International UK (2017) 'More than a quarter of UK women experiencing online abuse and harassment receive threats of physical or sexual assault – new research', Amnesty International, press release, 20 November. Available from: https://www.amnesty.org.uk/press-releases/more-quarter-uk-women-experiencing-online-abuse-and-harassment-rece ive-threats [Accessed 17 July 2019].

Banet-Weiser, S. (2018) *Empowered: Popular Feminism and Popular Misogyny*, Durham, NC: Duke University Press.

Banet-Weiser, S. and Miltner, K.M. (2016) '#MasculinitySoFragile: culture, structure, and networked misogyny', *Feminist Media Studies*, 16(1): 171–174.

Bartlett, J., Norrie, R., Patel, S., Rumpel, R. and Wibberley, S. (2014) *Misogyny on Twitter*, 10 May, London: Demos. Available from: https://demos.co.uk/project/misogyny-on-twitter/ [Accessed 30 December 2020].

Blunden, M. (2015) 'Caroline Criado Perez: how I won my banknote battle … and defied rape threat trolls', *Evening Standard*, 26 November. Available from: https://www.standard.co.uk/news/london/caroline-cria doperez-how-i-won-my-banknote-battle-and-defied-rape-threat-trolls-a3123956.html [Accessed 10 June 2019].

Cameron, D. (1985) *Feminism and Linguistic Theory*, London: Macmillan.

Citron, D.K. (2014) *Hate Crimes in Cyberspace*, Cambridge, MA: Harvard University Press.

Gannes, L. (2010) 'The short and illustrious history of Twitter #hashtags', *Old GigaOm* blog, 30 April. Available from: http://gigaom.com/2010/04/30/the-short-and-illustrious-history-of-twitter-hashtags [Accessed 17 May 2019].

Ging, D. and Siapera, E. (2019) 'Introduction', in D. Ging and E. Siapera (eds) *Gender Hate Online: Understanding the New Anti-Feminism*, Cham: Palgrave Macmillan, pp 1–18.

Halford, S., Pope, C. and Carr, L. (2010) 'A manifesto for web science?', in J. Erickson and S. Gradmann (eds) *Proceedings of the WebSci10: Extending the Frontiers of Society On-Line*, Raleigh, US, 25–26 April. Available from: https://eprints.soton.ac.uk/271033/ [Accessed 23 April 2022].

Hardaker, C. and McGlashan, M. (2016) '"Real men don't hate women": Twitter rape threats and group identity', *Journal of Pragmatics*, 91: 80–93.

Harris, B. and Vitis, L. (2020) 'Digital intrusions: technology, spatiality and violence against women', *Journal of Gender-Based Violence*, 4(3): 325–341.

Heffernan, V. (2018) 'Scrolling, rickrolling, and trolling', *Wired*, 12 March. Available from: https://www.wired.com/story/history-of-scrolling-rickrolling-and-trolling/ [Accessed 19 January 2019].

Henry, N. and Powell, A. (2018) 'Technology-facilitated sexual violence: a literature review of empirical research', *Trauma, Violence, & Abuse*, 19(2): 195–208.

Jane, E.A. (2014a) '"Your a ugly, whorish, slut": understanding e-bile', *Feminist Media Studies*, 14(4): 531–546.

Jane, E.A. (2014b) '"Back to the kitchen, cunt": speaking the unspeakable about online misogyny', *Continuum*, 28(4): 558–570.

Jane, E.A. (2016) 'Online misogyny and feminist digilantism', *Continuum*, 30(3): 284–297.

Jane, E.A. (2017) 'Gendered cyberhate, victim-blaming, and why the internet is more like driving a car on a road than being naked in the snow', in E. Martellozzo and E.A. Jane (eds) *Cybercrime and Its Victims*, Abingdon: Routledge, pp 61–78.

Jane, E.A. (2020) 'Online abuse and harassment', in K. Ross, I. Bachmann, V. Cardo, S. Moorti and C.M. Scarcelli (eds) *The International Encyclopedia of Gender, Media, and Communication, Volume 2 (G–P)*, Hoboken, NJ: Wiley Blackwell.

Jiang, B. and Ormeling, F. (2000) 'Mapping cyberspace: visualizing, analysing and exploring virtual worlds', *Cartographic Journal*, 37(2): 117–122.

Kastrenakes, J. (2019) 'Twitter says it now removes half of all abusive tweets before users report them', *The Verge*, 24 October. Available from: https://www.theverge.com/2019/10/24/20929290/twitter-abusive-tweets-automated-removal-earnings-q3-2019 [Accessed 7 December 2020].

Lumsden, K. and Morgan, H. (2017) 'Media framing of trolling and online abuse: silencing strategies, symbolic violence and victim blaming' *Feminist Media Studies*, 17(6): 926–940.

Malpas, J. (2009) 'On the non-autonomy of the virtual', *Convergence: The International Journal of Research into New Media Technologies*, 15(2): 135–139.

Mantilla, K. (2015) *Gendertrolling: How Misogyny Went Viral*, Santa Barbara, CA: Praeger.

McLean, J. and Maalsen, S. (2013) 'Destroying the joint and dying of shame? A geography of revitalised feminism in social media and beyond', *Geographical Research*, 51(3): 243–256.

Mead, R. (2014) 'The troll slayer', *The New Yorker*, 25 August. Available from: https://www.newyorker.com/magazine/2014/09/01/troll-slayer [Accessed 30 December 2020].

Murthy, D. (2018) *Twitter: Social Communication in the Twitter Age* (2nd edn), Cambridge: Polity Press.

Noble, S.U. (2018) *Algorithms of Oppression: How Search Engines Reinforce Racism*, New York: NYU Press.

O'Sullivan, P.B. and Flanagin, A.J. (2003) 'Reconceptualizing "flaming" and other problematic messages', *New Media & Society*, 5(1): 69–94.

Penny, L. (2013) *Cybersexism: Sex, Gender and Power on the Internet*, London: Bloomsbury.

Phillips, W. (2015) *This Is Why We Can't Have Nice Things: Mapping the Relationship Between Online Trolling and Mainstream Culture*, Cambridge, MA: MIT Press.

Repko, A.F. and Szostak, R. (2020) *Interdisciplinary Research: Process and Theory* (4th edn), Thousand Oaks, CA: Sage.

Salter, M. (2018) 'From geek masculinity to Gamergate: the technological rationality of online abuse', *Crime Media Culture*, 14(2): 247–264.

Schmidt, A. and Wiegand, M. (2017) 'A survey on hate speech detection using natural language processing', in L.-W. Ku and C.-T. Li (eds) *Proceedings of the Fifth International Workshop on Natural Language Processing for Social Media*, Stroudsburg, PA: Association for Computational Linguistics, pp 1–10.

Spender, D. (1996) *Nattering on the Net: Women, Power and Cyberspace*, Ontario: University of Toronto Press.

Statista (2020) 'Distribution of Twitter users worldwide as of October 2020, by gender', *The Statistics Portal*, 29 November. Available from: https://web.archive.org/web/20201031070841/https://www.statista.com/statistics/828092/distribution-of-users-on-twitter-worldwide-gender/ [Accessed 23 April 2022].

Twitter (2020a) 'Twitter rules and policies: hateful conduct policy'. Available from: https://help.twitter.com/en/rules-and-policies/hateful-conduct-pol icy [Accessed 1 December 2020].

Twitter (2020b) 'An update on our continuity strategy during COVID-19', updated 1 April. Available from: https://blog.twitter.com/en_us/topics/company/2020/An-update-on-our-continuity-strategy-during-COVID-19.html [Accessed 7 December 2020].

Twitter Investor Relations (2019) 'Q3 2019 letter to shareholders', 24 October. Available from: https://s22.q4cdn.com/826641620/files/doc_financials/2019/q3/Q3-2019-Shareholder-Letter.pdf [Accessed 15 December 2020].

Twitter Safety (2020) 'Expanding our policies to further protect the civic conversation', 10 September. Available from: https://blog.twitter.com/en_us/topics/company/2020/civic-integrity-policy-update.html [Accessed 7 December 2020].

Waseem, Z. and Hovy, D. (2016) 'Hateful symbols or hateful people? Predictive features for hate speech detection on Twitter', in *Proceedings of the North American Chapter of the Association for Computational Linguistics (NAACL) Student Research Workshop*, Stroudsburg, PA: Association for Computational Linguistics, pp 88–93. Available from: https://doi.org/10.18653/v1/N16-2013 [Accessed 1 January 2021].

Web Foundation, The (2020) 'The impact of online gender-based violence on women in public life', 25 November. Available from: https://webfoundation.org/the-impact-of-online-gender-based-violence-on-women-in-public-life/ [Accessed 29 December 2020].

Wu, B. (2015) 'A moment that changed me – Gamergate', *The Guardian*, 21 August. Available from: https://www.theguardian.com/commentisfree/2015/aug/21/gamergate-sexism-games-industry-women-trolls [Accessed 11 December 2020].

Zhang, Z., Robinson, D. and Tepper, J. (2018) 'Detecting hate speech on Twitter using a convolution-GRU based deep neural network', in A. Gangemi, R. Navigli, M.-E. Vidal et al (eds) *ESWC 2018: The Semantic Web, Presented at the European Semantic Web Conference*, Cham: Springer, pp 745–760.

PART III

Transnational and Political Spaces

8

Not the Wild West: Femonationalism, Gendered Security Regimes and Brexit

Alexandra Fanghanel

Introduction

On New Year's Eve of 2015 the streets of Cologne, Germany were flooded with revellers making the most of the celebrations. That night, in the main square, there unfolded a series of attacks on women in this public space. The men who were responsible for the attacks – which included groping, molestation and pickpocketing – were, as was widely reported, migrant Black men who were 'not German' (see Brenner and Ohlendorf, 2016; Weber, 2016a, 2016b; Kapur, 2018).

Later on in that year, in the UK, the British public would vote in a referendum which would ask them to respond to the question: 'should the United Kingdom remain a member of the European Union or leave the European Union?' Eventually, 52 per cent of those who voted would choose to leave.

Discourses surrounding the analysis of both these events position them as crisis points for both the political left and the political right in Europe. One discourse that symbolically ties these two seemingly distinct events together, however, and which will be the focus of this chapter, is the spectre of the rape of the nation and the latent menace of the body of the Black Other.

In their 1998 collection, Featherstone and Lash suggest that the traditional notions of the nation, and of national territory, have been troubled by the advances of globalization, of which this refugee crisis, and the politics of Europe, becomes one expression. Clashes of culture, they suggest, exceed national borders, and create a new spatialized logic that calls into question a traditional notion of nation which relies, for its very existence, on the certainty of a border, or a territory, and a bounded population. The debates that we see play out in this chapter expose how this antagonism between what is with us and what is not, emerge. Across the political spectrum, rhetoric about the White female body[1] – violated by the Black Other – has been mobilized as the symbol and the crucible through which a vision of nationhood is forged.

Bringing these spatialized, sexualized understandings of the nation-as-territory to bear on debates about rape culture – or the normalization of sexual violence against women – helps us to see how the anxieties expressed in response to this crisis become complicit with gendered security regimes, which then become state-sanctioned expressions of violence. In this chapter I examine how this happens and what it means for a nationhood that emerges, in part, through this manifestation of rape culture.

The rape of the nation?

Before we do that, let us return to the main square in Cologne, and try to understand more about how attacks on these women became transliterated into the rape of a nation, and how the sexually molested White female body would play a part in the future of Europe.

At the time of the Cologne attacks, there was much confusion about the events that were taking place. As the investigative work of Brenner and Ohlendorf (2016) demonstrates, even several months after the incident, there remained considerable ambiguity about the unfolding events of the night. For some, the New Year's Eve festivities were raucous and bawdy, but otherwise not dangerous, for others, the volume of crime reported that night suggested it was an incidence of organized crime. For the police – who according to Brenner and Ohlendorf were overwhelmed and unable to respond to all the criminal incidences that night – things got totally out of hand; for women who were robbed and sexually harassed at the train station and in the square that night, it was a living nightmare.

The level of ambiguity and uncertainty was reflected in policy, police and public responses to the events. Weber (2016a, 2016b) and Boulila and Carri (2017) confirm the observations made by Brenner and Ohlendorf (2016) about racialized and gendered responses that emerged at all these levels in Germany. It is not my intention to rehearse those observations here. Instead, it is helpful to return to some of the initial misapprehensions that emerged in the aftermath of the events in the centre of Cologne in 2015, and to bring them into a dialogue with contemporary and emerging anxieties of the nation, played out on the bodies of White women.

In the aftermath of the New Year's Eve attacks in Cologne, 1,168 crimes were reported to police, of which 493 were incidences of sexual assault.

The men accused were said to be of non-German origin, speaking Arabic, 'looking North African', and not 'of European appearance' (reported in Huggler, 2016). The refugees who had entered the country during 2015's 'long summer of migration' (during which thousands of people seeking asylum in Europe walked through Europe to settle in places like Germany; see Georgi, 2019: 88–89) were blamed. The attacks fuelled calls from the centre right, the far right and some left-wing parties to close the German borders to this influx of people – mostly Black men – seeking asylum. As police investigations developed over the course of 2016–2017, 52 men were identified and arrested. Three were convicted.

The dearth of convictions was due, in part, to elements of German law that required women to be able to identify their attackers, which in the circumstances was unrealistic. The police themselves found it hard to distinguish the identities of the attackers on security cameras in the square. Unidentifiable, indistinguishable bodies foster the impression that it was a swarm of undifferentiated Black bodies who had entered Germanic lands and who had attacked 'their' women, an impression that would nurture a racist gendered security regime which would resonate around Europe.

Indeed, it is worth noting that the significance of the *place* of the attacks – around the cathedral in the main square of the city – symbolically strikes at the heart of anxieties around the nation. As Puwar (2004) has observed, public squares tell stories of nationhood, of history, of politics and of populations. In the context of Cologne, this cathedral is the heart of the Catholic administration of Cologne (Garraio, 2021: 135). It is a UNESCO World Heritage Site and one of the most popular tourist attractions in Germany. It is an expression of religious fervour, of architectural prowess and of imperial glory. It is the synecdoche of the nation.

More than this, as a site of national importance, in the time-space of New Year's Eve revelry, where young and old, male and female, gathered to drink, socialize with friends, and move freely, it *also* becomes a synecdoche of Western liberalism: a Western liberalism that the attacks by non-German men symbolically come to menace.

As we know, space is gendered, racialized and political. While the nation is symbolically tied to the feminine, as we shall soon see, public space such as this square is discursively constructed as a masculinized space (Korac, 2020: 78). Historically, women have been excluded from having rights to the city and from occupying public space in ways that were unencumbered by burdens of harassment or the stigma of sex work (Wilson, 1992; Lefebvre, 1996; Mort, 2000). Indeed, much of the rhetoric around fear of crime turns on this imagination of public space as dangerous, laced with latent menace of male sexual violence against women (Fanghanel, 2016; Fanghanel and Lim, 2017). Yet, within a Western and liberal imagination of public space, women should, and do, have access to public space on the same terms as do men. So, when they are harassed in it, and that harassment is enacted by the body of the Black foreigner – the Other – that menace is figured as happening not just against women, and 'liberal' gender norms in Germany but against liberal imaginations of the nation (Korac, 2020).

Coding the crisis

The anxieties about the Cologne attacks reverberated throughout Germany. The government's local, national and international responses are well document by Weber (2016a, 2016b), Kapur (2018) and Boulila and Carri (2017). They reverberated through responses across Europe (Sager and Mulinari, 2018). For the remainder of this paper, I want to turn attention to how this crisis, and anxiety around security and the female body was put to work in the UK context in discourses around the Brexit vote, also of 2016.

To do this, I conducted an in-depth discourse analysis of newspaper stories published in British newspapers that mentioned the Cologne attacks in the year afterwards. Using the LexisNexis database, and the key words 'Cologne attacks', I analysed every article that was returned with these search terms. A total of 349 newspaper articles were analysed in this way, with dates ranging from 4 January 2016 to 15 January 2017, from 31 different media sources. I coded for reports that outlined the facts of the evening (or tried to), reports that rehearsed European nation-building discourses, reports that related the Cologne attacks to UK nation-building, reports that merged the Cologne attacks and the ongoing refugee crisis in Europe, and reports that linked discourses about the Brexit vote to the Cologne attacks. From this analysis, I was able to build a timeline of the evolution of discourses about the Cologne attacks and their significance in the UK.

The discourses that I focus on here are those that tied the events in Cologne to anxiety about the British nation, and to its future in Europe. I do this to demonstrate how the female body is put to work, in a denigrated manner, in the services of the creation of the nation and how this gendering of the nation fuels a contemporary rape culture.

Using British media sources to examine the ways that the events in Germany are made to resonate with events in the UK helps us to see how racist discourses converge with anxiety about gendered violence to forge an emetic boundary of fearfulness around bodies that are like us, and those on the borderlands, those who are 'out there', haunting, spectral, ready to attack the female body, and through this, the nation.

Woman as nation

Ideologies of the nation that rest on the sexualization of the female body are nothing new. We can see them engraved into the architecture of sites of power in the British capital. The 19th-century Foreign and Commonwealth Office in London, UK, is one such seat of racialized, colonial power. Situated at the heart of the city, adjacent to the Houses of Parliament, and attached to the Treasury Building, the Foreign and Commonwealth Office was described by its architect, George Gilbert Scott, as 'a kind of national palace or drawing room for the nation'.[2] Embodying the colonial British nation into the very fabric of the building, these days passers-by can marvel at the allegorical figures of five continents of the world – Europe, Africa, Asia, America, Australasia – that are represented by the figures of bare-breasted women within the spandrels around the windows of the first floor of the building. Of the allegorical industries – science, art, agriculture, government, education, law, manufacture, commerce, literature – only 'government' and 'education' are represented by masculine figures. The rest are principally bare-breasted women adorned in a classic style.

Elsewhere, William-Adolphe Bouguereau's 1883 allegorical painting entitled *The Motherland* (*Alma Parens* in the original) depicts the bare-breasted Marianne – symbol of the French nation – surrounded by nine naked, or nearly naked, children, several of whom are looking at her imploringly, climbing onto her, trying to suckle at her breast. The skin tone of the children is suggestive of their different ethnicities. And given the name of the painting, it is possible that body of the central figure – the mother – is the 'land' that nourishes otherwise poor, destitute dependencies: an idealist, colonialist, archaic imagination of colonial dynamics laid bare.

It is notable that in these two examples the body of the woman as nation is *allegorical*. The etymology of the word 'allegory' describes a 'figurative treatment of an unmentioned subject' or the 'description of one thing under the image of another'. That these are allegories means that the female body 'stands in' for expressions of nationhood. She is a symbol of a wider construction of the nation. Abundant, fertile, maternal, giving, able; in *The Motherland*, she is a nation that feeds, that supports and sustains more vulnerable dependencies. In 19th-century architecture, she represents the nation: she showcases its talents. Apply this to equally allegorical imagery used during the Second World War to stoke up racist sentiments about the danger posed by the body of the ethnic, enemy Other: allegories that we would now also call propaganda. Here, during the Second World War, Japanese propaganda figuring Japanese men as the 'yellow peril' abducting or torturing White women circulated to fuel racist, and ultimately dehumanizing sentiments about the so-called 'Asian menace'.

Imagery using sexual violence as an allegory of the menace to the nation is repeated in different contexts, even into the present day and the case we are currently considering here. Nowhere is this more explicit than on the covers of magazines such as the Polish *wSeici* (February 2016), and the German

Focus (8 January 2016) and *Süddeutsche Zeitung* (8 January 2016) published in the aftermath of the Cologne attacks. On their front cover, *Focus* depicted the body of a naked White woman covered with black, sticky-looking handprints. The text 'are we tolerant or are we blind?' is written across her on what resembled the ticker tape that police might use to cordon off a crime scene. The conservative Polish *wSeici* magazine featured a woman dressed in the European flag, screaming as Black men's hands try to rip her clothing off her, restrain her arms, and pull her hair; 'the Islamic rape of Europe' reads the headline. Once more, we find the naked and distressed female body becomes an allegorical and symbolic expression of anxiety about the nation (Jazmati and Studer, 2017).

Securitizing gender: securitizing nation

When the body of woman-as-nation is menaced by the sexualized encroachment of Others 'out there', we witness a number of discursive, political responses. As Kapur (2018: 86) notes, we see the rise of Orientalist discourses that cast the body of the other as an atavistic, barbaric outsider against whom we have to protect 'our' women (and in the context of international militarized action, sometimes 'their' women; see Banwell, 2020). These narratives accompany femonationalistic imperatives that mobilize apparently pro-feminist stances to drive anti-immigrant – and Islamophobic – campaigns (see Farris, 2012: 187). For Farris (2012), femonationalistic discourses make nationalistic claims about protecting the values of the nation – notably the feminist values of the nation – from others who do not protect the rights of women. Femonationalism might be associated with the political practices of the populist right-wing, but its premises – that 'we' are feminist and must guard against 'them' who are not – are also espoused by those on the political left, as we shall see later.

This sort of apparently benevolent feminist ideology can be used to nurture what Sager and Mulinari (2018: 151) describe as 'care racism'; the practice of enforcing racist ideologies and policies, or of iterating racist discourses in the name of care. Caring for our own – here of caring for 'our' women – becomes the guise behind which this sort of racism is able to thrive. We see this in the context of UK responses to the events in Cologne, and indeed, in the imperative to guard against the threat of this sexualized violence against women through stoking racist anti-immigration sentiment.

This imperative towards safety comes at a price, of course. I have already discussed the problem of securitizing female bodies elsewhere (Fanghanel, 2019). Here, the function of mobilizing a gendered security regime – that is, using the threat of gendered violence to justify exclusionary or aggressive spatialized security practices against Others – is to cast the body of the Black male as a threat to the nation in the name of saving women.

The implications of gendered security regimes are that they discursively cast the female body as a problem to be solved. That is, it is women whose safety must be secured, and women whose bodies become the locus for actions against would-be perpetrators. They also iterate imperialist discourses against Black men as invaders of the nation. We must ask: who is safety for? What should the price of that safety be? And by whom should the safety be secured? How does weaponizing safety in public space like this help to build the UK nation?

Reversing a hundred years of female liberation?

In the UK press, the events of the Cologne attacks started to be reported on 6 January 2016. Initial reports focused on the facts as they emerged, and then swiftly rehearsed the international responses to the attacks, from Slovakia (8 January 2016) and other parts of central and eastern Europe (8 January 2016). Meanwhile, reports of so called 'copycat' attacks in Sweden, Austria, Finland and Switzerland, and other parts of Germany started to be reported. Quickly, the spread of these attacks started to be represented as a swarming unknowable mass – like the hands that grab at the white skin of women – whose originary actions in Cologne appear to act as a crucible for an epidemic, or infestation by Black, foreign, stateless men's acts of violence against women who belong to the nation; transforming the city of Cologne, in the words of a council official Judith Wolter, into a 'no-go area for women' (Charlton and Calderwood, 2016). International responses to the Cologne attacks also provoked far right anti-immigrant rhetoric and stoked the popularity of anti-Islamist groups such as *Legida/Pegida* (Patriotische Europäer gegen die Islamisierung des Abendlandes [Patriotic Europeans Against the Islamicization of the Occident]) and *Alternative für Deutschland* [Alternative for Germany]. The emergence of these groups from the events of Cologne, and the subsequent crisis of Europe debates are analysed elsewhere (Weber, 2016a; Kapur, 2018). Here, my intention is to turn attention to the way that these events and their reporting reverberated into anti- and pro-Brexit discourses in the UK.

Though arguments in support of the UK leaving the European Union were based on an array of potential reasons, one dominant driver in popular rhetoric was anxiety about immigration and the erosion of the sovereignty of the nation. Just three weeks after the attacks, former defence secretary Liam Fox addressed a cross-party meeting for the campaign to leave the EU: 'Insecurity for our country comes from open borders and uncontrolled migration. … Germany has discovered in Cologne and other places exactly what it can mean when you do not know who you have allowed into your country. That for me is the real security issue at risk in this referendum' (cited in Daily Mail, 2016).

The porousness of space and populations becomes what is at risk here (Featherstone and Lash, 1998). The risk of 'what it can mean' to have 'open borders' is always, and only, sexual violence. Fox euphemistically points to the latent menace of the 'black peril' (Jazmati and Studer, 2017). Nigel Farage goes further. Prolific among the commentators associated with the Brexit referendum was Farage: a political personality whose ability to drive forward a 'leave' decision on the Brexit referendum despite never having held an elected office speaks only to the hubris of politicians in power around him at this time.

Speaking at an anti-EU event in south Wales three months after the Cologne attacks, Farage reportedly states:

> We've been through a hundred years of female emancipation and liberation and now the mistakes of Mrs Merkel are threatening all of that.
>
> What we saw outside that train station in Cologne on New Year's Eve was truly and genuinely shocking. If you allow the unlimited access of huge numbers of young males into the European continent who come from countries where women are at best second-class citizens, don't be surprised if scenes that we saw in Cologne don't happen more often. ...
>
> Do we want those young men within five years to have EU passports and to be able to come to our country and to reverse a hundred years of female liberation and to change our entire way of life? No! ...
>
> It is the job of the British Government to make our own laws, to control our own borders and it's about time we started putting the interests of our own people first. (Farage reported in Dathan, 2016)

A skilled orator, Farage deftly lays the menace towards 'hundreds of years of female emancipation and liberation' in the hands of 'huge numbers of young males'. Rehearsing the atavistic imaginary of the menacing Other whose women are 'at best second-class citizens', Farage makes 'our own borders' the terrain around which anti-European sentiment is played out.

The party that Farage created and whom he represented at this anti-European event is not a feminist party. Indeed, Farage himself has explicitly distanced himself from feminist politics (LBC, 2018), and in different contexts has been associated with archaic and hetero-patriarchal imaginings of gender and sexuality. Rather, this form of strategic feminism works to place Farage's 'own people' as the defenders of women's rights over the islands of the UK. Indeed, in a femonationalistic move that positions what is in 'our borders' as a safe haven for women, where women's rights are respected, Farage makes the emancipation and liberation of women a constituent element of what it is to be British, and what it is thus to reject the European Union.

The narrative about the importance of protecting 'our own' women by securing the borders of the nation also works to figure the nation as liberal, tolerant of the rights of women, and set against the illiberal – and thus dangerous – Other. Sexism and gender violence become figured as something that is 'out there' from which, if we can 'control our borders' we can protect ourselves.

This liberal claim to equality and female emancipation as a feature of the UK nation is not limited to the polemical rhetoric of those on the far right. Indeed, in the aftermath of the Cologne attacks, and in the context of requiring the female spouses of migrants to the UK to learn English, the then Prime Minister David Cameron (cited in White, 2016) stated, that 'in Britain, men are not frightened of women's success, it is celebrated proudly'; men who celebrate women are figured as properly British, men who are 'afraid' of women's successes are neither properly British, nor are they – discursively at least – performing successful British masculinity. The gendered and nationalistic line is once more drawn around what does, and does not, make a good British national identity.

From a more assimilative perspective, the columnist David Aaronovitch suggests that if:

> any groups of young white men conducted a mass sexual assault ... in a Western city, the outrage would have been immediate and thunderous. ... It is not absurd to worry about young men whose perception of women was formed in the relative backwardness of severely patriarchal societies. What, we would have been asked, is it about our society that permits such a thing to happen? That allows young men to believe that they can and should act in this way? ... It is not absurd to worry about young men – often poor, often bored, often deprived of family life and family restraints – whose perception of women was formed in the relative backwardness of severely patriarchal societies. (Aaronovitch, 2016)

Aaronovitch suggests that if it were 'our' men who were attacking 'our' women, we would react with horror, wondering how such a thing could have happened. Yet here, I argue that Aaronovitch's rhetorical plea of 'what is it about our society that permits such a thing to happen? That allows young men to believe that they can and should act in this way?' might well be asked precisely in the context of the Cologne attacks. If the perpetrators of the Cologne attacks herald from this 'backward' and 'patriarchal' society, what is it about what they encounter in 'our society' that leads them to think that they can and should act in this way 'here'?

It is not clear to me that the Cologne attacks have not been met by an 'outrage' that is both 'immediate and thunderous', nor is it clear that if 'young white men' attacked 'their own' women, that such an outrage would be forthcoming. Instead, the turning of the debate around the notion of archaic patriarchy, of a fixed cultural, indoctrinated misogyny, obscures consideration of the fact that it might be the structural sexism of the society in which the attacks took place that fostered the circumstances for the attacks to unfold.

Aaronovitch goes on to explain that there is gender parity in Europe, that women are considered to be 'as good as men' and not subordinate to them, they do not dress especially modestly, they are not considered to be inferior as they are in 'severely patriarchal societies'. Is it that this liberalism perhaps provoked these attacks? Or that the attacks were an expression of anger about the relative freedom of women in Europe? For Aaronovitch the solution is 'mandatory courses in citizenship and Western values'. An integrationist approach to be sure, and one that can be positioned contra Farage. Yet, it is one that continues to enshrine an imaginary of a gendered security regime in which Western cultures are the unproblematic answer to the problem of men 'out there'.

The Wild West

Against Aaronovitch's critique of liberal attitudes to racism, the Cologne attacks, and the way they express a racialized, nationalistic, gendered security regime, came the comments of Jess Phillips, a left-wing Labour Member of Parliament for Birmingham Yardley, who stated in response to an TV audience question about immigration and the Cologne attacks that: "There is violence against women and girls that you are describing, a very similar situation to what happened in Cologne could be described on Broad Street in Birmingham every week where women are baited and heckled" (cited in Doyle and Duell, 2016). The notion that the events of Cologne were not exceptional, that they could happen – that they *did* happen – weekly on the streets of the UK's second city was met with outrage.

Phillips continued: "We have to attack what we perceive as being patriarchal culture coming into any culture that isn't patriarchal and making sure we tell people not to be like that. But we should be careful in this country before we rest on our laurels when two women are murdered every week" (cited in Doyle and Duell, 2016).

While Phillips leaves open the possibility that the reason why men attack women in public space is because they are coming from a patriarchal culture into a culture that is not patriarchal, the crux of her objection to making the link between the Cologne attacks and immigration is that gender violence happens in the UK, too. Feminist emancipation and gender equality are not the universal given than discourses such as those of Farage, Cameron and Aaronovitch might suggest it is. Or rather, that theirs is an idealist misreading of the status quo for women in the UK; that it is not true that the UK is a safe space for women.

Phillips's comments were widely reported in the press, and the condemnation of them from people who lived and worked in Birmingham was robust. Whether or not Phillips is correct in this assessment of gender violence and the streets of Birmingham – the constituency she represents – is not the focus of this argument, here. Rather, what these comments and the responses to them illustrate, is the way that gender violence, public space, and security forge a sense of nationhood that is played out on women's bodies.

Police, business owners and journalists rejected Phillips's comments. Calls were made for her to resign. An entrepreneur stated that Birmingham was "not like the Wild West" and that sexual harassment was "not an institutionalised part of what goes on there" (cited in Turner, 2016). West Midlands Police said that the events of Cologne were "a million miles" from what happens in Birmingham (cited in Turner, 2016).

What would it mean for the events of Cologne to be figuratively or politically 'a million miles' away from a Saturday night in Birmingham? It would mean that they happen 'out there', that they are beyond the borders of the nation – both physically and psychically.

The West that is wild is clearly not the sort of West that commentators such as Aaronovitch suggest that immigrants should be assimilated to. This West describes a frontier-like ambience. Historically rooted in the 19th century and describing the westward settlement of White people across North America, the Wild West is associated with lawlessness, ruthlessness and disorder. This is what critics of Phillips's statement have in mind when they reject her claim that what happened in Cologne is not exceptional to Cologne, that it could be perpetrated by British men. A place that was 'not the Wild West' would be one that was orderly, law-abiding and settled. That which is wild is untamed and unruly: savage. These rejections delimit, once more, who is with us, and who is against us, using the threat of gendered violence as the point through which this distinction can be made.

Beyond Brexit

The interweaving of these political and media discourses as they respond to the attacks in Cologne and interact with the crisis of nationhood that accompanied discourses about Brexit in the UK helps us to see how ethnonationalism and contemporary rape culture is nurtured in the service of a certain form of nation-building. Acting as a crucible for racialized anxiety about Europe-in-crisis that positions the law-abiding and pro-feminist 'West' against the backward and patriarchal lands and cultures the perpetrators of the attacks are figured to have come from, these acts of violence also cast the female body – under perpetual, latent menace of sexual violence from the Black Other – as a symbol of the nation.

145

The female body comes to stand in for the values of the British nation: liberated, unveiled, equal. The sullying of the female body at the hands of the Other becomes transliterated onto fear of the soiling of the nation. The gendered security regime that casts woman as always-already to be protected from the hands of these Others mobilizes the types of emetic nationalistic discourses that fuelled, in part, pro-Brexit discourses.

An ideology of nationhood that relies on a thriving rape culture in order to mobilize itself does not protect women, or men, in the way that it pretends to. Rather, it normalizes that female bodies would fear sexualized attacks by male strangers, and that to protect against this given, a pro-nationalist, masculinist, racist and exclusionary project is the only way out. Benevolent, femonationalistic sexism becomes the tool which drives this agenda.

As I observed earlier, the coalescing of the female body and the body of the nation is nothing new. That fear of gendered violence should be used to stoke isolationist sentiment as nation-building should perhaps not surprise us, even if it should still trouble us. The dehumanization of the Other – cast as swarm, as dirt, as invader – and of women whose bodies stand in for the nation – as White, as vulnerable, as needing defence – enshrines, rather than dismantles racism and gender violence within the fabric of the nation. Mobilizing a gendered security regime as an alibi for this practice becomes simply one more way to nurture a rape culture which normalizes violence and the threat of violence against women.

Conclusion

Here, I have focused on the specific case of discourses from across the political spectrum which deal with Brexit. But it should be clear that there are manifestations well beyond this that are a cause for concern. We see them across the UK, Europe and beyond. Rather like Featherstone and Lash (1998) with whom we started, Chantal Mouffe (2012: 638) makes a plea for Europe to be figured as a pluriverse – as a series of plural universes and democracies that enable differences to be recognized and to be reached across in order to create a world worth living in, rather than one which seeks to erase or demonize difference as a source of fear, as something against which to protect our borders. While we continue to see the rise of populist discourses in the UK, the US, Brazil and other democracies around the world, striving across difference, refusing the emetic, uncoupling the body of the woman from the nation is not a concern we can do away with.

Notes

[1]   Certainly not all the women who were attacked in Cologne that night would be White, or even German women, and not all attackers were foreign or Black. However, the framing of the events along these lines dominated discourses about them. Thus, it is the discourses

that position this dualism and which then fuel anti-immigration and benevolent sexism in the building of the nation.

² https://www.gov.uk/government/history/king-charles-street

References

Aaronovitch, D. (2016) 'Liberal denial of the misogynistic cultures that many migrants come from will only make their assimilation harder', *The Times*, 14 January. Available from: https://www.thetimes.co.uk/article/migrants-must-learn-to-live-by-our-values-zwc99t82x [Accessed 1 July 2021].

Banwell, S. (2020) *Gender and the Violence (s) of War and Armed Conflict: More Dangerous to be a Woman?*, Bingley: Emerald.

Boulila, S.C. and Carri, C. (2017) 'On Cologne: gender, migration and unacknowledged racisms in Germany', *European Journal of Women's Studies*, 24(3): 286–293.

Brenner, Y. and Ohlendorf, K. (2016) 'Time for the facts. What do we know about Cologne four months later?', *de Correspondent*, 2 May. Available from: https://thecorrespondent.com/4401/time-for-the-facts-what-do-we-know-about-cologne-four-months-later/1073698080444-e20ada1b [Accessed 1 July 2021].

Charlton, C. and Calderwood, I. (2016) 'Groped between the legs and a firework thrown into a hoodie: brave female victims reveal the horrifying details after attacks by sex mob of 2,000 "North African and Arab" men in Cologne', *Mail Online*, 6 January. Available from: https://www.dailymail.co.uk/news/article-3386673/Women-Cologne-lockdown-council-admits-no-longer-safe-wake-African-Arab-mob-s-rapes-declares-upcoming-carnival-no-area-females.html [Accessed 24 April 2022].

Daily Mail (2016) 'Cologne sex mobs will arrive in Britain if we stay in the EU: former defence secretary Liam Fox warns women will be at risk of gang rape if UK does not sever ties with Europe', *Mail Online*, 23 January. Available from: https://www.dailymail.co.uk/news/article-3413552/Senior-Tory-MP-Liam-Fox-claims-Britain-greater-risk-Cologne-style-sex-attacks-migrants-remains-EU.html [Accessed 1 July 2021].

Dathan, M. (2016) 'Cologne-style mass sex attacks could happen in Britain if we stay in the EU, warns Nigel Farage', *Mail Online*, 30 March. Available from: https://www.dailymail.co.uk/news/article-3515239/Cologne-style-mass-sex-attacks-happen-Britain-stay-EU-warns-Nigel-Farage.html [Accessed 1 July 2021].

Doyle, J. and Duell, M. (2016) '"How dare you describe Birmingham in this way": locals' fury at Labour MP Jess Phillips for likening Cologne sex attacks to her own constituency on a Saturday night', *Mail Online*, 29 January. Available from: https://www.dailymail.co.uk/news/article-3422133/Cologne-style-sex-attacks-happen-weekly-Birmingham-Labour-MP-says-women-baited-heckled-weekend-city-centre.html [Accessed 1 July 2021].

Fanghanel, A. (2016) 'The trouble with safety: fear of crime, pollution and subjectification in public space', *Theoretical Criminology*, 20(1): 57–74.

Fanghanel, A. (2019) *Disrupting Rape Culture: Public Space, Sexuality and Revolt*, Bristol: Bristol University Press.

Fanghanel, A. and Lim, J. (2017) 'Of "sluts" and "arseholes": antagonistic desire and the production of sexual vigilance', *Feminist Criminology*, 12(4): 341–360.

Farris, S.R. (2012) 'Femonationalism and the "regular" army of labor called migrant women', *History of the Present*, 2(2): 184–199.

Featherstone, M. and Lash, S. (eds) (1998) *Spaces of Culture: City, Nation, World*, London: Sage.

Garraio, J. (2021) 'Cologne and the (un) making of transnational approaches to sexual violence', *European Journal of Women's Studies*, 28(2): 129–144.

Georgi, F. (2019) 'The role of racism in the European 'migration crisis': a historical materialist perspective', in V. Satgar (ed) *Racism After Apartheid: Challenges for Marxism and Anti-Racism*, Johannesburg: Witts University Press, pp 96–117.

Huggler, J. (2016) 'German women report string of sexual assaults by "Arab and North African men"', *The Telegraph*, 5 January. Available from: https://web.archive.org/web/20170331140809/https://www.telegraph.co.uk/news/worldnews/europe/germany/12082366/German-women-report-string-of-sexual-assaults-by-Arab-and-North-African-men.html [Accessed 24 April 2022].

Jazmati, Z. and Studer, N. (2017) 'Racializing "Oriental" manliness: from colonial contexts to Cologne', *Islamophobia Studies Journal*, 4(1): 87–100.

Kapur, R. (2018) *Gender, Alterity and Human Rights: Freedom in a Fishbowl*, Cheltenham: Edward Elgar.

Korac, M. (2020) 'Gendered and racialised border security: displaced people and the politics of fear', *International Journal for Crime, Justice and Social Democracy*, 9(3): 75–86.

LBC (2018) 'Nigel Farage: why I won't identify as a feminist', 29 January. Available from: https://www.lbc.co.uk/radio/presenters/nigel-farage/nigel-farage-why-i-wont-identify-as-a-feminist/ [Accessed 1 July 2021].

Lefebvre, H. (1996) 'The right to the city', in H. Lefebvre (ed) *Writings on Cities*, Oxford: Blackwell, pp 63–182.

Mort, F. (2000) 'The sexual geography of the city', in G. Bridge and S. Watson (eds) *A Companion to the City*, Oxford: Blackwell, pp 307–315.

Mouffe, C. (2012) 'An agonistic approach to the future of Europe', *New Literary History*, 43(4): 629–640.

Puwar, N. (2004) *Space Invaders: Race, Gender and Bodies Out of Place*, New York: Berg.

Sager, M. and Mulinari, D. (2018) 'Safety for whom? Exploring femonationalism and care-racism in Sweden', *Women's Studies International Forum*, 68: 149–156.

Turner, C. (2016) 'Labour MP faces calls to resign after comparing Cologne attacks to Birmingham night out', *The Telegraph*, 30 January. Available from: https://www.telegraph.co.uk/news/politics/labour/12131320/Labour-MP-faces-calls-to-resign-after-comparing-Cologne-attacks-to-Birmingham-night-out.html [Accessed 1 July 2021].

Weber, B. (2016a) 'The German refugee 'crisis' after Cologne: the race of refugee rights', *English Language Notes*, 54(2): 77–92.

Weber, B. (2016b) '"We must talk about Cologne": race, gender, and reconfigurations of "Europe"', *German Politics and Society*, 34(4): 68–86.

White, M. (2016) 'Cameron should try telling the City that women aren't "second-class citizens"', *The Guardian*, 18 January. Available from: https://www.theguardian.com/politics/blog/2016/jan/18/david-cameron-migrants-learn-english-women-second-class-citizens-ftse-boardrooms#comment-66972090 [Accessed 1 July 2021].

9

Transnational Regimes of Family Violence: When Violence Against Women Crosses Borders

Anja Bredal

Introduction

Violence against women is often highlighted as a global phenomenon, which then means that it affects women in all societies. However, despite recognition of the global nature of gender-based violence, little research to date has considered violence occurring in transnational contexts. This chapter contributes to this burgeoning research field through an analysis of how gendered abuse in a family context may include transnational elements and transcend national borders.

The empirical basis of this chapter is qualitative interviews with abused women and judgments in criminal cases on domestic violence, both of which involve more than one country in some way or other. The following questions are explored: how can individuals' and families' connections to several countries be utilized in perpetrators' control of and abuse against victims? Do transnational contexts offer specific tools or tactics of abuses? In particular, the chapter highlights the resources and structures that produce what is called a transnational opportunity structure for violence. Building on theories that conceptualize gender-based violence in regime terms (Stark, 2007; Katz, 2016), the chapter seeks to understand the particularities and dynamics of violence in transnational contexts. Following on this the concept of *transnational family violence regime* is suggested, to capture the spatiality, range and continuity of the regime as well as the dynamic mechanisms inherent in it.

Violence against women of immigrant background

Violence against women with an immigrant background living in the Global North has received increasing attention over the years. Recently, this research has focused on phenomena such as honour-based violence (Idriss and Abbas, 2011; Gill et al, 2014), forced marriage (Gill and Anitha, 2011), and violence in an extended family context (Rew et al, 2013; Lidman and Hong, 2018; Bredal, 2020). This literature sheds light on both specific motives for violence and specific social logics, for instance how the abuse may involve more than one perpetrator and more relations than that between intimate partners. While empirical data reveal transnational dimensions, these have rarely been the subject of in-depth analysis or theoretical development.

There are some exceptions, however, the first of which pertains to research on partner abuse in marriage migration. A key concern is how the immigration country's residence requirements may prevent women in violent marriages from leaving their abusers because they will then lose their residence permit (Thiara et al, 2011). This research shows how abusive men exploit immigration rules that make the women's residence status depend on their being married for several years. This chapter argues that studies on the interplay between perpetrators' strategies and state regulation should not only include the legislation of the immigration country but also that of other states and the dynamics between them.

Another notable exception from the methodological nationalism of domestic violence research applies to recent studies on 'transnational abandonment of women' which denotes the 'dumping' of wives in their country of origin (Lodhia, 2010; Rudra and Dasgupta, 2011; Bajpai, 2013; Bhattacharjee, 2013; Roy et al, 2019; Anitha et al, 2018, 2021). These studies are about South Asian women who marry men of South Asian descent living in Europe and North America, and who are subsequently abandoned in or returned to their home countries against their will. This happens because the husband or his family want the woman to live there or because he divorces her, often without informing her, while making sure her residence permit is withdrawn. As an abandoned wife, the woman is exploited by her in-laws or left to the stigma and economic disadvantage of living as a divorced woman. Anitha et al (2018, 2021) show how such abandonment is part of a broader repertoire of violence, where immigration regulation contributes to the dynamic. They propose that this practice should be defined as a form of violence against women. The present analysis is inspired by this research but suggests that a broader perspective is needed to capture the scope of what will be called transnational regimes of violence.

Transnational migration and family studies

This study is informed by insights from and critical perspectives on transnational migration and family studies. A key finding in studies on transnational migration is that people maintain and develop connections across several nation states (Fouron and Glick Schiller, 2001; Levitt and Glick Schiller, 2004). While some ties are strong and pervasive, involving frequent interaction, others are weaker with more episodic contact. On a concrete level, the exchange may include, for example, travel, electronic communication, marriage, financial investment, political participation, dual citizenship and other formal affiliations. A key point is the critique of the methodological nationalism inherent in research that takes the boundaries of the nation state for granted (Wimmer and Glick Schiller, 2002).

An oft-quoted phrase defines transnational families as 'families who live separately but who create and retain a sense of collective welfare and unity, in short "familyhood"', even across national borders' (Bryceson and Vuorela, 2002: 3). Normalizing transnational life appears to be an ambition of much research on transnational families, demonstrating that being a mobile, and at times also a divided, family is not necessarily a negative thing. To the extent that negative aspects are highlighted, the focus is often on external factors, typically on families who are dispersed due to poverty or immigration regulation. The fact that 'internal' family conflict and abuse can also be part of transnational social fields (Levitt and Glick Schiller, 2004) has received less attention. More generally, transnational studies have been accused of a positive bias, emphasizing possibilities and empowering outcomes. Feminist scholars, among others, have pointed out that there is nothing inherently transcendent or liberating about transnationalism (Pratt and Yeoh, 2003: 160) and empirical studies show a complex picture as to whether patriarchal gender orders change, are reproduced or even strengthened when people live transnational lives (Yeoh and Ramdas, 2014; Mahler and Pessar, 2001; Pessar and Mahler, 2003; Pratt and Yeoh, 2003). This study follows suit by focusing on what Hearn has conceptualized as transpatriarchies which is defined as 'the structural tendency and individualised propensity for men's transnational gender domination' (Hearn, 2015: 78).

Conceptualizing domestic violence as regime

The analysis presented here is part of an effort to move from incident-based understandings of gender-based domestic abuse – that have been criticized for misrepresenting the phenomenon and its impact – to more comprehensive approaches. Examples in the literature include conceptualizations in terms of violence continuums (Kelly, 1987; Cockburn, 2014) and regimes (Stark, 2007; Katz, 2016). While regime thinking seems mostly geared at grasping the totality of the abuse, including different tools and tactics available to the perpetrator, the continuum approach also refers to the continuity between contexts, time and space – which is of particular importance for the present study. The idea of *conducive contexts*, which was originally developed by Kelly (2007, 2016) to capture 'the interplay between the immediate and transnational conditions that created the sympathetic environment for trafficking' (Chantler and McCarry, 2020: 91) has further worked as a sensitizing concept throughout the analysis. While Chantler and McCarry use the term in their analysis of forced marriages, this chapter asks whether transnationality may work as a conducive context for domestic violence more broadly.

Mahler and Pessar's conceptual framework, *gendered geographies of power* (Mahler and Pessar, 2001; Pessar and Mahler, 2003) has also informed the analysis. It represents a promising line of thinking to grasp the spatiality of family violence and has been developed with the aim of understanding how transnational spaces and practices are hierarchically organized along different intersecting and interacting dimensions such as gender, class, ethnicity and legal affiliation with states. The framework is inspired by Massey (1994) who emphasizes how people's social positioning not only affects their access to resources and mobility in transnational spaces, but also the possibility for them to influence these conditions (Mahler and Pessar, 2001: 447). People are differently positioned when it comes to access to and power over the flow and connections between places, says Massey. While some initiate mobility, others are objects of mobility, and some are trapped by it (in Mahler and Pessar, 2001). As Anitha et al point out (2018), the concept of gendered geographies of power is useful for understanding how gender operates simultaneously on several spatial and social scales, for example the body, the family or the state, in transnational terrains.

Drawing on these concepts, the following analysis explores how gender-based family violence is perpetrated, endured and facilitated transnationally.

Methodology

The analysis is based on two data sets, one consisting of qualitative interviews and the other of criminal judgments. The interview material is from an ongoing study of women's experience of violence from male partners and in-laws comprising interviews with 97 women living in Norway. The women were recruited via Facebook and different services. The interviews were inspired by the teller-focused interview approach (Hydén, 2014) – which works well in interviews on topics that may be difficult to articulate, such as family violence. All interviews were recorded and transcribed. About a quarter of the interviewed women have immigrant backgrounds from Afghanistan, Bosnia, Iraq, Iran, Pakistan, Somalia, Syria, Chechnya and

Turkey. The interviews that comprised transnational elements of family violence were identified and subjected to further analysis.

The case-law material consists of judgments from criminal cases about violence in immigrant families, where it appears that the violence has partly taken place abroad or there are other transnational aspects. Some of this material was collected in previous research projects, while the main bulk was obtained through searches in the Lovdata Pro database. Lovdata Pro contains all reasoned decisions from the Norwegian Supreme Court and courts of appeal, and selected decisions from the district courts. The search criteria included the domestic violence provision in the old and new penal code (§219 of the Penal Code of 1902; §§282, 283 of the Penal Code of 2005, effective from 2015), combined with the jurisdiction provisions, §12 and §5 respectively.[1] In addition, the following search words were used: 'abroad', 'jurisdiction', 'Pakistan', 'Iraq' and some other major immigration countries. After supplementing with lower court judgments obtained from court administrations, the legal material consists of a total of 47 judgments representing 25 cases from the period 2009–2019, most of which are from the last five years. This chapter only refers to final judgments where the accused was found guilty. While the legal assessment is not the topic of this chapter, the material is used as data about the nature of transnational violence.

Using a thematic, explorative approach (Braun and Clark, 2006), the judgments and interviews were read systematically with the purpose of identifying elements and dimensions relating to transnationality. This process of analysis identified three key themes, which will be presented in the next part of this chapter: (1) transnational elements in regimes of violence, (2) how abuse and control cross national borders and (3) transnationality as a conducive context. For purposes of anonymization, judgment case numbers and country of origin have been omitted. Quotes in Norwegian have been translated to English by the author, and expression has been slightly edited for readability.

Analysis

Transnational elements in a regime based in one country

This first thematic concerns what can be called a transnational toolbox. The research data describes physical, material and psychological violence, including threats, that are part of an extensive pattern of control and abuse over time. While these cases have much in common with domestic violence regimes in general, there are also some particularities that may be identified as transnational elements. This is pertinently illustrated in the interview with Samina. She had come from Pakistan to Norway after marrying a Norwegian-Pakistani man and they lived with his parents and siblings in an extended household. Both Samina and her son were subjected to physical violence and psychological degradation by her husband and in-laws who cooperated in controlling her. She was not allowed to have her own phone or computer, and she was monitored when she spoke with her family in Pakistan. While these are typical control tactics in a domestic violence regime, for women like Samina the control is particularly effective since they literally have no social network outside the home and their potential support networks are based in another country. Furthermore, she and the other women interviewed were prevented from attending language courses and scared away from seeking help through misinformation and intimidation. In particular, the women interviewed had been told that the child protection services would remove their children if they shared anything with 'Norwegians'.

One judgment also described how the woman had been told that she would be raped and sent back to Pakistan by the police if she contacted them. Once there, she would be 'sold to a brothel where she would be raped every night'. This is one of several cases where the threats play on a combination of the victim having poor knowledge of Norwegian conditions and that she knows what can happen in the country of origin, for example that police officers may be corrupt and abusive against so-called shameless women. Similarly, another judgment described a father who had threatened his daughter that he would take her to their country of origin 'where she would be "slaughtered" ... and thrown at a well-known rubbish heap in [the capital], where women who, for example, have sex before marriage are thrown away after they are killed'. Furthermore, he would 'force her to marry an elderly man, and tear her passport so that she did not return to Norway' (case X).

Such threats of moving the victims to their country of origin against their will are repeated in the material. When wives are concerned, it varies whether or not they are threatened with divorce, and to what extent the perpetrators plan to keep the children. Threats of expulsion, or what Anitha et al (2018) call abandonment, become particularly effective when the woman comes from a community that stigmatizes divorced and single women. As known from other studies, wives with temporary residence permits are particularly vulnerable but abandonment also affects women and children with permanent residence or even Norwegian citizenship.

Another element in the transnational toolbox is when perpetrators threaten to or actually reveal information – true or false – about the victim to her family in the country of origin. These threats are often about alleged sexual transgressions, as for example in this quote from a judgment: 'the accused had spread rumours that she had run away and that she was with another man'. Furthermore, threats of violence may be directed at a third party, as described in a judgment where a man told his wife he would kill her brother in Pakistan and an ex-husband threatened to kill the woman's uncle in India. Samina had also received threats against her close kin in Pakistan. She considered the danger to be real, because her in-laws in Pakistan were capable of violence or would pay someone to harm her family.

Violence crossing national borders

A second transnational thematic is that violence and control are exercised in and across several countries. This topic involved situations where the perpetrator and victims lived together and moved between countries – violence on the move – and cases where they lived in different countries – violence from afar. As a third variety, the move itself can be used by the perpetrator to maintain control and is thus a key abusive tactic in itself.

Violence on the move typically involved families that alternate between living in Norway and in the country of origin. In the previously mentioned case X, their mobility was partly caused by the child protection services taking an interest in the family. According to the judgment, the man had abused both his wife and children, including sexual abuse against a daughter. In accordance with their transnational lifestyle, the violence had taken place during extensive stays in Norway, their country of origin and a third country. However, violence on the move may also include holidays and other short-term travel.

Yet another variety is when the abuser follows the victim to another country, as in the court case of a man convicted of extensive control of and sexual abuse against a daughter since she was four or five years old until she became an adult. The control was about preventing her from having contact with boys, especially during her teens. He delivered and picked her up at school, checked her mobile and computer regularly, and generally restricted her social life. When she moved abroad to study, he continued the control from Norway. Skype and mobile data showed that he had contacted her several times every day to ensure 'that she was in the apartment when she did not have tuition, and … that she did not have contact with men'. He also visited regularly, for up to a month at a time, subjecting her to severe sexual abuse several times a day. The young woman explained that 'the situation was more demanding in [country 2] because they were always alone'.

An example of *violence from afar* is from a judgment where a woman of Norwegian majority background was married to a man from another country. According to the judgment, he used gross violence against her and their children for over 30 years, including in periods when they lived in Norway, and he stayed in his country of origin or other countries. It is described that he was angry, threatening and verbally abusive 'through daily conversations on the phone and Skype'. Furthermore, 'he demanded to know where everyone was and what they were doing. He often threatened to come home and punish them'. This behaviour instilled a constant fear in his wife and children that he would come home suddenly. Interestingly, the court explicitly described the abuse in terms of a regime across national borders and over time: "As a result of the aggrieved party having lived under the defendant's regime with a combination of unpredictable rage and psychological violence and other abuse, it gradually took little to maintain the regime the defendant had created. The abuse has been a common thread throughout their lives". Another example from a court case describes a similar regime but in the reversed geographical direction; the man was based in Norway while his wife and children lived in their country of origin. Both when he visited them and via telephone contact, he maintained 'a regime in which the victims lived under a constant fear of violence and abuse even while living in [country]'.

Forced movement as an abusive tactic in itself is when the perpetrators take victims to the other country and keep them there against their will. There are several examples of such enforced relocation and detention in the legal material. In a judgment on a family, the man was convicted of violence against his wife and children over a 15-year period, in both countries. At one stage he had decided that they all would move back to their country of origin, luring and pressuring his wife and children to join him there on an alleged holiday. Consequently, he confiscated their passports and airline tickets, retaining them in the country by means of threats, violence and deprivation of liberty. They lived with his family who helped him maintain control, including when he travelled to Norway. Both in the present judgment material and in the findings of other studies (Lidén and Bredal, 2017; Norwegian Ministry of Health, 2020) there are examples of young women who are sent out of Norway by both parents, to be controlled and disciplined by relatives in their country of origin, typically as punishment for, or to prevent, a breach of chastity norms. If the girl has been raised in Norway, she may find herself in a similar situation as the isolated immigrant wives in Norway. She may not speak the language or know her whereabouts in the country of origin. Moreover, gender segregation norms will restrict young women's mobility and chances of seeking help outside the family.

While the interview material includes more examples of threats than of actual abandonment of wives, the problem of abandonment is well known from special services set up to combat forced marriage and so-called honour-based violence in Norway, including the national expert team and 'integration counsellors' at Norwegian foreign missions (Lidén and Bredal, 2017; Den Norske Ambassade i Islamabad, 2017; Norwegian Ministry of Justice and Public Security, 2017). Some of the implications will be drawn out in the next section.

Transnationality as a conducive context

A third theme is transnationality as a conducive context. Three dimensions can be identified in the interviews and judgments.

First, the data show how a transnational lifestyle entails access to resources in two or more countries. They can be material resources in the form of capital, housing and other property, and social skills such as mastering the language and knowing the system. Human resources are frequent in the data, and typically involves relatives who help enforce the regime of control and violence. This may be because they support the perpetrators in their desire for control, or mainly based on family loyalty or financial dependency. Some have their own motives for controlling the woman or children, for example to use a daughter-in-law as a domestic worker, or to ensure that the granddaughter does not harm family honour. Another motive could be their interest in the children, as described in a judgment where a man was convicted of violence against his wife and children, which included luring them to and retaining them in their country of origin after a holiday in a third country. In connection with the woman's attempt to flee back to Norway with her sons, a conflict arose at the airport between members of the husband's and her own family. It was described in the judgment that the two families had agreed, without involving the woman, that she would be allowed to travel but that the boys would stay.

Second, perpetrators can find support in informal and formal norms in their country origin. In the data, social norms are often favourable to male perpetrators and their kin group, in particular in classic patriarchal societies (Kandiyoti,1988; Therborn, 2004). As we have seen, threats against women can be based on how women in general and 'indecent' women in particular are treated in the other country. Furthermore, men may have stronger legal rights by virtue of their gender and the role of husband and father, while women and children have weaker legal protection. For instance, in some countries, men can prevent their wives from leaving the country by issuing a travel ban, and patriarchal family laws favour the father and his family in custody cases. In addition, the legislation on domestic violence and protection of victims may be weak and enforcement may be inefficient or corrupt. For example, in a judgment where a man held his wife and children in their country of origin against their will, he had obtained a written statement from the local police that he had not subjected them to violence. It is described that he got this without the police investigating the case or even talking to his wife and children. It may seem that he tried to exploit women and children's weaker legal protection in the other country, to strengthen his position in the Norwegian court case. Furthermore, as Anitha and colleagues (2018) point out, men will often have more financial resources to use the judicial system. Citizenship as well is a resource in that the authorities are obliged to safeguard the rights of their own citizens. For women and children, however, citizenship may be detrimental to the extent that their legal rights are weak, as when a married woman is trapped inside the country because the authorities are obliged to enforce her husband's travel ban.

However, and as a third dimension, although the sociolegal framework may be more overtly patriarchal in the family's country of origin, regulations of the host country should also be taken into account, as well as the dynamic between jurisdictions. While the impact of residence rules on abused immigrant women has already been mentioned, another example is found in recent studies of transnational abandonment of wives. This literature reveals how some men strategically choose between divorce legislation, in their efforts to get rid of or further control their wives. As Bajpai (2013) and others show, some men choose the liberal divorce rules of Western countries to their advantage, after sending their wife back to their country of origin. While for instance Indian law requires that both spouses be present in court for a divorce to be valid, many Western countries have *ex parte* divorce, which means that the other party does not have to be involved in – or even know about – the judicial procedure (Anitha et al, 2018). When the woman is finally informed, she often has little opportunity to assert her rights with regard to property, maintenance and child custody. Thus, this is an apt example of how legal regulations that are associated with women's rights at divorce in one national context – as is the case of *ex parte* divorce in Norway's marital law – may become a patriarchal tool in a transnational context, substantiating the need for an intersectional and transnational lens in understanding how the law operates and impacts on different women.

In apparent contrast, Wærstad (2017) finds that some men of Pakistani descent in Norway choose a Pakistani divorce when they deceive and return their wives. The reasons and outcome are the same in both cases, however, as also in these cases the man chooses the most favourable alternative, that is the Pakistani rules on property division and custody. Wærstad finds that the Norwegian authorities then approve these foreign divorces without ensuring that the women are informed, contrary to administrative law. Thus, they are prevented from seeking legal advice at the Norwegian Embassy and possibly also free legal aid, in the case that they managed to return to Norway. They are not made aware of their right to apply for family reunification with their children if the children remain in Norway. According to Wærstad, the reason given for exempting from the duty to inform, is simply that it is seen as 'obviously unnecessary'. Thus, by effectively excluding these women from the law, the state not only legitimates but even assists these perpetrators in forcibly displacing women.

Discussion

This chapter has shown how some husbands, fathers and parents-in-law use transnational tools and spaces to abuse and maintain control over their wives, children and daughters-in-law. This can be while the perpetrator and victims are located in the same geographical place, when they live apart or when they move between nation states together. In many cases, the geographical scope of violence is about families living distinctly transnational lives. This may be voluntary for all parties and as such a conditional fact, resulting in the violence also moving. However, mobility can also be a more instrumental part of the abuse, if the perpetrators move and restrain the victims against their will. Moreover, the perpetrators exploit their own and the victims' sociolegal connection to several countries to control, threaten and harm. By physically moving their bodies from one country to another, the perpetrators not only prevent the victims from seeking help but also manipulate legal frameworks to their advantage, producing specific vulnerabilities associated with entrapment.

In this way, the regime of violence extends across national borders, where it involves collective groups on both the perpetrator's and the victim's side, as well as several regulative frameworks, both formal and informal, in a transnational structure of opportunity. The term *transnational family violence regime* is proposed to conceptualize such practices. The intention of the concept is to capture the spatiality, range and continuity of the regime as well as the dynamic mechanisms inherent in it.

The chapter argues that research on gender-based violence has been dominated by methodological nationalism. As demonstrated in the preceding analysis, a national perspective on transnational violence and control will not only give a limited picture but a distorted one. In the effort to grasp the full extent and dynamic of transnational violence regimes, one promising theoretical approach is found in Pessar and Mahler's theory of gendered geographies of power (Mahler and Pessar, 2001; Pessar and Mahler, 2003). They point to a split between research on transnational migration that has privileged the state, and research on gender and migration that has focused on the family. Analyses of gendered geographies of power should include both levels or arenas, they argue. This is amply illustrated in the preceding analysis of transnational violence regimes. The residence requirement for marriage migrants is a pivotal example of how state regulations not only directly impact on the power relations within the married couple, but also play into the hands of abusive partners. In this chapter, a similar dynamic has been highlighted in connection with abandonment and divorce. It has been shown how the *ex parte* rules, which treat the couple as two independent individuals free to divorce each other, are exploited by abusive men who forcibly move their wives to another country, preventing them from accessing information and enforcement of their legal rights. By defining such information as obviously unnecessary the Norwegian state actively contributes to the entrapment of these women. Thus, in Chantler and McCarthy's (2020: 101) words, Norwegian authorities contribute to 'bolster conducive contexts'.

This study demonstrates how the strategic dislocating of women's bodies is instrumental in preserving (trans)patriarchy in families. Adding to Anitha et al's (2018, 2021) pioneering research, it confirms that transnational abandonment is a topical issue among immigrant women in the Global North, also in Norway. However, the data show that it not only affects women as wives, but also children of both sexes, especially teenage girls who challenge chastity norms. Furthermore, the analysis supports Anitha et al's conclusion that such abandonment should be seen as violence and abuse. However, rather than defining transnational abandonment as a *form* of violence against women, further research should focus on 'how abandonment is embedded within a pattern' of violence and control 'exacerbated by the power asymmetries that operate in transnational contexts' (Anitha et al, 2021).

Conclusion

Theoretically, this chapter engaged with key conceptualizations of family violence in terms of regime, continuum and conducive contexts. The intention of introducing the concept *transnational regimes of family violence* is not to suggest a new form of violence but to extend previous understandings. Hopefully, the concept should encourage studies that look for a broader range of tools and tactics in a wider spatial field, as well as transnational and multilevel dynamics and opportunity structures.

Note
[1]   For an English version of the Penal Code of 2005: https://lovdata.no/dokument/NLE/lov/2005-05-20-28

References
Anitha, S., Roy, A. and Yalamarty, H. (2018) 'Gender, migration, and exclusionary citizenship regimes: conceptualizing transnational abandonment of wives as a form of violence against women', *Violence Against Women*, 24(7): 747–774.
Anitha, S., Roy, A. and Yalamarty, H. (2021) 'Transnational marriage abandonment: a new form of domestic violence and abuse in transnational spaces', in J. Devaney, C. Bradbury-Jones, R.J. Macy, C. Øverlien and S. Holt (eds) *The Routledge International Handbook of Domestic Violence and Abuse*, Abingdon: Routledge, pp 340–355.
Bajpai, A. (2013) 'Across the high seas: abuse, desertion, and violence in transnational marriages in India', *Violence Against Women*, 19(10): 1246–1262.
Bhattacharjee, S.S. (2013) 'Distant silences and default judgments: access to justice for transnationally abandoned women', *University of Pennsylvania Journal of Law and Social Change*, 16(1): 95–110.
Braun, V. and Clarke, V. (2006) 'Using thematic analysis in psychology', *Qualitative Research in Psychology*, 3(2): 77–101.

Bredal, A. (2020) 'Minoritetsnorske og majoritetsnorske kvinners erfaring med partnervold', in A. Bredal, H. Eggebø and A.M.A. Eriksen (eds) *Vold i nære relasjoner i et mangfoldig Norge*, Oslo: Cappelen Damm Akademisk, pp 47–65.

Bryceson, D. and Vuorela, U. (eds) (2002) *The Transnational Family: New European Frontiers and Global Networks*, Oxford: Berg.

Chantler, K. and McCarry, M. (2020) 'Forced marriage, coercive control, and conducive contexts: the experiences of women in Scotland', *Violence Against Women*, 26(1): 89–109.

Cockburn, C. (2014) 'A continuum of violence: gender, war and peace', in R. Jamieson (ed) *The Criminology of War*, Farnham: Ashgate, pp 357–377.

Fouron, G. and Glick Schiller, N. (2001) 'All in the family: gender, transnational migration, and the nation-state', *Identities*, 7(4): 539–582.

Gill, A.K. and Anitha, S. (2011) *Forced Marriage: Introducing a Social Justice and Human Rights Perspective*, London: Zed Books.

Gill, A.K., Strange, C. and Roberts, K. (eds) (2014) *'Honour' Killing and Violence: Theory, Policy and Practice*, Basingstoke: Palgrave Macmillan.

Hearn, J. (2015) *Men of the World: Genders, Globalizations, Transnational Times*, London: Sage.

Hydén, M. (2014) 'The teller-focused interview: interviewing as a relational practice', *Qualitative Social Work*, 13(6): 795–812.

Idriss, M.M. and Abbas, T. (eds) (2011) *Honour, Violence, Women and Islam*, Abingdon: Routledge, pp 16–28.

Kandiyoti, D. (1988) 'Bargaining with patriarchy', *Gender and Society*, 2(3): 274–290.

Katz, E. (2016) 'Beyond the physical incident model: how children living with domestic violence are harmed by and resist regimes of coercive control', *Child Abuse Review*, 25(1): 46–59.

Kelly, L. (1987) 'The continuum of sexual violence', in J. Hanmer and M. Maynard (eds) *Women, Violence and Social Control*, Basingstoke: Macmillan, pp 46–60.

Kelly, L. (2007) 'A conducive context: trafficking of persons in Central Asia', in M. Lee (ed) *Human Trafficking*, Cullompton: Willan, pp 73–91.

Kelly, L. (2016) 'The conducive context of violence against women and girls', *Discover Society*, 30. Available from: https://archive.discoversociety.org/2016/03/01/theorising-violence-against-women-and-girls/ [Accessed 8 June 2021].

Levitt, P. and Glick Schiller, N. (2004) 'Conceptualizing simultaneity: a transnational social field perspective on society', *International Migration Review*, 38(3): 1002–1039.

Lidén, H. and Bredal, A. (2017) *Fra særtiltak til ordinær innsats. Følgeevaluering av handlingsplanen mot tvangsekteskap, kjønnslemlestelse og alvorlige begrensninger av unges frihet*, Oslo: Institutt for samfunnsforskning [Department of Social Research], Report 2017:1. Available from: https://samfunnsfo rskning.brage.unit.no/samfunnsforskning-xmlui/handle/11250/2445678 [Accessed 24 April 2022].

Lidman, S. and Hong, T. (2018) '"Collective violence" and honour in Finland: a survey for professionals', *Journal of Aggression, Conflict and Peace Research*, 10(4): 261–271.

Lodhia, S. (2010) 'Brides without borders: new topographies of violence and the future of law in an era of transnational citizen-subjects', *Columbia Journal of Gender & Law*, 19(3): 703–745.

Mahler, S.J. and Pessar, P.R. (2001) 'Gendered geographies of power: analyzing gender across transnational spaces', *Identities*, 7(4): 441–459.

Massey, D. (1994) *Space, Place and Gender*, Minneapolis: University of Minnesota Press.

Den Norske Ambassade i Islamabad [The Norwegian Embassy in Islamabad] (2017) Arbeidet med konsulær-, utlendings-, politi- og integreringssaker ved ambassaden i Islamabad: Erfaringer, utfordringer og anbefalinger [Casework on consular services, immigration, police and integration at the Embassy in Islamabad], Islamabad: Royal Norwegian Embassy in Islamabad.

Norwegian Ministry of Health (2020) *'Det var ikke bare ferie': Rapport fra ekspertgruppe om unge som etterlates i utlandet mot sin vilje*, Oslo: Departementenes sikkerhets- og serviceorganisasjon. Available from: https://www.regjerin gen.no/no/dokumenter/det-var-ikke-bare-ferie/id2703623/ [Accessed 24 April 2022].

Norwegian Ministry of Justice and Public Security (2017) *The Right to Decide About One's Own Life: Action Plan to Combat Negative Social Control, Forced Marriage and Female Genital Mutilation 2017–2020*, Oslo: Norwegian Ministry of Justice and Public Security. Available from: https://www.regj eringen.no/contentassets/e570201f283d48529d6211db392e4297/action-plan-the-right-to-decide-about-ones-own-life-2017-2020.pdf [Accessed 8 June 2021].

Pessar, P.R. and Mahler, S.J. (2003) 'Transnational migration: bringing gender in', *International Migration Review*, 37(3): 812–846.

Pratt, G. and Yeoh, B. (2003) 'Transnational (counter) topographies', *Gender, Place & Culture*, 10(2): 159–166.

Rew, M., Gangoli, G. and Gill, A. (2013) 'Violence between female in-laws in India', *Journal of International Women's Studies*, 14(1): 147–160.

Roy, A., Anitha, S. and Yalamarty, H. (2019) '"Abandoned women": transnational marriages and gendered legal citizens' *Australian Feminist Studies*, 34(100): 165–181.

Rudra, U. and Dasgupta, S.D. (2011) *Transnational Abandonment of South Asian Women: A New Face of Violence Against Women*, Manavi Occasional Paper No 6, New Brunswick, NJ: Manavi.

Stark, E. (2007) *Coercive Control: How Men Entrap Women in Personal Life*, Oxford: Oxford University Press.

Therborn, G. (2004) *Between Sex and Power: Family in the World, 1900–2000*. London: Routledge.

Thiara, R.K., Condon, S.A. and Schröttle, M. (eds) (2011) *Violence Against Women and Ethnicity: Commonalities and Differences Across Europe*, Opladen: Barbara Budrich.

Wærstad, T.L. (2017) *Protecting Muslim Minority Women's Human Rights at Divorce: Application of the Protection against Discrimination Guarantee in Norwegian Domestic Law, Private International Law and Human Rights Law*, Oslo: Nomos.

Wimmer, A. and Glick Schiller, N. (2002) 'Methodological nationalism and beyond: nation-state building, migration and the social sciences', *Global Networks*, 2(4): 301–334.

Yeoh, B.S.A. and Ramdas, K. (2014) 'Gender, migration, mobility and transnationalism', *Gender, Place & Culture*, 21(10): 1197–1213.

10

Between NGO-ization and Militarization: Women's Rights in the Fragile Geographies of Niger

Kristine Anderson

Introduction

Since the early 2010s, the security, political and symbolic interests of a diverse group of actors have converged upon the Sahel region of West Africa. Niger, a country in this region, has become a space in which a diverse cohort of foreign security forces, state and non-state armed actors, and humanitarian and development non-governmental organizations (NGOs) and United Nations (UN) agencies find themselves operating in overlapping spaces. This chapter examines how the concurrence of a humanitarian infrastructure that often seeks to speak on behalf of women and girls (NGO-ization) and increased foreign and state-led military action (militarization) within fragile spaces in Niger impacts women's agency and their experience of gender-based violence (GBV). This chapter questions what happens to women's agency within spaces that are increasingly characterized by concurrent NGO-ization and militarization. This chapter first contextualizes Niger within the larger Sahelian space, visiting the ways the Sahel has been conceptualized. It then argues that Niger represents a space characterized by both NGO-ization and militarization. It explores these two dynamics through the case studies of the Tillabéry region, bordering Mali and Burkina Faso, and the Diffa region bordering Nigeria and Chad, arguing these spaces to be productive of GBV and obstructive to women's meaningful economic, political and civic participation[1] and therefore contributing to the spiralling fragility of the country.

Situating Niger within the Sahelian space

The spatial characteristics of the Sahel are ambiguous, and the region's fluid boundaries have defied colonial and postcolonial attempts at classifying it into a neat territory with delineated borders on the basis of bioclimatic characteristics. Derived from the Arabic word for 'shore', the Sahel has often been confused (or conflated) with the great desert that laps its metaphorical shoreline to the north, and has often taken on the social, political, security and geographical characteristics conferred upon the Sahara by the academic and common imagination alike.

The Sahel can be defined as 'a strip of semi-arid land stretching from the Atlantic Ocean to Chad, characterised by steppe vegetation, and limited by 100–200 and 600–700 mm of average annual rainfall' (Walther and Retaillé, 2010: 3). Moving beyond this zonal conception, Walther and Retaillé (2021: 2) conceptualize the Sahel as a 'space of circulation in which uncertainty has historically been overcome by mobility', one in which multiple actors have moved across fluid spaces and borders throughout time, irrelevant of territorial control and climactic changes. Bøås and Strazzari (2020: 2), rejecting what they call 'geographical determinism', define the region as a 'social space' that 'expands and shrinks in line with political, social, and economic trajectories that are impacted by ecological changes'.

Situating Niger within this space, it stands as something of a quintessential Sahelian country per Western conceptualizations, one in which the security, political and economic interests of global actors have grown in prominence and urgency in the 2010s onwards.

NGO-ization in Niger

Niger gained greater prominence on the international stage during the Sahelian famine in the 1970s, when the ensuing humanitarian crisis brought a large number of Western humanitarian actors into the region. Mann (2014: 11) argues that the rise of the NGO in the Sahel came to change the meaning of government by 'prying open a new political space of imported initiatives, controlled distribution, and constrained sovereignty', a space that NGOs would later expand during the post–Cold War period of democratic transitions in Africa. During this time, images of the plight of Sahelian people were brought to the global stage by foreign media, contributing to the Western notion of the Sahel as a space of suffering in need of intervention.

The alphabet soup of NGOs and INGOs (international NGOs) present in Niger and its neighbours have continued to battle the ongoing afflictions of poverty, malnutrition and poor education – and have also taken on the cause of women and girls. In pace with Niger's rising geostrategic topicality, international consternation around the plight of women and girls in Niger (and the Sahel more broadly) has increased. This concern is not unjustified given Niger's poor performance on gender equality indicators: Niger sits at 154 out of 162 countries on the Gender Inequality Index, due to low rates of participation in the formal labour force and politics, educational inequalities, and sky-high rates of child marriage, maternal mortality and adolescent births (UNDP, 2020: 5–6).

As with poverty, malnutrition and other social issues, women's and girls' rights have increasingly been subsumed under the mandate of the NGO. A cursory Google search of women and girls in Niger yields a list of media articles depicting the travails of women and girls, and various efforts aimed at saving and empowering them by NGO actors.[2] This placement of women and girls' rights into the NGO space raises concerns around the NGO-ization of women's participation. Broadly defined as the reshaping of larger social movements and their discourses into the depoliticized units of NGOs, scholars have criticized NGO-ization as reflective of a neoliberal thrust that de-emphasizes the state and views the NGO as the primary mechanism for social change and basic service delivery. Shivji (2006: 35), for example, asserts that NGO discourse reduces African people to 'subject matter of papers on strategies for poverty reduction, authored by consultants and discussed at stake-holders workshops in which, the "poor" are represented by NGOs'. Thus, while NGOs may be driven by well-meaning political or moral intentions, they function largely to respond to demands of primarily Western donors.

A key characteristic of the NGO-ized space is its effect of mapping Western, neoliberal notions of rights and participation onto Sahelian women and girls. This is illustrated well by an October 2020 statement released by the Gender-Based Violence Area of Responsibility (GBVAR et al, 2020) (a global coordinating body for humanitarian GBV interventions) and other NGOs that accompanied a side event to the Ministerial Roundtable on the Central Sahel led by the Area of Responsibility, the United Nations Population Fund, and two INGOs. At this event, these actors sought to 'amplify the voices and priorities of girls from Burkina Faso, Mali and Niger offering [a] unique opportunity to learn from first-hand-experience and receive recommendations from the affected girls' (GBVAR et al, 2020: 2), to bring greater donor and government attention (and resources) to GBV interventions. The event included the testimonies of three 'Sahelian girls', one from each of the three concerned nations, whose testimonies are presented in the event summary as their recommendations to regional governments, donors, and development and humanitarian actors for how they may empower and help girls like them. Even while this event addressed very real challenges and was couched in the language of participation and empowerment, there is a distinct sense that the voices of the girls have been somehow processed or repackaged: it is difficult to imagine an adolescent girl would request donor governments to 'support integrating actions that strengthen the self-esteem of girls through intergenerational dialogues or role models' (GBVAR et al, 2020: 3).

Militarization in Niger

Increasingly, the Sahelian space (and Niger) are seen as spaces defined by security, or rather, its absence. Walther and Retaillé (2010: 6) point to the depiction of the Sahel as a 'dangerous' area predominant in geopolitical discourse. Frowd and Sandor (2018: 70–71) describe the Sahel as 'heavily securitized in both discourse and practice', portrayed by African and Western actors as a space of 'crisis, uncertainty, illicit flows, and terrorism', all of which justify the use of 'military interventions, capacity-building projects, regional intelligence coordination, international policing operations, and law enforcement training to better govern (in)security in this space'.

There is no denying, since the early 2010s, that there has been a proliferation of violence and insecurity into the country – and in its wake, a range of security actors. Niger's Forces de Défense et Sécurité (FDS, or Security and Defence Forces) – comprising the military, the police, the National Guard and the gendarmerie – are mobilized to quell crises on multiple fronts. Most prominent of these are the wars being waged (and largely lost) to extinguish extremist non-state armed actors in the western border areas with Burkina Faso and Mali, and against militants in the Boko Haram crisis in the south-east on the borders with Chad and Nigeria. Elements of Niger's FDS are also implicated in implementing components of controversial border management policies, most prominently in the northern region of Agadez, a historical crossroads for migration both intra-regionally and towards North Africa.[3]

Simultaneously, a number of foreign security-focused missions have established or have upscaled their presence in Niger, under different mandates.[4] Many fall under the broad category of capacity-building missions providing non-combat support in the form of equipment, training, intelligence and other behind-the-scenes activities aimed nominally at strengthening the capacity of the FDS to stem terrorism and criminality, secure borders and provide protection to civilians. The EU Capacity Building Mission (EUCAP) Sahel Niger mission is a prominent example, established in 2012 through the EU's Strategy for Security and Development in the Sahel. EUCAP is firmly rooted in the assumption that 'development and security are mutually supportive' and its mission to Niger aims 'to strengthen Niger's internal security sector and its capacity to counter the various security threats', which it accomplishes through activities grouped around the four pillars of 'training, mentoring, strategic advice, and provision of equipment and infrastructure support' (EUCAP Sahel Niger, 2020). The EUCAP mission frames its work around what it calls a 'people-centred security concept', touting its training-of-trainers approach and its collaboration with UN agencies, civil society, and local and national authorities.

Other foreign security actors present in Niger and its neighbours project a decidedly more military character, being engaged in direct operations and/or playing a strong role in intelligence gathering. The G5 Sahel Joint Force is a partnership between Niger, Burkina Faso, Mali, Mauritania and Chad, created in July 2017 to counter the security threats facing the Sahel. The G5 was formed amid handwringing and debate among its Western backers (primarily the US and France), and its added value in stemming terrorism has been questioned (Berger, 2019).

Additionally, the French Opération Barkhane forces carries out anti-insurgency operations in Niger as part of a wider Sahel campaign against terrorism. Barkhane's footprint in Niger is most perceptible on the western borders with Mali and Burkina Faso, a restive triangle known as Liptako-Gourma region that straddles the three countries. France's regional military involvement has intensified since Opération Serval in 2012–13 temporarily removed Islamists from northern Mali, and the follow-up mission continues nearly a decade later. France's military expansion has been contentious given its heavy colonial past in West Africa, which has not been helped by the loss of the lives of 10,000 West Africans and the displacement of more than 1 million; France and its West African partner forces have suffered significant losses as insecurity intensifies (Maclean, 2020). The US has additionally input significant resources into Niger, having built a massive and costly drone base in Agadez and maintaining a large percentage of its total military personnel deployed in Africa in Niger as of 2020 (Turse, 2020).

This influx of foreign actors in the name of security, coupled with the intensified deployment of security forces in fragile border regions, has led to Niger being labelled a militarized space in an increasingly militarized Sahel.[5] The extensive list of security actors *in situ* is not the sole indicator of militarization: a generous share of Niger's public budget goes to military and security expenditures, which like other Sahelian countries has largely shown a pattern of growth during the 2010s and beyond (World Bank, 2021). Security is also increasingly a driving force for foreign policy in the region of Western powers, evidenced by policies around migration, environment and climate change, and development.[6]

In light of this evident militarization, it is important to examine the impacts on women and girls observed by feminist scholars. Enloe (1983) asserts that patriarchy legitimizes and reinforces militarization and argues that militarization permeates women's daily lives at all levels of society, in the household and in states, markets and institutions. Elveren and Moghadam (2019: 11) use quantitative methods to shed light on the correlation between higher rates of militarization and gender inequality and reduced female labour force participation, concluding that militarization 'reinforces a masculinized social order ... more likely to wage war or encourage conflict, with their predictable effects on the physical security of women and girls, not to mention their overall wellbeing'. Peksen (2011: 458) demonstrates the militarization of society occasioned specifically by foreign military interventions can increase the incidence of GBV, stating that 'foreign intervention might escalate the problem of the suppression of women by making them frequent targets of sexual abuse, harassment, and physical violence'.

In short, militarization can augment the quotidian violence that women and girls experience and create new risks; in this sense, militarization occasions the (further) retreat of women and girls from the public sphere.

Locating women and girls within hybrid NGO-ized and militarized spaces

This chapter now examines the case studies of Tillabéry and Diffa to problematize the impacts of the hybrid NGO and security space on women and girls. NGO and security actors have come to dominate and redefine these spaces according to neoliberal and militarized (and fundamentally masculine) ideals that render these spaces less safe for women and girls, and narrowing space for their meaningful participation in society. This increase in violence against women and girls and their retreat from the public sphere is an essential driving force of the unravelling of the country. There are two large dynamics at play within these spaces of concurrent NGO-ization and militarization: the overt securitization of NGO projects and discourse (including/particularly those around gender), and the distinct blurring of roles between the NGO actor and the security actor.

Regarding the first dynamic, while NGOs are not necessarily far greater in number than during their rise in the 1970s, there is a securitization of their discourse and work, which is increasingly framed and/or justified in terms of its contribution to security. Thus, a food security intervention must demonstrate how it tackles the root causes of irregular migration, or women and girls' community-based groups are given the task of confronting extremist ideology among youth or facilitating civilian dialogue with security actors.

Moving to the second dynamic, in Tillabéry and Diffa it has become difficult to distinguish the security actor from the NGO actor. In these spaces in which militarization is largely seen as the solution to fragility, open collaboration between NGO actors and security actors has even become more formalized: the Nigerien armed forces have been trained by INGOs and UN agencies on protection, and foreign and national military actors attend coordination meetings with humanitarians in the name of protecting civilians within shared spaces of operation. There is not simply a thematic blurring of boundaries; in some instances, this collaboration between the security actor and the NGO actor is visible, risking public confusion over the actual agendas and added value of (largely foreign) security and aid actors.[7]

Tillabéry

On the Nigerien side of the troubled Liptako-Gourma region, Tillabéry is a prime site of the security traffic jam of the Sahelian space coupled with intense NGO interest – and spiralling violence. In Tillabéry, collaboration between NGO and security actors is formally mediated through the Civilian–Military strategic coordination (CMCoord) structure, joining representatives of the state, UN agencies, INGOs and military actors. Despite a mutual acknowledgement that members are not always on the same page with regards to means and ends to protection, collaboration has largely been accepted as an uncomfortable necessity for nominally different actors working side by side. Illustrating this, a document coming out of the Ministerial Round Table on the Central Sahel organized in late 2020 by Germany, Denmark, the EU and the UN outlines concerns related to civilian–military coordination in Niger and the 'unwanted proximity' between military and humanitarian actors in Tillabéry, pointing to the imposition of mandatory military escorts for humanitarian actors, the subversion of humanitarian to security imperatives, and the human rights abuses committed by FDS that came to light in 2020 (UN OCHA, 2020).

The apparent frustration expressed from the humanitarian side of the CMCoord table appears contradictory in light of the collaboration between security actors and NGO actors in the region. Tillabéry has, since the early 2010s, been one in a handful of key intervention sites for large donor funds that seek to redress security issues by strengthening dialogues between civilian populations and security and state actors through humanitarian and development frameworks. The United Nations Peacebuilding Funds are one such example. Having heaped over $33.5 million into Niger and cross-border projects since 2013, the Funds are premised on the idea that 'socio-economic empowerment of youth and women at risk of conflict' on the country's border regions will tackle poverty and conflicts over resources, reckoned to be the 'root causes' of instability and extremism (United Nations Peacebuilding Fund, 2018). A recent iteration of the Peacebuilding Funds in Tillabéry included a component aiming to empower 'women and youth' who received training in human rights and conflict resolution and livelihoods support, and participated in dialogues with security forces and state actors. This suite of activities was seen as complementary to capacity-building of the security forces conducted by EUCAP, a partner with the Funds. While the effort to step up women's inclusion in security matters is not to be dismissed, this project followed a rather familiar formula of soft activities that tend to have ambiguous outcomes. One questions where the agency of women is located in this project, particularly as the conflation of women and youth obscures the diverse experiences of both heterogenous groups, rendering them into securitized units and seeking to (re)order them to fit more neatly into the logic of this neoliberal, securitized space.

Furthermore, the revelation later in 2020 of human rights violations against civilians committed by the FDS in one of the project's sites, Ayorou commune,[8] point to the fragility of the assumptions around which NGO and security actors build their interventions. In Tillabéry, women and girls do not appear to be widely subject to the abductions, forced recruitment and enslavement that have characterized the Boko Haram crisis in Diffa explored later. Here, Tillabéry's relation to the state and its history as a space of political, social and economic marginalization comes into play. The resilience of extremist groups within Liptako-Gourma has been attributed to their ability to respond to the grievances of both men and women against the abuses of power and marginalization perpetrated against them by the state and its security forces. Thus, despite the fact that women and girls may not fully agree with, or may even suffer from, the restrictive versions of Islam imposed by armed groups, in some cases these extremist groups may in fact be better able to provide a more culturally accessible space for women to seek recourse for the marginalization and structural violence they suffer, including the quotidian forms of GBV – particularly domestic violence, denial of rights and opportunities, and early marriage perpetrated largely within domestic settings (Raineri, 2018, 2020). As such, in Tillabéry the attempt to remould space according to Western notions of peace and security and their accompanying forms of activism does always not provide leeway for women and girls to express and enact their actual needs and ambitions, nor does it appear to curb violence in the public or private spheres. Another stark illustration of this came to light in 2021, when Chadian soldiers stationed in Tillabéry as part of the G5 Sahel forces were found guilty of raping local women, including an 11-year-old girl (Le Monde Afrique, 2021).

Diffa

Diffa is the region in Niger most affected by crisis in the Lake Chad Basin occasioned from 2009 by the armed group popularly known as Boko Haram, a movement that has in many ways framed its identity and strategies around women and girls (Matfess, 2017). At its beginning in Borno state in north-east Nigeria (a region with which Diffa shares both borders and long-standing historical and cultural ties), Boko Haram exploited a number of grievances commonly held by women (including their exclusion from religious education and the social obstacles to securing desirable marriages) as well as generalized resentment of state corruption and disinterest in local needs felt by both men and women (International Crisis Group, 2016). Diffa has been deeply fragilized over years of living in the crossfire of Boko Haram and the counterinsurgency, during which time trust in the state and security institutions has been deeply degraded (International Crisis Group, 2017).

While Diffa has not seen the international security traffic at the same intensity as Tillabéry, the zone is a highly militarized and NGO-ized space. Like Tillabéry, Diffa is a priority region for humanitarian/development projects grounded in Western notions of security, often combining the familiar set of soft skills trainings and sensitizations for community leaders, youth and women, dialogues between FDS and civilians, and trainings for state and security actors. In Diffa, there is a particular interest in persons who have returned from Boko Haram, including women. This reflects broader trends – as the Boko Haram crisis has drawn international attention to the group's abuses of and impacts upon women and girls in the Lake Chad Basin – and in particular a sensationalist preoccupation with the sexual violence suffered by women and girls abducted by the group, as well as the group's deployment of women and girls as suicide bombers. Both military and humanitarian/development interventions in the Lake Chad region have invoked (particularly sexual) violence against women and girls in their discourse and framing: it was in part the kidnapping of schoolgirls in Chibok in Borno state in Nigeria in 2014 that spurred Western donors to support the Nigerian military to upscale its military response, along with stepping up their humanitarian and development assistance to neighbouring Niger, Chad and Cameroon.

One such example is the European Commission's Instrument Contributing to Stability and Peace, which funds a number of peacebuilding projects framed in security and has spent over €37 million in Niger. In 2016, the Nigerien Ministry of the Interior launched an amnesty plan for Boko Haram returnees, hoping that a less institutionalized approach would coax more group members to defect. The Instrument funded an INGO to work with the state on reintegration through a project engaging 'civil society groups, religious and women's leaders ... to deradicalise former Boko Haram fighters and sympathisers, help them acquire the social and professional skills they need for a peaceful, civilian life'(Search for Common Ground, 2019). The project website features success stories of three beneficiaries, including that of a young woman who experienced abduction and victimization by Boko Haram (including a forced marriage to a combatant). It describes her harrowing escape and subsequent empowerment and reintegration in Diffa through the project, quoting her in its narration of her story:

> '[Boko Haram] started killing and raping. We all fled. They caught me and forced me to go their hiding place in the middle of the bush. Overnight, I became their wife. ... [During my escape] the thorns cut my legs and feet, but all that mattered was reaching the place where

I could tell myself: this is it, I am saved ... the [project] activities and the psychologist have helped me to express myself and live among others. ... Today, I am happy.' (Search For Common Ground, 2020, author's translation)

Certainly, such efforts to address the psychosocial well-being of returnees are justified, and the focus on integration rather than punishment is to be lauded. Yet such discourse demonstrates a preoccupation with sexual violence suffered by returnees (many of whom have suffered punishing stigmatization when their association with the group has been made public); it furthermore risks oversimplifying the diverse motivations and experiences of women returnees from Boko Haram, rendering them as subjects of security and intervention rather than persons with their own agency and ambitions. Finally, it also overlooks the fact that structural violence and oppression of women and girls in the Lake Chad region has in fact driven some women to look *towards* Boko Haram as the best available option to them to pursue a desire for participation, agency and autonomy in the absence of other viable options (Matfess, 2017). More broadly, this type of discourse has underlined and justified the construction of the Lake Chad region into a space dominated by the values of a hypermasculine militarized response that has often wrought havoc on civilian communities, and the NGO-ized values that may overlook the complex motivations of women and girls, choosing instead to see them as units of victimhood and/or empowerment.

Conclusion

The two examples of Tillabéry and Diffa expose the fragility of women's rights within the space of concurrent NGO-ization and militarization. As militarization fundamentally sees violence as the solution to insecurity and constrains women's and girls' access to the public sphere, at the same time, NGO-ization fails to provide recourse for the quotidian and structural forms of violence women and girls suffer from, or the struggles of daily life in an increasingly difficult environment.

This is not to say that women's activism in Niger is non-existent, nor that efforts to empower women and girls in security or other sectors are inevitably insincere or ineffective. In Niger, the efforts of women activists in both government and civil society account for Niger's relative (if uneven) advancement in policy and normative frameworks around women's rights in the last several decades (Kang, 2015). There also is a history of community-based formal and informal women's groups that, while they may not always be framed by Western notions of empowerment, represent a form of positive support and participation for many. Similarly, the work done by NGOs and INGOs in strengthening women's access to and control of rural livelihoods has – when well-executed – been a form of empowerment that speaks to the ambitions of many women and girls.[9] Interventions that work *through* rather than *over* existing forms of women's participation are likely to provide positive space for women and girls to cultivate their actual ambitions.

But as this chapter has explored, the most fragile geographies of Niger lying on the borders of other Sahel states are increasingly defined by the interests of NGOs and security actors, interests that are often mapped onto women and girls. In both cases, the fact that some women and girls may find more space within the ideologies espoused by extremist groups to enact their ambitions and seek recourse for structural violence and marginalization speaks to the inadequacy of these well-meaning models to provide a viable alternative. The solution is not to abandon efforts to empower women and girls and provide support to survivors of GBV: rather, there would ideally be space for other forms of participation to grow and flourish. The current paradigm risks a longer-term foreclosure on women's meaningful agency and participation, exerting serious implications for Niger's future in light of the fact that research on conflict and peace processes in fragile societies draws convincing linkages between women's marginalization and poor outcomes for long-term stability.[10] Without a larger paradigm shift in these spaces, it is unrealistic to expect meaningful improvements for women and girls in Niger, nor for the long-term stability of the whole country.

Notes

[1]   Women's participation is a broad term understood differently in different contexts. This chapter takes as a point of departure Arnsteins's understanding of citizen participation as 'the redistribution of power that enables the have-not citizens, presently excluded from the political and economic processes, to be deliberately included in the future' (1969: 216). Positioning women and girls as 'have-nots', their meaningful participation thus equates to reclaiming of power in the economic, social and political spheres.

[2]   See, for example, Searcey (2019) and Filipovic (2017).

[3]   This chapter does not consider the region of Agadez, about which much as been written. See, for example, Boyer (2019).

[4]   This chapter does not attempt to provide a mapping of all security-focused foreign missions in Niger. It is difficult to characterize these missions as a whole, given the relative diversity of their specific thematic focuses and the different means by which they pursue these.

[5]   Wilén (2019: 3) states:

> Niger's relative stability in this region, in combination with its strategic location as a transit point for migrants going to Europe, has made it an attractive partner for Western states fighting terrorism and illegal migration.
>
> This geostrategic location and the Nigerien president's willingness to host foreign troops have made Niger one of the most militarised states in the Sahel, with hundreds of troops from several different Western Partner Nations.

6   For example, Walther and Retaillé (2010: 15–20) note:

> The regional dimension of the terrorism threat is also at the heart of the
> initiatives developed by France after Operation Serval. ... Military strategies
> implemented by the United States and France since the 2000s seem to
> suggest that the Sahel is the epicentre of a large theatre of operations that
> virtually knows no boundaries.

7   While there are no representative statistics available on Nigerien public opinion towards
foreign security forces, anecdotal evidence suggests there is suspicion regarding the
opacity of foreign forces, and frustration as insecurity intensifies. A civil society actor
interviewed by the author in early 2020, for example, pointed out that during attacks on
armed forces there are far more casualties among the Nigerien FDS than foreign forces
(Author Interview with Madame R, 26 January 2020).

8   According to Amnesty International (2020), in Tillabéry, FDS members carried out
arbitrary arrests, forced disappearances and executions of civilians.

9   Author interviews with Madame H, 30 January 2020; Madame R, 28 January 2020; and,
Madame S, 6 February 2020.

10 For example, Buvinic et al, 2013 demonstrate that women's political representation
tends to be lower in pre-conflict contexts, and that increased involvement in civil and
political life post-conflict has proven to be a positive outcome for violent conflicts.
Davies and True 2015 compare the SIGI (Social Institutions and Gender Index) gender
equality scores of a number of contexts affected by conflicts between 2012 and 2015,
concluding that gender discrimination in these conflict countries tends to be higher
than the global average of the SIGI scores, suggesting that high levels of GBV in a
non-conflict context represent a risk factor for conflict in non-conflict contexts, or a
return to violent conflict.

References

Amnesty International (2020) 'They Executed Some and Brought the Rest
with Them': Human Rights Violations by Security Forces in the Sahel, Report
no AFR 37/2318/2020, London: Amnesty International. Available
from: https://www.amnesty.org/en/documents/afr37/2318/2020/en/
[Accessed 7 June 2021].

Arnstein, S.R. (1969) 'A ladder of citizen participation', Journal of the American
Planning Association, 35(4): 216–224.

Berger, F. (2019) 'West Africa: shifting strategies in the Sahel', International
Institute for Strategic Studies, 1 October. Available from: https://www.iiss.
org/blogs/analysis/2019/10/csdp-west-africa-sahel [Accessed 7 June 2021].

Bøås, M. and Strazzari, F. (2020) 'Governance, fragility and insurgency in
the Sahel: a hybrid political order in the making', International Spectator,
55(4): 1–17.

Boyer, F. (2019) 'Sécurité, développement, protection: Le triptyque
de l'externalisation des politiques migratoires au Niger', Hérodote,
172(1): 171–191.

Buvinic, M., Gupta, M., Casabonne, U. and Verwimp, P. (2013) Violent
Conflict and Gender Inequality: An Overview, Policy Research Working Paper
No 6371, Washington, DC: World Bank.

Davies, S.E. and True, J. (2015) 'Reframing conflict-related sexual and gender-based violence: bringing gender analysis back in', *Security Dialogue*, 46(6): 495–512.

Elveren, A.Y. and Moghadam, V. (2019) *The Impact of Militarization on Gender Inequality and Female Labor Force Participation*, Working Paper No 1307, Giza: Economic Research Forum. Available from: https://erf.org.eg/publi cations/1307/ [Accessed 24 April 2022].

Enloe, C. (1983) *Does Khaki Become You? The Militarization of Women's Lives*, London: Pluto Press.

EUCAP Sahel Niger (2020) 'EUCAP Sahel Niger European Union Capacity-Building Civilian Mission', EEAS (European External Action Service), 30 November. Available from: https://eeas.europa.eu/csdp-missions-operations/eucap-sahel-niger/89305/eucap-sahel-niger-europ ean-union-capacity-building-civilian-mission_en [Accessed 7 June 2021].

Filipovic, J. (2017) 'How do you get girls to school in the least educated country on earth?', *The Guardian*, 15 May. Available from: https://www. theguardian.com/global-development-professionals-network/2017/may/ 15/niger-girls-education-challenge-un [Accessed 7 June 2021].

Frowd, P.M. and Sandor, A.J. (2018) 'Militarism and its limits: sociological insights on security assemblages in the Sahel', *Security Dialogue*, 49(1/ 2): 70–82.

GBVAR (Gender-Based Violence Area of Responsibility), UN Population Fund, CARE International and Plan International (2020) *Gender-Based Violence: Girls' and Women's Rights in the Central Sahel – Summary Report*, October. Available from: https://reliefweb.int/sites/reliefweb.int/files/ resources/wcaro-gbv-sahel_summary_en.pdf [Accessed 7 June 2021].

International Crisis Group (2016) *Nigeria: Women and the Boko Haram Insurgency*, Africa Report No 242, December, Brussels: ICG. Available from: https://www.crisisgroup.org/africa/west-africa/nigeria/nigeria-women-and-boko-haram-insurgency [Accessed 7 June 2021].

International Crisis Group (2017) *Niger and Boko Haram: Beyond Counter-Insurgency*, Africa Report No 245, February, Brussels: ICG. Available from: https://d2071andvip0wj.cloudfront.net/245-niger-and-boko-haram-beyond-counter-insurgency.pdf [Accessed 16 May 2022].

Kang, A.J. (2015) *Bargaining for Women's Rights: Activism in an Aspiring Muslim Democracy*, Minneapolis: University of Minnesota Press.

Le Monde Afrique. (2021) 'Des soldats tchadiens du G5 Sahel responsables de viols au Niger', 5 April. Available from: https://www.lemonde.fr/afri que/article/2021/04/05/des-soldats-tchadiens-du-g5-sahel-responsables-de-viols-au-niger_6075601_3212.html [Accessed 7 June 2021].

Maclean, R. (2020) 'Crisis in the Sahel becoming France's forever war', *New York Times*, 29 March. Available from: https://www.nytimes.com/2020/03/29/world/africa/france-sahel-west-africa-.html [Accessed 7 June 2021].

Mann, G. (2014) *From Empires to NGOs in the West African Sahel: The Road to Nongovernmentality*, New York: Cambridge University Press.

Matfess, H. (2017) *Women and the War on Boko Haram: Wives, Weapons, Witnesses*, London: Zed Books.

Peksen, D. (2011) 'Foreign military intervention and women's rights', *Journal of Peace Research*, 48(4): 455–468.

Raineri, L. (2018) *If Victims Become Perpetrators: Factors Contributing to Vulnerability and Resilience to Violent Extremism in the Central Sahel*, London: International Alert. Available from: https://www.international-alert.org/sites/default/files/Sahel_ViolentExtremismVulnerabilityResilience_EN_2018.pdf [Accessed 7 June 2021].

Raineri, L. (2020) *Dogmatism or Pragmatism? Violent Extremism and Gender in the Central Sahel*, London: International Alert. Available from: https://www.international-alert.org/publications/dogmatism-or-pragmatism-violent-extremism-gender-central-sahel [Accessed 7 June 2021].

Searcey, D. (2019) 'A quiet revolution: more women seek divorces in conservative West Africa', *New York Times*, 6 January. Available from: https://www.nytimes.com/2019/01/06/world/africa/niger-divorce-women.html [Accessed 7 June 2021].

Search for Common Ground (2019) 'Reintegrating Boko Haram detainees and repentants'. Available from: https://www.sfcg.org/reintegrating-boko-haram-detainees-and-repentants/ [Accessed 16 May 2022].

Search for Common Ground (2020) 'Je veux retourner dans ma communauté apporter ma contribution'. Available from: https://www.sfcg.org/wp-content/uploads/2019/08/EEU012-Goudoumaria-Ya_koura.pdf [Accessed 7 June 2021].

Shivji, I.G. (2006) 'The silences in the NGO discourse: the role and future of NGOs in Africa', *Africa Development*, 31(4): 22–51.

Turse, N. (2020) 'Pentagon's own map of US bases in Africa contradicts its claim of "light" footprint', *The Intercept*, 27 February. Available from: https://theintercept.com/2020/02/27/africa-us-military-bases-afri com/ [Accessed 7 June 2021].

UN OCHA (United Nations Office for the Coordination of Humanitarian Affairs) (2020) 'Humanitarian Access and Civil–Military Coordination', 11 October. Available from: https://www.unocha.org/sites/unocha/files/201019%20Niger%20T3%20final%20English%20Version.pdf [Accessed 7 June 2021].

UNDP (United Nations Development Programme) (2020) 'The next frontier: human development and the anthropocene', Briefing note for countries on the 2020 Human Development Report, New York: United Nations. Available from: http://hdr.undp.org/sites/all/themes/hdr_theme/country-notes/NER.pdf [Accessed 7 June 2021].

United Nations Peacebuilding Fund (2018) 'The Peacebuilding Fund in Niger'. Available from: https://reliefweb.int/report/niger/peacebuilding-fund-niger [Accessed 7 June 2021].

Walther, O. and Retaillé, D. (2010) *Sahara or Sahel? The Fuzzy Geography of Terrorism in West Africa*, CEPS/INSTEAD Working Paper No 2010-35. Available from: https://papers.ssrn.com/sol3/papers.cfm?abstract_id=1803996 [Accessed 7 June 2021].

Walther, O. and Retaillé, D. (2021) 'Mapping the Sahelian space', in L. Villalón (ed) *The Oxford Handbook of the African Sahel*, Oxford: Oxford University Press, pp 15–34.

Wilén, N. (2019) *Belgian Special Forces in the Sahel: A Minimal Footprint with Maximal Output?*, Africa Policy Brief No 26, Brussels: Egmont Royal Institute for International Relations. Available from: http://www.egmontinstitute.be/belgian-special-forces-in-the-sahel-a-minimal-footprint-with-maximal-output/ [Accessed 7 June 2021].

World Bank (2021) 'Military expenditure (% of GDP) – Niger'. Available from: https://data.worldbank.org/indicator/MS.MIL.XPND.GD.ZS?end=2019&locations=NE&start=1975&view=chart [Accessed 7 June 2021].

PART IV

Institutional Spaces

11

Neither Seen Nor Heard: State-Sanctioned Violence Against Women Prisoners in Australia

Debbie Kilroy, Tabitha Lean and Suzi Quixley

Introduction

'Unlike other incarcerated battered women who have come forward to reveal their impressions of prison, I do not feel "safer" here because "the abuse has stopped". It has not stopped. It has shifted shape and paced itself differently, but it is as insidious and pervasive in prison as ever it was in the world I know outside these walls.'

Marcia Bunney, prison activist, US, cited
in Cook and Davies, 1999: 28

Similarly to the situation in the US illustrated through Marcia Bunney's statement, state-sanctioned violence against women and girls plays a central role in legitimizing and perpetuating gender-based violence in 'Australia'.[1] While this occurs at all levels of the carceral state – in prisons, police cells and other institutions of surveillance and control – this chapter will largely focus on gender-based violence in women's prisons.

Prisons sit outside the binary of public/private space. In prison, women are emotionally, socially and geographically isolated. They become 'invisiblized' as we 'lock them up and throw away the key', preferring to keep women who have offended the sensibilities of the state at arm's length from the rest of society. This places women prisoners in the peculiar situation of being unseen by community (because anyone outside the prison system has very little access to them) yet always seen (due to the heavily surveilled architecture of prisons). This praxis enables carceral authorities to largely function with impunity. The unique intersection of these physical environments and their social context creates a space in which women prisoners are largely rendered powerless and voiceless.

Prisons are violent places. This chapter demonstrates how the state's deployment of prisons as punishment renders it complicit in the violation of women. This is no accident: the prison system is functioning exactly as intended. Far from 'rehabilitating' prisoners, prisons are an essential part of maintaining the social status quo and keeping marginalized and disadvantaged women 'in their place'. Given the massive over-representation of Aboriginal and Torres Strait Islander women in prisons, and the higher penalties imposed on them at all levels of the criminal legal system, prisons also perpetuate race-based violence and play a critical role in maintaining and enforcing colonial authority.

Worldwide, prisons replicate women's past experiences of violence (Cook and Davies, 1999). The following shows how women's human rights are violated on a daily basis as they are subjected to multiple forms of violence, abuse and neglect at the hands of the carceral state in Australia. This despite the fact that routine prison practices such as strip-searching, solitary confinement and some forms of restraint are inconsistent with the United Nations Convention Against Torture and Other Cruel, Inhuman, or Degrading Treatment or Punishment (OHCHR, 1984) and other international agreements.

In Australia, like the US (Cook and Davies, 1999), the distinctive features of prisons perpetrate and perpetuate violence against women. This chapter explores how the invisibility of prisons in Australia masks the harm they do, and the silence about the treatment of women behind bars demonstrates the state's disregard for prisoners' lives. It draws heavily on empirical evidence from Australian women with lived prison experience and Sisters Inside workers with criminalized women in Queensland.[2]

Brief profile of women prisoners in Australia

The number of prisoners in Australia has increased by nearly 50 per cent since 2000 (Justice Reform Initiative, 2020). Over the same period, women's imprisonment has grown exponentially, with Aboriginal and Torres Strait Islander women prisoners being the fastest-growing cohort (HRLC and CTR, 2017). In Queensland, for example, the number of women in prison has more than tripled in two decades: in 2000 there were a total of 273 women prisoners (5.8 per cent of the prison population) and by 2018–2019, 869 women were in prison (9.7 per cent of the prison population). (CYPP, 2013; Productivity Commission, 2020) The gender disparity in imprisonment growth rates was particularly evident between 1998 and 2007, when the prison population in Queensland increased by 20 per cent among men compared with 99 per cent among women (Office for Women, 2009 cited in CYPP, 2013).

It is impossible to overstate how overwhelmingly disadvantaged women prisoners are. Their opportunities in life begin with location – most live in a small percentage of postcodes. In Victoria, for example, 6 per cent of postcodes account for 50 per cent of all prisoners (CPD, 2020). Women prisoners represent the most socially, culturally and economically marginalized populations in Australian society. The literature universally recognizes that the vast majority have a history of poverty; homelessness and housing insecurity; unemployment; poor educational outcomes; poor health; unaddressed trauma; and surveillance and control by the state (CPD, 2020). Many were in state care or prison as a child. A significant proportion also live with an intellectual or learning disability, mental health and substance abuse issues – often a result of their history of trauma and failures of the state (Quixley and Kilroy, 2011).

Repeated Australian studies since the turn of the century have found that the overwhelming majority of women prisoners have lived experience of sexual, physical or emotional abuse as adults and/or children, and that most were victims of multiple forms of violence (HRLC and CTR, 2017). Up to 98 per cent of women prisoners have experienced physical abuse, up to 89 per cent have experienced sexual violence, and 57–90 per cent have survived childhood sexual assault (Stathopoulos et al, 2012). In addition to domestic and family violence, many women and girls experience high rates of violence at the hands of police and 'carers' in the child 'protection' system. Women and girls defending themselves against violence become targets of law enforcement (Boxall et al, 2020) – a phenomenon that is increasingly being referred to as the 'sexual abuse to prison pipeline' (Martin, 2017). Violence, particularly in First Nations communities, often escalates because 'women may choose not to report abuse, violence or substance misuse out of fear that they, or a family member, will die in custody' (AHRC, 2020: 268).

Focus on Aboriginal and Torres Strait Islander women

> Imprisonment entrenches the disadvantage and poverty that criminalises Aboriginal and Torres Strait Islander women in the first place.
>
> Aboriginal and Torres Strait Islander Social
> Justice Commissioner in AHRC, 2020

Aboriginal and Torres Strait Islander women are massively over-represented in Australian prison populations. In 1991, there were 121 First Nations women in Australian prisons (17 per cent of the women's prison population). By 2016, there were 1,062 First Nations women in prison (34 per cent of the women's prison population). First Nations women are now imprisoned at 21 times the rate of other women, enter the justice system at a younger age and are nearly twice as likely to return to prison (LCA, 2015; HRLC and CTR, 2017).

Entry to the 'justice' system often begins in early childhood: a history of childhood imprisonment is an indicator of adult criminalization.[3] For example, a New South Wales Bureau of Crime Statistics and Research study of children before the Children's Court for the first time found that 90 per cent of Aboriginal and Torres Strait Islander children, compared with 52 per cent of other children, went on to appear before an adult criminal court during the follow-up period (Aboriginal and Torres Strait Islander Justice Commissioner, 2009). First Nations children (age 10–17) account for 5 per cent of Australian children, but 59 per cent of the child prison population (Justice Reform Initiative, 2020) and 78 per cent of 10–13-year-old prisoners (Hurst, 2021). In 2018–2019 they were 22 times more likely than other children to be imprisoned (AIHW, 2020a).

Early criminalization is closely associated with involvement with the child 'protection' system. First Nations children were 17 times more likely than other children to be under the supervision of both the child 'protection' and youth 'justice' systems in the same year (AIHW, 2019). First Nations girls are particularly vulnerable with 71 per cent of these girls (compared with 49 per cent of First Nations boys) in the youth 'justice' system in 2018–2019 having been in both systems (AIHW, 2020b). The United Nations Special Rapporteur on the Rights of Indigenous Peoples was distressed by the number of children moving from out-of-home care to prison, and raised concerns about the punitive nature of Australian children's prisons their role in perpetuating intergenerational cycles of violence, trauma, poverty and crime (AHRC, 2020). With 80 per cent of First Nations women prisoners believed to be mothers of dependent children (Behrendt et al, 2009 cited in HRLC and CTR, 2017), too often children are removed by authorities due solely to their mother's imprisonment (with no evidence of abuse or neglect of the children).

Aboriginal and Torres Strait Islander women prisoners generally face the same social and economic disadvantages experienced by other criminalized women, but at significantly higher rates. First Nations women are 34 times more likely to be hospitalized as a result of family violence (AIHW, 2015) and 10 times more likely to die of assault, as other women (Braybrook, 2019). First Nations women prisoners are more likely to be a victim of violent crime than other women prisoners (ADCQ, 2006). The harm of imprisonment for First Nations women is immeasurably compounded by the ongoing effects of colonization: First Nations women continue to be punished for surviving when they fail to confirm to colonial expectations, making their very existence a form of radical resistance.

The starting point to this punishment occurs in the community. It has been widely recognized that First Nations communities are over-policed, and First Nations women are more likely to be imprisoned for minor crimes than other women. For example: 'in 10 areas in NSW with high Indigenous populations, Aboriginal women were locked up for intoxication at 40 times the rate of non-Aboriginal women and ... detention for outstanding warrants was ... 16.5 times (the rate) for Aboriginal women' (Newnam, 2008). Over-policing does not reduce crime or make communities safer: rather, it widens the net and draws more people into carceral systems. Many low-level crimes that typically remain untargeted and undetected in other communities result in charges for women living in First Nations communities. Greater interaction with the police also increases the risk of women facing additional charges such as resisting arrest and assaulting police. Racist over-policing applies equally in urban areas, where many First Nations women report being targeted by police (AHRC, 2020).

Evidence of systemic racism continues at all levels of the criminal legal system. First Nations women are more likely to be arrested, charged, detained, imprisoned on remand and sentenced to imprisonment for the same offences. They are less likely to receive a non-custodial sentence or parole (HRLC and CTR, 2017).

The nexus between criminalization and gender-based violence

The nexus between family violence and criminalization has long been established. Family violence has been connected to many women's crimes (Victorian Department of Justice, 2006) with 80 per cent of women prisoners in one study believing their criminalization was a direct consequence of family violence (NSW Aboriginal Justice Advisory Council, 2001).

The effects of repeated trauma are well documented and often include mental health and substance abuse issues and ultimately, for a few, reactive violence. Many criminalized women, particularly Aboriginal and Torres Strait Islander women, fear contacting police in relation to domestic violence – fears that are realized when the woman herself is arrested. This is hardly surprising, given the experiences of women such as Ms Dhu. Ms Dhu was a 22-year-old Yamatji woman who died in in Port Headland, Western Australia, in 2014. Police arrested her when called to a domestic violence incident at her home. When she couldn't pay outstanding fines she was imprisoned. Three days later, she died in horrendous pain in a concrete police cell of septicaemia stemming from a domestic violence injury. Ms

Dhu was taken to hospital three times, but medical staff (like the police) accused her of faking her pain. According to the Coroner, Ms Dhu had received 'unprofessional and inhumane' treatment from the police (including repeated verbal abuse and being dropped and hitting her head on the floor), and deficient treatment from staff at the hospital. No one ever faced charges in relation to Ms Dhu's death (Langton, 2016).

Sisters Inside has worked alongside women prisoners from remote communities who have called the police for family violence assistance and have instead been charged with a related or unrelated crime, or been arrested for an outstanding warrant on a minor matter. Too often, the gender basis of domestic violence is not recognized by authorities, particularly in states such as Queensland where the legislation originally intended to protect women is expressed in gender neutral terms. This allows police the discretion to demonize women. Many First Nations women from remote communities are issued a domestic violence order (DVO) by police, break the order (for example, when the order affects their ability to care for their children or leaves them homeless) and are then quickly charged with breaches of the order. Breach of DVOs is now among the top ten reasons for women's imprisonment in Queensland.[4] It is not unusual for 20 per cent of the (mainly First Nations) women prisoners on remand in Townsville to be charged with domestic violence–related crimes.[5] These same women are often survivors of extreme violence.

There is a pervasive emerging myth that First Nations women are becoming more violent. The available ABS (2020) data shows increases in convictions for violent crimes (for example, assaults, grievous bodily harm). What these data fail to distinguish is the number of these convictions that reflect breaches of unreasonable DVOs; women's actions to protect themselves or their children; and reactive violent crimes (Boxall et al, 2020). A First Nations woman prisoner in Canberra reflects the experiences we hear regularly at Sisters Inside:

> 'Those people in these systems, are just stupid. Pedos get no jail, I stick up for myself with a bloke who bashed me for 15 years, and I go to jail for 6 months. White men abuse us, and we go to jail. If someone hits me I'll stick up for myself, they expect us to just take it, "she must of deserved it". ... "Black slut".' (Cited in AHRC, 2020)

In the authors' experience, the supposed increase in violent crimes by First Nations women reflects increased opportunities for police to act on sexist and racist values. We are unaware of any increase in aggressive violent offences by First Nations women – only in the number of women who are charged, particularly following prolonged family violence.

Prisons are designed to isolate

Prisons were designed by men, for men. Prison design is predicated on the stereotype of the dangerous male prisoner and, more absurdly, on the assumption that women prisoners are equally dangerous. Prisons are designed to securely lock away 'criminals', far from their families and communities. Prisons function under the illusion that this will contribute to 'rehabilitation'.

Women's prisons are largely modelled on men's prisons (and were often originally built as men's prisons). In 2018–2019, secure places accounted for 84 per cent of prison design capacity in Australia (Productivity Commission, 2020). Further, this secure capacity was overused in most jurisdictions. In Queensland, for example, open places operated at 82 per cent of capacity and secure places at 108 per cent of capacity in 2018–2019 (Productivity Commission, 2020). Despite the minor 'crimes' for which women are imprisoned (and the reality that 37 per cent of women prisoners are untried), 79 per cent of the built capacity for women prisoners in Queensland is in high-security prisons, and only sentenced women have access to low-security facilities (ABS, 2020; Queensland Corrective Services, 2021). This, despite recognition of the different needs of women prisoners by all Australian governments:

> The management and classification of female prisoners should reflect their generally lower security needs, but their higher needs for health and welfare services, and for contact with their children. (Clause 1.43, *Standard Guidelines for Corrections in Australia* [State and Territory Governments, 2012])

Too often, individual women are formally classified as low security, but are forced to live under high-security conditions, because they are located in a high-security prison.

Geographic isolation

The location of Australian women's prisons facilitate family breakdown, isolation and therefore, intergenerational criminalization. Since the 1990s, prisons in capital cities have been increasingly relocated to the city margins and nearby regions. Queensland is a good example of this.

In the mid-1990s all women prisoners in Queensland were held in the Boggo Road prison, which was six kilometres from the Brisbane central business district and located on major public transport routes. Children living in Brisbane could relatively easily visit their mother in prison. However, in 1999, women were moved to the new Wacol prison precinct. The Brisbane Women's Correctional Centre is a high-security prison: 23 kilometres from the CBD, and a 23-minute walk from the nearest public transport. The only alternative to walking is to book a seat on an occasional charity bus service. Both a low-security facility (Numinbah) and a recently opened high-security prison in Gatton are 100 kilometres from Brisbane. Neither is accessible by public transport. A convoluted mix of public transport and charity bus travel often requires two to four hours' travel by up to four separate buses and/or trains. Imagine managing this with a child, or two, or three ... beginning around 4 am, then having to wait at the prison for at least an hour before visiting time.

The only other major Queensland women's prison is 1,300 kilometres north in Townsville. This appears more accessible to visitors, being only 12 kilometres from Townsville city, with a bus service available. However, this 'accessibility' pales into insignificance when you consider its distance from most women's homes and families. Typically, 80 per cent of women prisoners in the Townsville prison are Aboriginal and Torres Strait Islander women. A significant proportion of these women are imprisoned more than 1,000 kilometres away from their home community. Most remote communities are deeply impoverished, and the ability for mothers and children to stay connected by digital or physical means is severely limited.

Yet, in Queensland, there are at least 60 men's prison locations spread widely throughout the state. These reflect a mix of security levels and include work camps in remote areas near high First Nations populations (ADCQ, 2019). It is easier for children to retain contact with their father than their mother.

In addition to the practical difficulties, mothers are forced to consider the burden of visits on their child – the cost of transport, time lost from schooling and the risk of further trauma. Trauma can result from a variety of factors including austere, institutional visiting spaces; 'security' measures such as dogs and searching (including strip-searches of mother and/or child); the impact of forced separation at the end of visits; and restrictions on physical contact between mother and child (Baldwin and Epstein, 2017). It is hardly surprising that some mothers choose not to have visits with their children, and child 'protection' authorities commonly refuse to arrange visits. Each mother must decide whether the cost of visits outweigh the benefits, for themselves and their children.

Isolation from other prisoners

The higher the level of prison security, the greater the isolation (and consequent vulnerability to violence) faced by women prisoners. In secure prisons high-, medium- and low-security women often live together under virtually the same conditions of confinement: in the same housing units, attending programmes and recreation together, and having the same (lack of) freedom of movement within the prison. Women with a variety of classifications can be held in the most isolated areas such as single cells, protection, detention and mental health cells (Quixley and Kilroy, 2011).

Prisons were designed by the White 'worthy' wealthy for the 'unworthy' poor: they are designed to show the poor, particularly people of colour, their place. It is hardly surprising then, that women's previous experiences of disadvantage (including gender-based violence, poverty, mental health issues and cultural background) are treated as 'risk factors' when assessing their security level. As a result, women with no history of committing violent 'crimes' are often classified as high-security prisoners and placed in more isolated settings.

Prisons function as a training ground for continuing violence against women. Far from 'correcting' or 'rehabilitating' women, prisons retraumatize women and teach them to accept their place in life. This includes training women to believe that they deserve to be subject to violence. Women prisoners are required to unquestioningly obey any direction from an officer, no matter how unreasonable. With an expectation of acquiescence to male power, women are taught how to better conform to the demands of their perpetrators. Like a violent family setting, (often male) prison officers have enormous levels of arbitrary power, which they routinely exercise against women prisoners (for example, through inconsistent imposition of 'discipline'), with many First Nations women reporting being disproportionately targeted for punishment by prison officers (AHRC, 2020).

Prisons as the new 'missions'

Prison violence must be seen in the context of ongoing colonization. 'Australia' continues to be built on the genocide and dispossession of Aboriginal and Torres Strait Islander people. For First Nations women, even the very architecture of a prison perpetrates and perpetuates violence, given it occupies stolen ground.

Colonization is not a matter of history alone: colonial practices continue to be reflected in the many systems of surveillance and control imposed on First Nations. Continuing genocide is evident in the more than 470 deaths in custody of First Nations people since the Royal Commission into Aboriginal Deaths in Custody (1991), for which no one in authority has ever been convicted (Guardian Australia, 2021; Royal Commissions, 1991).

Since invasion, the Australian legal system has operated as a mechanism to order, control, regulate and dispose of First Nations lives and bodies (Wolfe, 2006). Colonialism continues to be reframed as 'protection' and 'recognition' – soft power concepts that mask the coercive realities of increasing child removals and imprisonment (Coulthard, 2014). The recent wave of coronial inquests, inquiries and royal commissions[6] has done nothing to change the structural racism that is the bedrock of Australia's criminal injustice system.

Throughout Australia's violent history, police and prisons have operated in the interests of the most powerful settlers. Prisons continue to play a critical role in state-sanctioned, colonial violence against First Nations people. Growth in the number of First Nations prisoners is no accident: it is happening by design, both literally and figuratively. The carceral state upholds capitalism, patriarchy and other systems of oppression. The prison industrial complex literally protects the state and its actors from penalty for violence.

As the number of First Nations prisoners grows, the similarity between prisons and missions becomes increasingly evident. During the first two centuries of colonization in Australia, First Nations people were rounded up and forced to live on missions. Similarly, contemporary prisons draw together large numbers of First Nations people, from unrelated family groups and Nations, and force them to live together under the control of White authorities. In the 'mission days', recalcitrant people were removed to prisons: today, they are removed to prisons with a higher level of security or, penalized in other ways such as being moved further from their Country and family.

Isolation enables torture

The capacity to exercise arbitrary authority, as far as possible away from the gaze of others, is fundamental to the functioning of carceral settings. The further removed from other prisoners and visitors in a prison, the more hidden women's interaction with prison officers and the greater their vulnerability to violence. Prison officers can make use of this isolation to assert their power over women.

Overt violence by prison officers is intrinsic to the functioning of women's (and children's) prisons and is repeatedly reported by women prisoners, civil society organizations, prison staff and investigative bodies (AHRC, 2020; Victorian Ombudsman, 2017; Royal Commissions, 2017; Human Rights Watch, 2018). Routine Australian prison practices are in breach of the United Nations Convention Against Torture (OHCHR, 1984) and other international instruments. These include use of excessive force (for example, four or five officers holding a woman down); ogling, touching or making lewd or humiliating comments about women's bodies; bullying women; sexually assaulting women; using bodily restraints such as straitjackets, body belts and handcuffs; shackling women to attend medical visits; and tying women to mattresses (Human Rights Watch, 2018; Victorian Ombudsman, 2017). Strip-searching and solitary confinement particularly retraumatize women with a history of abuse and contribute to increased incidents of self-harm (McCulloch and George, 2009).

Strip-searching is sexual assault by the state. While strip-searching is often justified as necessary for maintaining security, systemic justifications for the practice do not stand up to scrutiny.[7] Behaviour that is considered abhorrent (and illegal) in the wider community is routinely carried out by the state with impunity behind the closed doors of our prisons. Strip-searching is often deeply traumatizing for women with lived experience of gender-based violence, particularly when undertaken or observed by male officers (in contravention of the Bangkok Rules[8]: UNODC, 2010), and can be tantamount to torture. Routine strip-searching also reduces a woman's ability to engage with the wider world while in prison. For example, women are often required to undergo strip-searches before and/or after visits with their children, family members, friends and in some cases their lawyer (McCulloch and George, 2009).

Too often the cruelty of solitary confinement is obscured by the use of euphemisms such as 'separation', 'segregation', 'management units' or 'crisis support units'. COVID-19 has provided an opportunity to further torture women through so-called medical isolation. Women prisoners repeatedly report more frequent strip-searches and excessive use of force and restraint in these 'back' areas of the prison, where staff are even less open to scrutiny (Victorian Ombudsman, 2017). While women are alone in a cell, they are also under 24-hour surveillance and have zero privacy. They may be observed by male officers or any other man that happens to enter the area (Victorian Ombudsman, 2017). This is further exacerbated in mixed-sex prisons, where the most vulnerable women are sometimes kept in male maximum-security units (Ombudsman NT, 2017).

The stated purpose of solitary confinement is incongruous. Similar bleak cells are used for 'protection' and punishment – for penalizing women who exhibit both weakness (having 'mental health' issues) and strength (behaving in a way that displeases prison officers). This enables officers to make arbitrary decisions for their own convenience. The physical environment and women's treatment in solitary confinement is similar – whether she is being kept for hitting another woman, walking on the grass, threatening (or attempting) self-harm, or having newly arrived in prison on remand during a pandemic! Repeated reports by Australian human rights bodies have found conditions in solitary confinement unacceptable. In particular, they have raised concerns about the extended use of solitary confinement (sometimes for months or years) in contravention of internationally mandated time limits (Ombudsman NT, 2017; Victorian Ombudsman, 2017; Queensland Ombudsman, 2016; Office of the Chief Inspector, 2016).

Conclusion

During 2020, parliaments in several Australian jurisdictions considered legislating to 'protect' women against 'coercive control'. One member of parliament characterized coercive control as an insidious form of domestic abuse that can include a pattern of emotional abuse, isolation, sexual coercion, financial abuse, stalking, various types of intimidation and removing the victim's sense of self-worth (Dornin, 2020).

These characteristics equally describe the routine treatment of women prisoners in the 'care' of the state, in prisons and other statutory systems. Like any violent domestic setting, prisons serve to negate, criticize, humiliate, control, shame, accuse, blame and isolate women – while concurrently denying the state's role as a perpetrator of violence. The spatial design and geographic isolation of prisons play a key role in enabling this systemic violence.

We must think outside, and beyond, the prison bars. After decades of reform of prisons, police and the child protection system, we are still seeing the same issues. Reform of a broken system will never work. To truly address the routine violation of women prisoners we must confront the normalized violence and structural racism at the heart of our legal system.

Notes

[1]   'Australia' is used throughout this chapter for the sake of expediency. The authors neither accept the hostile and violent takeover of this country, nor recognize 'Australia' as a legitimate nation state.

[2]   Driven by criminalized women, Sisters Inside is an independent community organization which exists to advocate for the human rights of criminalized women, girls and their children, and works towards the abolition of prisons. To this end, Sisters Inside aims to reduce the number of women in prison, through providing services in response to the unmet needs of women and girls. (Too often, it was these needs that drove their criminalization.) Since 1992, Sisters Inside has worked to expose injustice in prisons and other coercive institutions, locally, nationally and internationally. For further details about the organization's values, policies, advocacy and service delivery see www.sistersinside.com.au

[3]   For example, a NSW Bureau of Crime Statistics and Research study of juveniles before the Children's Court for the first time found that 90 per cent of Aboriginal and Torres Strait Islander children, and 52 per cent of non-First Nations children, went on to appear before an adult criminal court during the follow-up period (cited in Aboriginal and Torres Strait Islander Justice Commissioner, 2009: 42)

[4]   Breach of domestic violence protection orders was the tenth most common offence type for women in Queensland prisons in both 2014–15 and 2015–16. In 2015–16, women in prison had 227 offences for these breaches on their records. (Data provided by Queensland Corrective Services, Performance and Reporting Unit to Sisters Inside on 13 December 2016 in response to an informal data request.)

[5]   Between February and August 2017, Sisters Inside's Supreme Court Bail program assessed 141 women on remand at Townsville Women's Correctional Centre. Through our assessments, we have identified that 28 women (almost 20 per cent of the women assessed) are remanded in custody for contraventions of DVOs.

[6]   Those focused on women and children include the Royal Commission and Board of Inquiry into the Protection and Detention of Children in the Northern Territory (Royal Commissions, 2017) and coronial inquests into the deaths in custody of Ms Dhu (2014), Rebecca Maher (2016), Aunty Tanya Day (2017) and Ms Wynne (2019), taken into police custody respectively for unpaid fines, 'protective custody', public drunkenness and mistaken identity (McGowan, 2019; McQuire, 2020).

7   Systemic justifications for strip-searching include preventing dangerous contraband from entering prisons and, ironically, protecting women from harm. For example, according to data disclosed to Sisters Inside under RTI request 180931 (28 February 2018), in 2017 women in Queensland prisons were strip-searched 16,258 times, with 0.01 per cent of searches finding any 'contraband' (mainly items such as unauthorized cotton buds, hair clips, clothing or tattoos).

8   Rule 19 reads: 'personal searches ... shall only be carried out by women staff who have been properly trained'.

References

Aboriginal and Torres Strait Islander Justice Commissioner (2009) *Social Justice Report 2009*, Sydney: Australian Human Rights Commission. Available from: https://www.hreoc.gov.au/Social_Justice/sj_report/sjrepor t09/index.html [Accessed 2 July 2021].

ABS (Australian Bureau of Statistics) (2020) Prisoners in Australia, Australian Bureau of Statistics. Available from: https://web.archive.org/web/2021070 2055141/https://www.abs.gov.au/statistics/people/crime-and-justice/ prisoners-australia/latest-release [Accessed 2 July 2021].

ADCQ (Anti-Discrimination Commission Queensland) (2006) *Women in Prison: A Report by the Anti-Discrimination Commission Queensland*, Brisbane: ADCQ. Available from: https://www.qhrc.qld.gov.au/resour ces/reports [Accessed 2 July 2021].

ADCQ (Anti-Discrimination Commission Queensland) (2019) *Women in Prison 2019: A Human Rights Consultation Report*, Brisbane: ADCQ. Available from: https://www.qhrc.qld.gov.au/resources/reports [Accessed 2 July 2021].

AHRC (Australian Human Rights Commission) (2020) *Wiyi Yani U Thangani Report*, Sydney: AHRC. Available from: https://humanrights. gov.au/our-work/aboriginal-and-torres-strait-islander-social-justice/publi cations/wiyi-yani-u-thangani [Accessed 2 July 2021].

AIHW (Australian Institute of Health and Welfare) (2015) *Australia's Welfare 2015* (Australia's Welfare Series No 12), Canberra: AIHW. Available from: https://www.aihw.gov.au/reports/australias-welfare/australias-welf are-2015/contents/table-of-contents [Accessed 2 July 2021].

AIHW (Australian Institute of Health and Welfare) (2019) *Young People in Child Protection and Under Youth Justice Supervision: 1 July 2014 to 30 June 2018*, Canberra: AIHW. Available from: https://www.aihw.gov.au/repo rts/child-protection/young-people-in-youth-justice-supervision-2014-18/ contents/table-of-contents [Accessed 2 July 2021].

AIHW (Australian Institute of Health and Welfare) (2020a), *Youth Detention Population in Australia 2019*, Bulletin 148, February, Canberra: AIHW. Available from: https://www.aihw.gov.au/reports/youth-justice/youth- detention-population-in-australia-2019/contents/table-of-contents [Accessed 2 July 2021].

AIHW (Australian Institute of Health and Welfare) (2020b) *Young People Under Youth Justice Supervision and in Child Protection 2018–19*, 15 October, Canberra: AIHW. Available from: https://www.aihw.gov.au/reports/youth-justice/young-people-in-child-protection/contents/summary [Accessed 2 July 2021].

Baldwin, L. and Epstein, R. (2017) *Short But Not Sweet: A Study of the Impact of Short Custodial Sentences on Mothers and Their Children*, Leicester: De Montfort University. Available from: https://dora.dmu.ac.uk/handle/2086/14301 [Accessed 2 July 2021].

Boxall, H., Dowling, C. and Morgan, A. (2020) 'Female perpetrated domestic violence: prevalence of self-defensive and retaliatory violence', *Trends and Issues in Crime and Criminal Justice*, No 584, Canberra: Australian Institute of Criminology. Available from: https://www.aic.gov.au/publications/tandi/tandi584 [Accessed 2 July 2021].

Braybrook, A. for Indigenous X (2019) 'I'd like to share a few uncomfortable truths: Australia's violent crisis', *The Guardian*, 21 February. Available from: https://www.theguardian.com/commentisfree/2019/feb/21/id-like-to-share-a-few-uncomfortable-truths-australias-violent-crisis [Accessed 2 July 2021].

Cook, S. and Davies, S. (eds) (1999) *Harsh Punishment: International Experiences of Women's Imprisonment*, Boston, MA: Northeastern University Press.

Coulthard, G. (2014) *Red Skin, White Masks: Rejecting the Colonial Politics of Recognition*, Minneapolis: University of Minnesota Press.

CPD (Centre for Policy Development) (2020) *Partners in Crime: The Relationship Between Disadvantage and Australia's Criminal Justice Systems*, December, Melbourne: CPD. Available from: https://apo.org.au/sites/default/files/resource-files/2020-12/apo-nid310032.pdf [Accessed 2 July 2021].

CYPP (Comparative Youth Penalty Project) (2013) 'Women in Prison Queensland 1970–2010', Sydney: UNSW. Available from: https://www.cypp.unsw.edu.au/women-prison-queensland-1970-2010 [Accessed 2 July 2021].

Dornin, T. (2020) 'Labor looks to outlaw coercive behaviour', *Canberra Times*, 2 December. Available from: https://www.canberratimes.com.au/story/7038352/labor-looks-to-outlaw-coercive-behaviour [Accessed 2 July 2021].

Guardian Australia (2021) 'The 474 deaths inside: tragic toll of Indigenous deaths in custody revealed', *The Guardian*, Australian edn, 9 April. Available from: https://www.theguardian.com/australia-news/2021/apr/09/the-474-deaths-inside-rising-number-of-indigenous-deaths-in-custody-revealed [Accessed 2 July 2021].

HRLC and CTR (Human Rights Law Centre and Change the Record) (2017) 'Over-represented and overlooked: the crisis of Aboriginal and Torres Strait Islander women's growing over-imprisonment'. Available from: https://www.hrlc.org.au/reports/2017/5/18/report-over-represen ted-and-overlooked-the-crisis-of-aboriginal-and-torres-strait-islander-womens-growing-over-imprisonment [Accessed 2 July 2021].

Human Rights Watch (2018) '"I needed help, instead I was punished": abuse and neglect of prisoners with disabilities in Australia, 6 February. Available from: https://www.hrw.org/report/2018/02/06/i-needed-help-instead-i-was-punished/abuse-and-neglect-prisoners-disabilities [Accessed 2 July 2021].

Hurst, D. (2021) 'More than 30 countries condemn Australia at UN over high rates of child incarceration', *The Guardian*, 21 January. Available from: https://www.theguardian.com/australia-news/2021/jan/21/china-attacks-australia-at-un-over-baseless-charges-as-canberra-criticised-for-keeping-children-in-detention [Accessed 2 July 2021].

Justice Reform Initiative (2020) *Jail is Failing: The State of the Incarceration Nation, a Briefing to Australia's Members of Parliament*, 6 September, Enmore, NSW: JRI. Available from: https://www.justicereforminitiative.org.au/resources [Accessed 2 July 2021].

Langton, M. (2016) 'Two victims, no justice: Ms Dhu, Lynette Daley and the alarming rates of violence against indigenous women', *The Monthly*, July. Available from: https://www.themonthly.com.au/issue/2016/july/1467295200/marcia-langton/two-victims-no-justice#mtr [Accessed 2 July 2021].

LCA (Law Council of Australia) (2015) *Addressing First Nations Imprisonment: National Symposium – Discussion Paper*, November. Available from: https://web.archive.org/web/20160313164813/https://www.lawcouncil.asn.au/lawcouncil/images/II_Discussion_Paper_23_11.pdf [Accessed 25 April 2022].

Martin, M. (2017) 'Advocates say Cyntoia Brown's case is part of the "sexual abuse-to-prison" pipeline', *KUOW*, 3 December. Available from: http://archive.kuow.org/post/advocates-say-cyntoia-browns-case-part-sexual-abuse-prison-pipeline [Accessed 2 July 2021].

McCulloch, J. and George, A. (2009) 'Naked power: strip searching in women's prisons', in P. Scraton and J. McCulloch (eds) *The Violence of Incarceration*, New York: Routledge, pp 107–123.

McGowan, M. (2019) 'Rebecca Maher inquest: death in custody could have been prevented if police called ambulance', *The Guardian*, 5 July. Available from: https://www.theguardian.com/australia-news/2019/jul/05/rebe cca-maher-inquest-death-in-custody-could-have-been-prevented-if-pol ice-called-ambulance [Accessed 2 July 2021].

McQuire, A. (2020) 'The families fighting for justice for Indigenous deaths in custody', *Marie Claire*, 21 August. Available from: https://www.mariecla ire.com.au/indigenous-deaths-in-custody-report [Accessed 2 July 2021].

Newnam, K. (2008) 'Aboriginal deaths in custody: protest to demand new justice', *Direct Action*, 4 September. Available from: https://web.archive. org/web/20200330120500/http://directaction.org.au/issue4/aboriginal_ deaths_in_custody_protests_to_demand_justice [Accessed 2 July 2021].

NSW Aboriginal Justice Advisory Council (2001) 'Holistic community justice: a proposal response to Aboriginal family violence', Sydney: NSW Attorney General's Department.

Office of the Chief Inspector (2016) *Chief Inspector Report: Brisbane Women's Correctional Centre Full-Announced Inspection Report, 16th to 20th November 2015*, published as Exhibit 23 to the Crime and Corruption Commission's Taskforce Flaxton, Fortitude Valley, QLD: Crime and Corruption Commission. Available from: https://www.ccc.qld.gov.au/ public-hearings/taskforce-flaxton/taskforce-flaxton-exhibits [Accessed 2 July 2021].

OHCHR (UN Office of the High Commissioner for Human Rights) (1984) *Convention against Torture and Other Cruel, Inhuman or Degrading Treatment or Punishment*, Geneva: United Nations. Available from: https://www. ohchr.org/en/professionalinterest/pages/cat.aspx [Accessed 2 July 2021].

Ombudsman NT (2017) *Women in Prison II – Alice Springs Women's Correctional Facility*, May, Darwin, NT: Ombudsman. Available from: https://www. ombudsman.nt.gov.au/WIP2_Vol2 [Accessed 2 July 2021].

Productivity Commission (2020) *Report on Government Services 2020*, Part C, Section 8: Corrective Services, 29 January, Melbourne: Productivity Commission. Available from: https://www.pc.gov.au/research/ongoing/ report-on-government-services/2020/justice/corrective-services [Accessed 2 July 2021].

Queensland Corrective Services (2021) *Queensland Corrective Services procedures, Appendix: Built capacity counts for corrective services facilities*, 4 February. Available from: https://www.publications.qld.gov.au/dataset/qcs-procedures/resource/af9b92ed-7f89-4aef-807b-5dce0d3c27c0 [Accessed 2 July 2021].

Queensland Ombudsman (2016) *Overcrowding at Brisbane Women's Correctional Centre: An Investigation into the Action Taken by Queensland Corrective Services in Response to Overcrowding at Brisbane Women's Correctional Centre*, September, Brisbane: Queensland Ombudsman. Available from: http:// www.parliament.qld.gov.au/Documents/TableOffice/TabledPapers/2016/ 5516T1587.pdf [Accessed 2 July 2021].

Quixley, S. and Kilroy, D. (2011) *Working with Criminalised and Marginalised Women: A Starting Point* (2nd edn), West End, QLD: Sisters Inside.

Royal Commissions (1991) *Royal Commission into Aboriginal Deaths in Custody*, Sydney: Australasian Legal Information Institute. Available from: http://www.austlii.edu.au/au/other/IndigLRes/rciadic/index.html [Accessed 16 June 2022].

Royal Commissions (2017) *Royal Commission and Board of Inquiry into the Protection and Detention of Children in the Northern Territory: Findings and Recommendations*, Canberra: Commonwealth of Australia. Available from: https://webarchive.nla.gov.au/awa/20181010003051/https://child detentionnt.royalcommission.gov.au/Pages/Report.aspx [Accessed 2 July 2021].

State and Territory Governments (2012) 'Standard guidelines for prisons', in *Standard Guidelines for Corrections in Australia* (revised edn), pp 16–36. Available from: https://justice.nt.gov.au/__data/assets/pdf_file/0009/238 185/aust-stand_2012.pdf [Accessed 2 July 2021].

Stathopoulos, M., Quadara, A., Fileborn, B. and Clark, H. (2012) *Addressing Women's Victimisation Histories in Custodial Settings*, ACSSA Issues No 13, December. Melbourne: Australian Centre for the Study of Sexual Assault. Available from: https://aifs.gov.au/publications/addressing-womens-victim isation-histories-custodial-settings [Accessed 2 July 2021].

UNODC (United Nations Office on Drugs and Crime) (2010) *The Bangkok Rules: United Nations Rules for the Treatment of Women Prisoners and Non-Custodial Measures for Women Offenders with their Commentary*, New York: United Nations. Available from: https://www.unodc.org/ documents/justice-and-prison-reform/Bangkok_Rules_ENG_22032 015.pdf (Adopted by the UN General Assembly on 21 December 2010) [Accessed 2 July 2021].

Victorian Department of Justice (2006) *Victorian Aboriginal Justice Agreement – Phase 2*, Melbourne: Victorian Department of Justice. Available from: https://www.aboriginaljustice.vic.gov.au/the-aboriginal-justice-agreement-phase-2 [Accessed 2 July 2021].

Victorian Ombudsman (2017) *Implementing OPCAT in Victoria: Report and Inspection of the Dame Phyllis Frost Centre*, Melbourne: Victorian Ombudsman. Available from: https://assets.ombudsman.vic.gov.au/ass ets/Reports/Parliamentary-Reports/1-PDF-Report-Files/Implementing-OPCAT-in-Victoria-report-and-inspection-of-Dame-Phyllis-Frost-Cen tre.pdf?mtime=20191217153438 [Accessed 2 July 2021].

Wolfe, P. (2006) 'Settler colonialism and the elimination of the native', *Journal of Genocide Research*, 8(4): 387–409.

12

'There Is Always a Reason for the Beatings': Interrogating the Reproduction of Gender-Based Violence Within Private and Public Spaces

Haje Keli

Introduction

The Kurdistan Region of Iraq, which includes the three Kurdish majority governorates in the north of the country, has, since 1991, steadily evolved into a semi-independent territory with its own regional government, security forces, region-specific laws and a high degree of economic autonomy. The territory's constitutionally recognized government, the Kurdistan Regional Government (KRG), is often compared favourably to the central government of Baghdad, and the region is frequently seen as a progressive semi-state, presenting economic opportunity and drawing global support (Danilovich, 2014: 160). The KRG's progressive reputation is partly due to its purportedly reformist outlooks on gender, based on the Law to Combat Domestic Violence of 2011 (Kurdistan Parliament, 2011), and the amendment to the Iraqi Personal Status Law passed in 2008 (Kurdistan Parliament, 2008), both of which are exclusive to the Kurdistan Region. This chapter reviews how the domestic violence (DV) law is implemented, not only through judicial outcomes, but also in how DV survivors are treated within public institutions.

My research has found that there is violence against women (VAW) perpetrated by law enforcement officers, legislators, practitioners and staff designated to assist DV survivors at the Directorate to Combat Violence Against Women (DCVAW), an institution of the KRG. Based on a year-long fieldwork (2014–2015), grounded on open-ended and semi-structured expert interviews (n = 36), focus groups (n = 20) and participant observation, this chapter is an ethnography of women's experiences of gender-based violence (GBV) within institutions designed to protect them. I argue that public institutions become a site for the reproduction of the family structure, thus blurring the lines between GBV in private and public space. Drawing on literature that conceptualizes the family in the Middle East, I demonstrate that the position of Kurds as a minority that disrupted Iraq's nation-making process resulted in oppression, which in turn, led to Kurdish society designating the private sphere as a space of patriarchal male authority and gender hierarchy immune to scrutiny. In contexts of conflict and turmoil, family and kinship are regarded as the only 'safe haven' (Moghadam, 2013: 114), and in Iraqi Kurdistan family became an influential point of power for the individual oppressed by the state (Alinia, 2013: 38). This chapter explains that, while Iraq's Kurds have now obtained self-governance, a great deal of power nonetheless remains within the family structure and, instead of assisting women, the Kurdistan Region's public institutions reproduce patterns of violence within in the family.

Conceptualizing GBV across the private and public: overlapping forms violence

Space has never been neutral and is always discursively constructed, ideologically marked and shaped by dominant power structures, and is produced and created through, among other things, gender discourse that cannot be understood outside its socially mediated perspective (Wrede, 2015: 11). In fact, space is constitutive to the construction of gender relations: the symbolic meaning of places, the gendered messages they convey, and the violence they conduct through exclusion all point to how space and place are not only themselves gendered, but that their very existence affect how gender is constructed and understood (Massey, 1994: 179). The spaces where violence takes place are also interrelated and co-constitutive. Space plays a crucial role in how GBV is discursively framed and whether or not the state responds to it (Bows and Fileborn, 2020: 299). In this context, DV, which occurs in the home, must be analysed alongside the violence to which DV survivors are exposed in the public sphere.

When we discuss the forms of violence found in different spaces, the binary between public and private should be challenged. First, the distinction between the spaces is itself gendered and used to legitimate violence and control and regulate sexuality (Duncan, 1996: 128). All space is not necessarily distinctly private or public and is subject to various territorializing and deterritorializing processes (Duncan, 1996: 129). Thus, discourse on the private/public divide plays a pivotal role in constructing the relationship between women and the state where gender inequality is (re)produced (García-Del Moral and Dersnah, 2014: 662).

Violence occurs principally in three contexts: the family, the community (social, economic, religious and cultural institutions) and the state (Schuler, 1992: 12). The family unit is a major site for violence where labour is divided unequally between the sexes and where members can control a woman's body and sexuality, abuse her emotionally, verbally and sexually, and physically confine her for not abiding by traditional gender norms (Schuler, 1992: 12–13).

It is crucial to note that when the chapter refers to the family unit or structure, it is not only referring to the nuclear family. In line with Kurdish culture and social norms, this chapter defines grandparents, uncles and cousins as part of what constitutes the family. Article 1 of the Law to Combat Domestic Violence defines family as: 'a group of individuals bound to each other by marriage or blood to the fourth degree and whoever is included in the family legally' (Kurdistan Parliament, 2011). A major underlying motive for structural GBV in public institutions is tied to the role and status of the family within Iraqi Kurdish society. Some states grant political privilege to the family as a unit and provide legal privilege within those families to men over women (Joseph, 1996: 6). In Iraq, and in most of the Middle East, an individual's relationship with the state was traditionally negotiated through a strong and interrelated kin group or family (Rassam, 1982: 95). This dynamic is particularly prominent within Kurdish society because Kurds, as an ethnic minority, posed a threat to the nation-building processes of the region, and thus the political structure of these states seldom benefited them (Alinia, 2013: 18). Consequently, in the Iraqi Kurdish context, family and kinship were often the only safe haven for individuals who faced state violence, causing the private sphere to become a crucial point of power for persecuted individuals (Alinia, 2013: 38). While Iraqi Kurds have benefited from relative self-determination and autonomy since 1991, the family in Iraqi Kurdistan remains a significant location for identity formation and identification and is also where political and economic power are distributed (Begikhani, 2005: 219). Families can mirror the structure of the state where, in modern times, the patriarchal power that once belonged to male heads of families is often consumed by governing institutions (Hunnicutt, 2009: 563–564).

Private space has been noted as the embodied and natural state, personal property, unpaid labour and intimacy, whereas public space is conceptualized as the disembodied, rational, justice, citizenship and the state (Duncan, 1996: 128). Private space is thus depoliticized, rendering women who are associated with it powerless, both towards the men they encounter in the private sphere and within governing institutions. My research disproves the perception of public space as an ungendered space that espouses rationality and justice, unaffected by patriarchal values that permeate the private sphere. In Iraqi Kurdistan, family norms are intertwined within the governing powers' own ideals of good citizens for the nation. Notions of respectability are tied to the construction of archetypical gender identities of a nation, and these identities socialize people into moral understandings of appropriate and inappropriate behaviour tied to ideals of propriety (Whitehead et al, 2001: 4). This allows the state and family to work symbiotically to the disadvantage of women.

While the home is often gendered as feminine, it is nonetheless also a space of patriarchal authority where the male head can violate and even negate the rights, autonomy and safety of women and children who inhabit the space with him (Duncan, 1996: 131). Remarking on the familiar expression 'A man's home is his castle', Duncan (1996: 131) succinctly points out that such a phrase highlights the connections between 'masculinity, patriarchal autonomy and how they are expressed in the spatial expression in the form of private property'.

Governing institutions transfer their authority to male heads of the household so these men can ensure control in the private sphere with regards to disciplining and punishing of women and youth, acts which become protected and 'almost sanctified under the norm of "privacy of the family"', and violence committed against women within the family becomes a private matter which the public sphere does not acknowledge or want to rectify (Ertürk, 2016: 136). In the context of my research, the authorities not only failed to intervene in family violence but also reproduced that violence within their own institutions. States reproduce patriarchy through nurturing patriarchal structures – the extended family provides welfare for their members, which provides safety for individuals, thereby relieving the public institution of its responsibility towards its citizens (Moghadam, 2013: 118).

Mr Yasin, the resident legal expert at the main office of DCVAW, warned me of the danger of falling out with one's family: "Family is a sacred institution. It is surrounded by sacredness. There is privacy and a secrecy that comes with dealing with issues regarding family. What happens in the family has to stay secret, whether it is a fight or any violence" (April 2015). Lieutenant Dilshad Rasul, a senior staff member at the Sulaymaniyah branch of the DCVAW, agreed with Yasin, emphasizing the importance of keeping DV a private issue and not escalating it to police or other official channels. The following section examines the consequences of women escalating such issues to official channels.

The other major locus of violence relevant to our context is the state because it can be violent through discriminatory laws and policies or through biased application of the law (Schuler, 1992: 12–13). Additionally, it can perpetuate violence: 'through *omission*, that is, by failing to take appropriate measure to protect vulnerable women' (Schuler, 1992: 15, emphasis in original). State institutions are conceptualized here as public space. Public space is not 'democratic', meaning that women and racialized men are often excluded against their will (Bondi and Domosh, 1998: 277). Thus, despite public space being understood as unbiased and rational (Duncan, 1996: 128), my research, like many other feminist works, demonstrates that governmental institutions are patriarchal and fail to provide DV survivors with assistance or some measure of justice. Women who face GBV seek support from state institutions, and when they are denied assistance, their experience of GBV extends from one sphere to another.

Subjugation of DV survivors is made official through legislation and implementation of law. In 2008, the regional authorities amended the Iraqi Personal Status Law of 1959 to grant additional legal protections to women (Kurdistan Parliament, 2008) and, in 2011, the region's parliament passed the Law to Combat Domestic Violence (Kurdistan Parliament, 2011), the first of its kind in Iraq. Prior to both of these laws, the DCVAW, a governmental institution within the KRG's Ministry of the Interior, was founded in 2007 and now has branches in the three Kurdish majority governorates administered by the KRG (Begikhani et al, 2015: 125). Women can register their complaints, speak to police officers and obtain legal advice at the directorate, which also publishes monthly reports containing the quantity and types of complaints recorded (DCVAW website).[1]

By law, the DCVAW is the competent authority to address DV cases (Article 3, Law No 8; Kurdistan Parliament, 2011). The Law to Combat DV defines domestic violence as any action, physical, sexual or verbal, including threats of GBV perpetrated by family, and details the many practices that are considered DV, including female genital mutilation, forced marriage, forced divorce, physical violence, marital rape, verbal violence, emotional violence and psychological violence (Article 1, Law No 8; Kurdistan Parliament, 2011). The punishment for committing DV is six months to three years imprisonment and a fine of one to five million Iraqi dinars (about £545–£2,700 or US$685–$3,400; Article 7, Law No 8; Kurdistan Parliament, 2011).

Significantly, the text of the law also spells out its 'founding reasons', stating that the law exists to protect the family unit from disintegration and thus promote reconciliation between its members, as according to the document, 'the family is the founding base for the society' (Law No 8; Kurdistan Parliament, 2011). Article 5 of the law maintains that a committee made up of competent members shall conduct reconciliation meetings between the perpetrator and the victim, with the goal of reconciling prior to a court case. In practice, survivors of DV are referred to the Official Reconciliation Committee to reconcile with their abusers, something proven to put women in great danger (DIS, 2018: 16), and the committee itself is known to blame the abused woman (DIS, 2018: 17). An 'informal justice system' in Iraqi Kurdistan has often been practised through talks between the respected individuals and the concerned parties, and the DCVAW, along with lawyers, judges, women's NGOs and shelters, still utilizes this method (Begikhani et al, 2015: 122). This coincides with previous research on Iraqi Kurdistan, which finds that the governing powers in the Kurdistan Region still view VAW, GBV and DV as family matters, and often resorts to informal family mediation instead of implementing the law (Al-Ali and Pratt, 2011: 347), demonstrating that the state privileges the power and status of the family. This is also articulated by the 'founding reasons' of the Law to Combat Domestic Violence, which clearly indicate that, while the law purports to provide protection to survivors of DV, it still prioritizes the family above the individual's safety.

GBV in the public sphere can also be located within the judiciary. In the Kurdistan Region, governing institutions have acted against the interests of women through legislation that creates space for mitigating sentences for those who act violently against women (Taysi and Minwalla, 2009: 100). In other cases, the law and sentencing are not enforced at all, contributing to structural violence against women on the governmental level (Taysi and Minwalla, 2009: 100). While men who commit acts of violence against women often receive lenient sentences, women who commit crimes are not met with the same consideration (Taysi and Minwalla, 2009: 114).

Women who seek justice for DV are faced with many challenges, such as the social shame and financial burden of divorce in addition to the fact that the law only allows for the victim to bring a suit to court (Puttick, 2015: 19). When women do report DV or bring a claim to court, widespread gender bias within the public spaces such as the police and legal system lead to outcomes in favour of the men (Puttick, 2015: 19). Public servants, who do not undergo any type of gender-sensitivity training, often privilege men's testimonies over women's, affecting the impartiality and detailed content of their written reports, which in turn can impact the judge's evaluation of the case (Puttick, 2015: 19).

While Alinia (2013: 118) claims there is a bias in the Iraqi Kurdish legal system that works in favour of the male perpetrators, others maintain that the situation is far more dire and point to corruption in the legal system in the form of systematic discrimination against women, particularly if the perpetrators are politically connected and wealthy (DIS, 2018: 17). The Kurdistan Region has long suffered from lack of implementation of rule of law, and most institutions, including legal institutions, need reform, which often only happens if particularly influential people initiate such reform (Taysi and Minwalla, 2009: 88).

'There is always a reason for the beatings': reframing victims as violators

After highlighting how the state legitimizes DV through legislation and the implementation of laws, it is beneficial to view how everyday forms of violence and humiliation within the DCVAW and other public contexts are utilized against DV survivors. During my fieldwork, I observed that DV survivors face subjugation and delegitimization at the hands of DCVAW staff through verbal violence, being disbelieved and exposed to judgement due to perceived immoral behaviour. During my fieldwork, I visited different branches of the DCVAW and spoke with social workers whose main duties were to assist and be the first line of contact for the beneficiaries of the directorate. During a visit, I overheard some of the social workers discussing a DV survivor, openly mocking her appearance and her accounts of abuse. After introducing me, the manager ushered me into their office and encouraged the five female social workers present to speak with me. While alone with them, I asked about the types of complaints they encounter. One staff member shared that DV survivors' complaints are related to "husband and wife issues" or "boyfriend and girlfriend issues", where the woman's family or husband/boyfriend are physically and verbally abusive and make threats against them. The social worker continued, "However, there is always a reason for the beatings" (May 2015). Prompted by me to elaborate she explained, "Well, she has, for instance cheated on him so he beats her" (May 2015). The remaining four women were looking at their colleague and nodded in agreement. When I responded that according to the law, there were no valid reasons for violence, she replied: "I know what you mean, but the women avoid telling us the whole story when they report the violence" (May 2015). Another staff member sat up in her office chair and raised her voice loud enough to command the attention of the entire room and exclaimed that women who seek help from the DCVAW are "bad because they use mobile phones, social media and the internet to form new relationships instead of taking care of their children like real mothers should" (May 2015).

The social workers' admonishment of women who have allegedly committed adultery is not uncommon in this context. Falsely accusing women of adultery in Iraqi Kurdistan is known to be a way to silence them and stop them from demanding their rights (Puttick, 2015: 19; Taysi and Minwalla, 2009: 106), and condemnation of women who commit adultery is widespread in Iraqi Kurdistan, to the point where many promote killing women who have committed adultery (Puttick, 2015: 19; Taysi and Minwalla, 2009: 106). While adultery is a crime according to the Iraqi Penal Code (Article 377, Law No 111, Iraqi Penal Code, 1969), and while Article 377 of the Iraqi Penal Code was amended in the Kurdistan Region in 2001 to hold men and women equally responsible for committing adultery (Puttick, 2015: 9; Danilovich, 2014: 160; Begikhani et al, 2015: 118), there is still a bias against women accused of adultery. The social worker's assertion reported earlier shows how there are, at best, only blurred boundaries between what state institutions and family have deemed immoral or illegal. Thus, private and public spaces mutually reinforce and co-constitute one another. As such, violence against women in the Kurdistan Region is perpetuated through the actions of the community and family, and, instead of modifying or contesting VAW through laws, the governing structures authorize it (Taysi and Minwalla, 2009: 100).

Accusations of sexual impropriety are not the only way to disrupt norms of patriarchal connectivity and upend the family unit. Beyan, a 32-year-old married teacher, explained that she stopped requesting assistance from the DCVAW because she was repeatedly vilified and demeaned by the directorate's staff. Her husband emotionally and physically abused her for years and she wanted to file a complaint against him, and she hoped an NGO would provide a safer space than the DCVAW. We met at the Women's Legal Assistance Organization, a non-governmental organization established to provide free legal assistance to women. She told me that she provided the DCVAW with a detailed testimony about her husband's violence, after which the staff asked her husband to provide his own account to the directorate. When Beyan returned to the DCVAW, staff told her how kind her husband was, and said they did not believe her story and they doubted she would have survived the severity of the abuse she claimed to have faced. Punished for having survived DV, her case workers then reproached her for keeping her salary from her husband, something he had told them during his interview with the case workers. While Beyan was seeking help for GBV – and GBV is an illegal act according to the law that provided the foundation for the DCVAW – the directorate's staff nonetheless found her to be the one guilty of breaking unofficial laws based in patriarchal values. She needed urgent help for DV, and the DCVAW responded by accusing her of financial infidelity. By admonishing women in a public space, the DCVAW intervenes in private space and upholds the violence perpetrated against women within the home. In this case, the public sphere became a site of violence itself by reproducing the patriarchal family space.

Beyond the DCVAW, other public institutions can also reinforce and reconfirm patriarchal ideals enacted within the family. Ashna, a 30-year-old divorced housewife, told me her husband was physically, emotionally, sexually and financially abusive. He monitored her and recorded her phone conversations, using one recording as supposed evidence of an alleged extramarital affair and sharing it with her family. At the time of our interview, Ashna had experienced homelessness as a result of her husband's abuse and successful campaign to destroy her reputation. She had only recently found a small house to rent through financial help from her brother, who lives outside of Iraq and is the only member of her family who has not disowned her. She has not seen her children since her now ex-husband evicted her from their home. When her husband filed to divorce her, his lawyer threatened that they would report Ashna for adultery if she did not sign divorce papers that indicated she relinquish custody of her four children and forfeit her right to spousal support. Ashna's own lawyer urged her to sign these divorce papers in order to avoid being accused of adultery. Ashna's attorney did not act in the best interest of her client – her legal counsel was aware that Ashna was being forced to sign divorce papers and nonetheless insisted Ashna go through with it. Returning to the social workers' claim, that women accused of adultery are not real mothers, it is clear that Ashna's own counsel holds similar sentiments. That points to the fact that rather than being a personal opinion, this view is an accurate representation of how public institutions in general views DV survivors.

While women staff at the DCVAW expose DV survivors to violence by ridiculing, gossiping about and disbelieving them, men also enact violence against the directorate's beneficiaries. Male staff violate DV survivors through comments, physical contact and intimidation tactics. Like public spaces during night-time, the DCVAW centres become spaces where men attempt to dominate women through various methods of intimidation such as aggressive behaviour, embarrassing/mocking women, verbal and physical harassment and focusing attention on women who are unaccompanied by men (Valentine, 1989: 388–389). Male staff toxify the space by applying these practices against survivors of DV and anyone who can be read as one of them. During a research trip to one of the DCVAW offices, a social worker led me to the legal advisers' room where I began speaking with some of the women seeking help. While seated next to one of the women, I noticed a male police officer had entered the room. Because I was speaking with the women, I ignored him despite noticing that he was trying to say something to me. I heard him repeating a phrase but continued listening attentively to the women's stories. As soon as the woman with whom I was speaking left, I finally heard what he was saying to me. He was verbally abusing me while laughing as three female staff members were awkwardly smiling. They looked uncomfortable but did not criticize him for repeatedly verbally abusing me. Realizing I was my only advocate, I asked the uniformed abuser: 'Did you really call me that?' The sneer on his face disappeared and he asked who I was. I responded that my identity was irrelevant and that he had no right to verbally assault anyone. He apologized and his behaviour towards me went from antagonistic to obsequious upon discovering that I was a researcher, and not a beneficiary of the DCVAW. Remarkably, a week prior to this incident, I was in his supervisor's office and the abusive officer greeted me and treated me respectfully. However, this time he coded me as a local woman in need of assistance against GBV and deemed me undeserving of basic respect and, rather, worthy of abuse.

While feminist theory is preoccupied with recognizing and equalizing power-relations between the researcher and the researched to empower marginalized voices, it is crucial to interrogate whether the researcher is *always* more powerful (Sharp and Kremer, 2006: 319), particularly if we approach the research context within an intersectional context. While I was a relatively privileged researcher based in London, I was still a Kurdish woman without political connections who conducted my fieldwork without a male chaperone or family members who could guarantee my respectability. I traversed city life without a private car and chauffeur, signalling a separation from the patriarchy to which I should be adhering. Thus, women's fear of violence in public space is not necessarily due to the space itself, but rather 'the way public space is used, occupied and controlled by different groups at different times' (Sharp and Kremer, 2006: 319). In the Middle Eastern context, women are afforded only restricted access to public spaces and are approached and observed more closely than men (Bagheri, 2014: 1294). Comments, harassment, verbal violence and intimidation are tools utilized by men in order to control women due to gendered perceptions of 'acceptable' behaviour (De Backer, 2020: 350). Though my experiences are less severe than my participants', we are all nonetheless entrenched within the same gendered continuum of violence that permeates private and public space. While I did not experience violence in the private sphere, I was assumed to have as I was mistaken for a DV survivor. As space is produced by gender discourse and its very existence affects how gender is constructed and understood (Massey, 1994: 179), it is clear why I was read both as a woman worthy of respect and as one deserving of abuse in the same public space. My connection to the police officer's superior afforded me respect and protection from violence, but my presence in a room full of DCVAW beneficiaries a few days later provided the officer with a different signal of my position in society, one interpreted as being far beneath the woman he previously saw in his boss's office.

Conclusion

This chapter illustrates how GBV intersects and overlaps across many contexts and spheres. The public sphere, through legislation, the judicial system and the DCVAW, reproduces the family unit and often acts as an extension of the violent family structure that women seek to escape. Following decades of war and conflict, the family as an institution has gained legitimacy and prominence in Iraqi Kurdish society, making it a site where economic and political power are distributed (Begikhani, 2005: 219) and where the male perpetrator of violence receives protection (Joseph, 1999: 14). While the

Kurdistan Region of Iraq has cultivated an image of gender equality and assistance for women through governmental institutions, the founding reasons for the Law to Combat Domestic Violence, the DCVAW and the judicial system all value the patriarchal family unity over the individual's well-being. This is seen through legislation, implementation and practice. The public and private sphere inform one another, where DV in the private sphere is a precursor for GBV within public institutions. Women's safety depends on the public sphere being actively involved in dismantling the harmful effects of patriarchy both within public and private space. As my research demonstrates, the state needs to invest in public institutions that can assist DV survivors and counteract violence in private spaces.

Note

[1] According to the directorate's website and field interview with head of Directorate, Ms Kurda Omer. While I had access up until the end of 2019, the DCVAW website has since blocked all non-Iraq IP addresses.

References

Al-Ali, N. and Pratt, N. (2011) 'Between nationalism and women's rights: the Kurdish women's movement in Iraq', *Middle East Journal of Culture and Communication*, 4(3): 339–353.

Alinia, M. (2013) *Honor and Violence Against Women in Iraqi Kurdistan*, New York: Palgrave Macmillan.

Bagheri, N. (2014) 'Mapping women in Tehran's public spaces: a geo-visualization perspective', *Gender, Place & Culture*, 21(10): 1285–1301.

Begikhani, N. (2005) 'Honour-based violence among the Kurds: the case of Iraqi Kurdistan', in L. Welchman and S. Hossain (eds) *'Honour': Crimes, Paradigms, and Violence Against Women*, London: Zed Books, pp 209–230.

Begikhani, N., Gill, A. and Hague, G. (2015) *Honour-Based Violence: Experiences and Counter-Strategies in Iraqi Kurdistan and the UK Kurdish Diaspora*, Farnham: Ashgate.

Bondi, L. and Domosh, M. (1998) 'On the contours of public space: a tale of three women', *Antipode*, 30(3): 270–289.

Bows, H. and Fileborn, B. (2020) 'Space, place and GBV', *Journal of Gender-Based Violence*, 4(3): 299–307.

Danilovich, A. (2014) *Federalism Studies: Iraqi Federalism and the Kurds – Learning to Live Together*, Farnham: Ashgate.

De Backer, M. (2020) 'Street harassment and social control of young Muslim women in Brussels: destabilising the public/private binary', *Journal of Gender-Based Violence*, 4(3): 343–358.

DIS (Danish Immigration Service) (2018) *Kurdistan Region of Iraq (KRI) Women and Men in Honour-Related Conflicts*, Copenhagen: DIS. Available from: https://www.ecoi.net/en/document/1450520.html [Accessed 10 July 2022].

Duncan, N. (1996) 'Renegotiating gender and sexuality in public and private spaces', in N. Duncan (ed) *BodySpace: Destabilizing Geographies of Gender and Sexuality*, Abingdon: Routledge, pp 127–145.

Ertürk, Y. (2016) *Violence Without Borders: Paradigm, Policy and Praxis Concerning Violence Against Women*, Bethesda, MD: Women's Learning Partnership.

García-Del Moral, P. and Dersnah, M.A. (2014) 'A feminist challenge to the gendered politics of the public/private divide: on due diligence, domestic violence, and citizenship', *Citizenship Studies*, 18(6/7): 661–675.

Hunnicutt, G. (2009) 'Varieties of patriarchy and violence against women: resurrecting "patriarchy" as a theoretical tool', *Violence Against Women*, 15(5): 553–573.

Iraqi Penal Code (1969) Law No 111 of 1969, July. Available from: https://www.refworld.org/docid/452524304.html [Accessed 10 July 2022].

Joseph, S. (1996) 'Gender and citizenship in Middle Eastern States', *Middle East Report*, 198: 4–10.

Joseph, S. (1999) 'Introduction: theories and dynamics of gender, self, and identity in Arab families', in S. Joseph (ed) *Intimate Selving in Arab Families: Gender, Self, and Identity*, Syracuse, NY: Syracuse University Press, pp 1–17.

Kurdistan Parliament (2008) Law Number 15, 2008: Law to Amend the Personal Status Law No 188 of 1959, Erbil: Kurdistan Regional Government, Iraq. Available from: https://www.parliament.krd/media/2498/%D9%82%D8%A7%D9%86%D9%88%D9%86-%D8%B1%D9%82%D9%85-15-%D9%82%D8%A7%D9%86%D9%88%D9%86-%D8%AA%D8%B9%D8%AF%D9%8A%D9%84-%D8%AA%D8%B7%D8%A8%D9%8A%D9%82-%D9%82%D8%A7%D9%86%D9%88%D9%86-%D8%A7%D9%84%D8%A3%D8%AD%D9%88%D8%A7%D9%84-%D8%A7%D9%84%D8%B4%D8%AE%D8%B5%D9%8A%D8%A9-%D8%B1%D9%82%D9%85-188-%D9%84%D8%B3%D9%86%D8%A9-1959-%D8%A7%D9%84%D9%85%D8%B9%D8%AF%D9%84.pdf [Accessed 10 July 2022]. Translation available from: https://govkrd.b-cdn.net/OtherEntities/High%20Council%20of%20Women%20Affairs/English/Publications/Laws/1.%20Act%20No.%2015%20of%202008%20The%20Act%20to%20Implement%20the%20Amended%20no%20188%20of%201959_%20Personal%20Status%20Law,%20in%20Kurdistan%20Region%20of%20Iraq.pdf [Accessed 10 July 2022].

Kurdistan Parliament (2011) Law Number 8, 2011: Law to Combat Domestic Violence, Erbil: Kurdistan Regional Government, Iraq. Available from: http://www.ekrg.org/files/pdf/combat_domestic_violence_english.pdf [Accessed 10 July 2022].

Massey, D. (1994) *Space, Place, and Gender*, Minneapolis: University of Minnesota Press.

Moghadam, V. (2013) *Modernizing Women: Gender and Social Change in the Middle East* (3rd edn), Boulder, CO: Lynne Rienner.

Puttick, M. (2015) *The Lost Women of Iraq: Family-Based Violence During Armed Conflict*, Minority Rights Group International. Available from: http://minorityrights.org/publications/the-lost-women-of-iraq-family-based-violence-during-armed-conflict/ [Accessed 10 July 2022].

Rassam, A. (1982) 'Revolution within the revolution? Women and the state in Iraq', in T. Niblock (ed) *Iraq: The Contemporary State*, London: Croom Helm, pp 88–99.

Schuler, M. (1992) 'Introduction: violence against women – an international perspective', in M. Schuler (ed) *Freedom From Violence: Women's Strategies from Around the World*, New York: UNIFEM, pp 1–45.

Sharp, G. and Kremer, E. (2006) 'The safety dance: confronting harassment, intimidation, and violence in the field', *Sociological Methodology*, 36(1): 317–327.

Taysi, T.B. and Minwalla, S. (2009) 'Structural violence against women in Kurdistan, Iraq', *KHRP Legal Review*, 15: 87–119.

Valentine, G. (1989) 'The geography of women's fear', *Area*, 21(4): 385–390.

Whitehead, J., Bannerji, H. and Mojab, S. (2001) 'Introduction', in H. Bannerji, S. Mojab and J. Whitehead (eds) *Of Property and Propriety: The Role of Gender and Class in Imperialism and Nationalism*, Toronto: University of Toronto Press, pp 3–33.

Wrede, T. (2015) 'Introduction to special issue "theorizing space and gender in the 21st century"', *Rocky Mountain Review*, 69(1): 10–17.

PART V

Space, Place and 'Justice'

13

Adaptations to Sexual Violence: Reduced Access to Opportunity Structures by Women Victimized by Sexual Abuse and Harassment

Suzanne Goodney Lea, Elsa D'Silva and Jane Anyango

Introduction

Sexual and gender-based violence is a global pandemic impacting one in three women around the world (Gaynair, 2013). This violence takes many forms, including non-verbal, verbal and physical violence, intimidation, and harassment in public and private spaces. These abuses generate from a patriarchal mindset that prioritizes men over women, portraying women and girls as vulnerable beings in need of protection from men – the irony being that the men who might protect too often become the predators. These stereotypes and sociocultural norms are reinforced by religion, culture, lack of education, media and influencers in a society (Madan and Nalla, 2016). Moreover, this patriarchal mindset also reinforces the belief that women are the cause of the harassment and therefore must stay silent when they are victimized, lest they bring shame and dishonour to themselves and their families.

The Safecity[1] reporting platform, which was launched in December 2012, has been crowdsourcing anonymous stories of sexual and gender-based violence to make visible the under-reported nature of these incidents. With a data set of now 40,000+ reports, it is insightful to study the patterns and trends within the data, based on location, time of day, day of week and so forth. This provides a better understanding of the context in which sexual and gender-based violence occurs and what might contribute to the location being the comfort zone of the perpetrator.

Through three case studies, one in New Delhi, India, and another in Mumbai, as well as one in Nairobi, Kenya, we offer here a deep dive into how the location and the cultural context contributes to sexual and gender-based violence, impacts the opportunity structure afforded women, and influences the kinds of solutions that have worked.

Case Study 1: Lal Kuan, New Delhi

Lal Kuan in New Delhi is an urban village with a lot of small and medium-sized enterprises. This means there is a large migrant population, comprising mainly males. Safecity's Lal Kuan campaign was initiated in 2015 to address sexual harassment in the public spaces of the village.[2] This campaign was a collaboration with a Plan India International Gender Resource Center (GRC) programme (Awaaz Uthao), established under the state government, which was launched in 2013 to address sexual violence against women in public spaces.

Lal Kuan is a predominantly low-income area, with less than a 50 per cent employment rate and more than 80 per cent of the population living below the poverty line. Fewer than 20 per cent of the women were literate, and awareness of sexual harassment and their rights was largely absent.

The campaign

Over a three-month period, the campaign received widespread coverage. It educated and enabled community members with the knowledge and tools to curb sexual harassment cases. It engaged over a thousand people, 20–25 per cent of them men, by encouraging people to report incidents but also by using direct engagement such as community dialogues, theatre acts, public art installations and sporting events. The campaign also marshalled the data that was collected to engage local municipal corporation and police authorities in addressing key infrastructural issues such as street lighting and public toilets that affected access to and engagement of these spaces.

Through several capacity-building developmental training events, awareness workshops on legal rights and focused discussions (one-on-one and group discussions), we created safe spaces for women and girls to speak up. Safecity organized capacity-building sessions for the women and girls to help them identify the spectrum of abuse – different forms of emotional, non-verbal, verbal and physical violence. They were encouraged to challenge harmful gender norms and stereotypes. They were also informed of their legal rights under Indian law. Four community collectives were formed to spread awareness on sexual harassment in the larger community.

These workshops were instrumental in building the confidence of the women and girls to break their silence regarding their experiences. More than 100 incidents of sexual harassment were reported on Safecity, and another

25 informal reports were received at the GRC. The data was analysed, hotspots were identified and the results were presented to the community. This allowed for a discussion about possible interventions and, importantly, engaged the community in the design of the interventions.

Twenty-five artists of the Asmita Theatre Group organized an afternoon of theatre performances in some of these sexual harassment hotspots. The gatherings attracted close to 300 community members, 40 per cent of them men. The performance focused on women's sexual harassment in public spaces and was followed by an open discussion to highlight the findings of Safecity's reporting platform. The objective was to increase awareness and community action in sexual harassment hotspots.

One of the hotspots identified was on an arterial main road connecting two densely populated blocks of Lal Kuan (E and G). This particular street had increasingly high incidents of sexual harassment with men staring and commenting at the women passing by. The presence of a tea stall gave men and boys an excuse to loiter for extended hours, commenting on and stalking women, making it uncomfortable for women to access this road and forcing them to use alternate longer routes.

Twenty-four girls and women in the 15–45 age group were invited to attend a workshop conducted by Shilo Suleiman of The Fearless Collective. The workshop's objective was to train women on using art and wall murals to disseminate strong social messages in public spaces. During the three-hour workshop, these women identified the location for the mural painting (next to the tea stall). Later, 15 of these women along with Shilo painted big staring eyes on the public wall facing the tea stall. The messages interspersed in the art were in English and Hindi and translated to 'Look with your heart, not with your eyes', 'We will not be intimidated by your gaze', 'We will speak up', 'We will break our silence' and so on.

This wall mural and its messaging was very powerful. The women and girls felt confident as the act of painting the mural itself was in defiance of social norms, and so they were able to express their feelings and challenge the perpetrators. As such, the act itself gave voice to their outrage and oppression. One woman, after being part of the collective, was able to address the domestic violence she was experiencing at home and went on to open her own little store. Another young girl, Sunita, said that the power of collective action to make neighbourhoods safer was an eye-opener for her and made her want to act. For the men, including the tea-stall owner, it made them more aware of how uncomfortable the leering was making the young women feel, evidenced by dialogues with the men. Most reported that it had just simply never occurred to them that their behaviour might have made the young women feel so uncomfortable. As such, this creative and inexpensive intervention immediately resulted in a reduction of cases of ogling, stalking and the discomfort faced by women in accessing this road.

In addition, several local stakeholders and institutions were pushed to act to improve the living conditions of the community and reduce the cases of sexual harassment by using evidence-based data. As a result of this joint effort, multiple public toilets were reopened, broken streetlights were repaired and the entire community was organized to come together to fight this issue. The community as a whole, especially the women, became aware of sexual rights and laws and started to report these issues via Safecity's reporting platform and local authorities. Extensive media coverage from the newspaper *DNA* further helped in spreading the word that combined community action can lead to improved living standards and a reduction in sexual harassment.

Key challenges

A range of challenges in responding to sexual harassment were identified via the Safecity interventions, but three factors stood out: culture; infrastructure; and simple awareness of the issues that women, especially, experience. The workshops and associated discussions, as well as reports by the girls, helped raise awareness about gender violence and also highlighted infrastructure to be addressed – as well as cultural challenges to be examined.

Lack of public infrastructure

The lack of public infrastructure presented a number of challenges. The first issue related to the absence of or disrepair of community toilets. The majority of households did not have indoor toilets, forcing women to access isolated, far away, and poorly lit public spaces to relieve themselves – usually late evenings or early mornings. During these times, several women faced sexual abuse such as groping, stalking or sexual assaults in these public spaces from local men.

The second major challenge related to the poor street lighting in the by-lanes of Lal Kuan. The lanes, connecting the different blocks of Lal Kuan, were poorly lit or not lit at all, restricting the mobility of women and putting them at risk of sexual abuse. A majority of the issues reported were stalking and groping. Poor lighting deters women from venturing far from their homes, and they report every effort to return home before it turns dark. This severely restricts the number of hours a woman or girl can spend in public space.

The design of infrastructure in many public places also promoted groups of men to loiter, congregate and, often, harass women. These were typically tea stalls on the road or trucker stops. One particular example is the trucker stop near Prehladpur Petrol Pump. This area was occupied by truck loaders (mostly men), stationed here through most parts of the day with bustling activity during the evenings and nights. Many women shared personal incidents of sexual harassment by these men, citing that these men were usually under the influence of alcohol, which notably impedes many people's inhibitions and, as such, may contribute towards them acting against social and cultural norms and mores – though in the cases of sexual violence, the social norms may support behaviour that generates the violence. The nature of the abuse reported at the truck stops and tea stalls was mostly staring and commenting. However, there were also a few unverified reports of sexual assault, rape, and the presence of an underlying prostitution and sex-work ring.

Cultural barriers

Patriarchal structures inform not only the oppressive attitudes and behaviours of men but also of women. Women were also engaged in perpetuating the hold of patriarchy as they too often internalize the belief that women are meant to be inferior to men and hence should accept everything associated to a second-tier status – including violence. This ideology prevented many interested women from engaging in the campaign and also made it difficult for Safecity to engage men as there were few sources of challenge to their behaviours.

Incidences of sexual violence have had far-reaching impacts on the women living in the area. As reported in our discussions within the community, these have affected women's and girls' daily choices and restricted them in living an independent, fear-free life. Families had great influence on their choices and perspectives on life. They were restricted in accessing public spaces especially due to the threat of sexual violence. The women and girls were also restricted and discouraged from participating in community events or from pursuing higher education as they would have to travel long distances by public transport. The women themselves had a strong sense of fear and apprehension in visiting public spaces. Notably, there was a trust deficit in the system to safeguard their rights. Patriarchal norms put that blame upon the women and put the onus of safety on them, so there was emotional and psychological trauma and shame inflicted upon them and contributed to a culture of silence. This meant there was poor or no reporting of experiences of sexual harassment and violence.

Case Study 2: Kibera, Nairobi

Kibera is the largest slum in Kenya and, indeed, the largest slum in all Africa. According to the 2009 Kenya Population and Housing Census, the population in Kibera is estimated to be 170,070. Most of Kibera's residents live in extreme poverty, earning less than $1 per day. The average house for four is about 24 square feet and is made out of mud, cardboard and tin – with no running water for a bathroom or kitchen.

In partnership with local NGO Polycom Development Project located in Kibera, which aims to engage girls in sports and ensure they can stay in school, we developed a programme[3] to introduce and train young people in the use the Safecity platform as a means to record and document sexual violence in public spaces. The training had two components: (1) understanding the nature of violence through crowd mapping and (2) creating a campaign methodology to use the data for change. Through various capacity-building exercises, the youth were equipped to design the campaign objectives and activities, to identify target groups to engage and stakeholders to strengthen the campaign's base, and to articulate outreach and mapping roles for each member of the team.

The campaign

Polycom Development Project had been working in 15 schools in Kibera where they had installed 'talking boxes' to collect anonymous stories from children about their experience of bullying and harassment. These locked boxes were placed in schools, and the Polycom Development Project staff would collect the stories every week and read them. Most of these stories were about teachers bullying children, beating them at the smallest provocation, touching them, punishing the girls for returning late from their toilet breaks and so on. This data helped understand the nature of the abuse so that Polycom Development Project could problematize these matters with schools so as to moderate rogue teachers but also to advocate on behalf of the girls for better toilet facilities. The existing toilets were not sufficient to accommodate all the girls, and the time allocated for breaks was too short. When the girls arrived back late in class, the teacher would ask them to lower their pants and would then cane them on their buttocks. This practice had to stop. And so, the number of toilets needed to increase.

Seeing the value of crowd mapping, Ms Jane Anyango, the Founder of Polycom Development Project, decided to digitize the existing data and crowdsource new data. This approach allowed for the stories to be seen as a data set rather than individual stories. It was thereby easier to cluster stories by type or location or day of week or category and to then study the recurring patterns and trends. In Kibera, there are no formal street names, and so Google Maps is ineffective. But the ability to cluster the data by descriptors like the 'Pentagon Bar', 'green hut', 'small mosque' and so forth was immensely helpful. Through the campaign, over 1,000 reports were filed and 15 hotspots identified.

One strategy that was adopted early on was the use of the term 'sexual harassment' instead of 'sexual violence'. This term was deliberately chosen because most households in Kibera were facing some kind of intimate partner or family violence and so, in order to get the community to buy-in to the project, they wanted to highlight that what was being crowdsourced and mapped was information related to events occurring outside the home.

Sexual harassment was described to participants, and its different forms were presented in a graphical manner that would be easy to understand by the school-aged girls. A sample Safecity's flier was customized to suit the Kenyan context and printed onto stickers and 'talking boxes' so as to help girls better understand different forms of sexual harassment so that they could more fully report upon their experiences.

The initial set of reports that was received was eye-opening. Many girls reported being shown pornography without consent and being exposed to men engaging in indecent exposure by flashing their genitalia at public bus stations. This was not necessarily happening only within Kibera but in different parts of Nairobi where the girls might have travelled. The girls were uncomfortable travelling because this kind of harassment was quite common. Until this campaign was undertaken, they did not speak up or share their experience. For the first time, many young girls felt they were heard as they were being asked to share their experiences and speak out in a safe space.

One of the hotspots identified was a street near a school. Young girls on their way to schools were being groped by men who were loitering around. The intention was to harass the girls. They would grab the girls, push them against the walls, and grope their bodies. Once the data was collected and analysed, the trends were presented to the youth participating in the campaign. The brainstorming for solutions resulted in a simple intervention. At the location where the men would loiter, the girls wrote messages like 'Respect our rights' on posters. This was quite effective in challenging the men and it resulted in a reduction of loitering.

Another hotspot was near a mosque where men would congregate and harass young girls. Polycom Development Project invited the religious leaders to examine the data. They were appalled and started incorporating educational messages into their sermons and conversations with young men. They discussed topics like sexual harassment, appropriate behaviour and consent. This was an effective strategy as it engaged elders and influencers like teachers and religious leaders within the community. Further, Polycom Development Project also used local community radio stations in Kibera to talk about the various issues the girls were facing and what could and should be done. This created further awareness and advocacy.

Another strategy was to understand who the perpetrators were and how to best educate them. Many of these young men were juvenile offenders for petty crimes like robbery. They had already experienced detention but did not want to repeat an offence. However, they were not aware that under Kenyan law, sexual harassment is a crime. So, when they were informed about the various sections of the law as well as the penalty for the crime which was either a fine or a jail sentence, they were on guard.

The effects of the campaign resulted in the girls becoming much more confident about their rights and speaking up against harassment. The community action also helped to challenge perpetrators with evidence-based data. Sometimes they did not even realize the harm they were causing. The strategies used to build general awareness within the community, such as radio, religious leaders' lectures and community-based discussions were also effective ways to engage men and boys so as to raise awareness of how common gender-based violence is and the impact it has upon women. This motivated community and religious leaders to step up to challenge abusive behaviours, which further helped to promote change. Polycom Development Project now has a project with the UN Population Fund in 45 schools using the talking boxes. The most significant result, however, was that laws were changed in Kenya to sanction perpetrators so as to better protect young girls.[4] The simple threat of a legal consequence is enough to deter many casual perpetrators, which is what most are when the culture tolerates such behaviour. Few perpetrators are truly predatory.

Key challenges

Lack of awareness

Many young girls were unaware of what sexual abuse might entail, or that they had rights to combat and challenge it. We find this often in many of our campaigns when we begin. The understanding of why even 'minor' harassment matters is often lacking. In fact, however, when harassment is tolerated, a climate is created which encourages and overlooks more serious offences such as groping, exposure and even rape. Perpetrators were also unaware of how their behaviour was impacting the young girls – or that it was inappropriate. Once religious leaders and public awareness began to problematize the behaviour, the perpetrators largely adjusted what they were doing. Many genuinely did not see to realize that what they were doing was abusive or criminal and, as such, impacting the daily lived experiences of the girls.

Cultural barriers

The cultural barriers began to quickly erode as the girls were engaged to both create and enact the campaign. They grew up amid the culture, and so they know its norms and practices, and they therefore did a really great job developing interventions that worked well. And their initiative made others more likely to support them, and hence the law change.

Case Study 3: Indira Naga, Mumbai

Located in Jogeshwari East, in the city of Mumbai, Indira Nagar is a large urban settlement that incorporates many smaller, under-resourced communities. Most of the families migrated from northern India, as well as rural Maharashtra and rural Karnataka. Primarily Hindu, there are communities representing multiple caste positions. There is a heavy influence of Shiv Sena and Maharashtra Navnirman Sena political parties in the area, with many mandals (community centres) consisting of young boys of the community. These groups are regarded as having social power in these communities and are often the cause of sexual harassment towards the girls in the area.

In 2015, in partnership with NGO Vacha, we engaged 20 girls aged 13–18 years in a workshop about mapping sexual harassment in their community.[5] The workshop began with a short discussion about sexual harassment. Since they had had a workshop on the same topic the previous day, the discussion focused on why sexual harassment takes place and on what factors tend to encourage it. Answering the first question, they said boys harass for fun, to prove their *mardangi* (manhood), or to keep women/girls in their place. They listed darkness, empty roads and extremely crowded spaces as factors that contribute towards harassment.

An exercise to list safe and unsafe spaces in the locality was facilitated, and what showed up was that there were more unsafe spaces listed than safe spaces. Some unsafe spaces listed were the school, the toilet, the temple and the maidan (playground). After the discussion, four groups of five girls each audited the physical spaces of the *basti* (locations) of Azad Nagar, MHADA (Maharashtra Housing and Area Development Authority), Indira Nagar and Jarna. They mapped the roads and noted any unsafe zones in those areas. After the walk, they drew out individual maps of those areas, marking unsafe zones as well as the reasons why they are considered unsafe. The reasons were then listed in the key on the map as dark, deserted, too much garbage, boys loitering around and so forth. Some of the key issues raised by workshop participants are illustrated through the following quotes from the workshop:

- "Boys do sexual harassment to prove their manhood to each other. They challenge each other to do so."
- "Deserted roads are scary, but sometimes harassment takes place in very crowded areas as well."
- "The area around my home is unsafe to me."
- "In many areas, boys sit in groups and stare at girls. They even pass comments."
- "We got stared at even when doing this mapping exercise."
- "I am scared to go in certain places in the *basti*."

The campaign

After conducting a workshop and the mapping exercise with the adolescent girls in the community, the girls together created a survey based on the Safecity reporting form. In addition to the existing questions of the 'what, when and where' of incidences of sexual violence, the girls added questions such as what action was taken after the incident, with whom the girl shared this incident, and what the repercussions of this incident were on the girl and her behaviour. The answers to this survey shine a light not only on the prevalence of sexual violence in and around the community but also on the perceptions towards this violence and how important it is to talk about public space and girls' rights to access them.

The survey was conducted over a few months and included a sample of 100 girls between the ages of 10 and 20 years. The data revealed the following trends:

- Out of the 100 girls, 96 said that they have experienced some form of sexual violence. Most of these incidents had been in the form of comments, rude stares and whistling within public spaces (our mapping platform mainly addresses public harassment and violence, though COVID-19 has prompted us to add domestic violence and cyberstalking, which occur in private spaces but have become so epidemic as to necessitate public engagement). However, there were also cases of touching, groping and of rape. The 96 percentage points resonated the findings of Gaynair (2013), which found that 95 per cent of Indian women and girls have experienced at least once some form of sexual harassment or assault.
- Most of the respondents reported that these incidents took place nearby, especially on the roads near their home. Many also reported facing sexual harassment near their colleges and schools.
- On being asked about the repercussions of an incident of sexual violence, most respondents spoke about how they had to change the route they normally took. This effect might not seem significant at first, but if one understands its implications as how the onus of violence is placed on the girl as well as how such an experience may affect her access to spaces, we can see how sexual harassment leads to structural violence as girls and women 'adapt' by altering their lives to 'adjust' to conditions that are patently abusive (Gaynair, 2013). Why should the victim be the one to have to adjust her actions? Further, if one takes into account the fear that makes these girls change their route, we also see how sexual harassment can affect one's mental health.
- Another fact to be noted from these findings were that some girls were made to drop out of school/college, and one girl was even married off. These show the severity of implications that sexual harassment has

on the lives of young women. Even as they are victimized, the brunt of the 'punishment' or response falls upon the girl herself (Allen and Vanderschuren, 2016).

Given all this, it becomes even more disheartening to see how the girls responded with regard to action taken, or with whom they shared the information with. Fifty-seven girls took no action, and those who did, mainly shared the incident with someone they knew well. Only one girl made a police complaint. Through this data we can glimpse the lack of reporting that is associated with sexual harassment. A few girls even responded that they did not take any action at all – not even telling anyone. If they did share the incident, they mostly preferred to speak to a friend or teacher over family members, especially male relatives. This creation of silence around the issue allows for it to perpetuate, and it creates an environment of fear.

Thirty-two adolescent girls aged between 10 and 18 years from Indira Nagar took part in a focus group discussion on the issue of sexual harassment in their community. The facilitators asked the group to share their experiences of harassment. The older girls, who had already started work on this issue, seemed more comfortable with sharing their experiences. The younger ones were hesitant but felt strongly about working against sexual harassment.

During the discussion several places in the region were marked 'unsafe', and, in most areas, the problem was groups of boys that sit in those spaces. They made comments at girls, stared and sang songs. Some even grabbed hold of the girls' hands. In the garden and in other open spaces, there were mostly boys and hardly any girls. This encouraged boys to harass girls, so that, when the number of boys largely outnumbered the girls present, the girls felt unsafe.

Strategies for solutions

Discussion with parents

Vacha and Safecity conducted a meeting with the parents of the girls who were a part of the campaign. The main agenda for the meeting was to discuss the campaign with the parents and develop a support group within the community. The meeting was attended by women who had left their housework for this meeting. The meeting was also attended by representatives of the Mahila Mandal (women's group) of the community. After introducing attendees to the campaign, the facilitators led a short session explaining sexual harassment and why it was important to work against it within the community. The session was delivered in a question-and-answer format and clarified the many myths around this issue, such as how dressing in a particular way does not in fact lead to more harassment or how putting more restrictions on girls in an effort to stop harassment misses the more appropriate target: those who perpetrate the harassment. Many women shared their experiences and fears about public spaces, and they came to agree as to the need to speak out against the many forms of violence against women and girls. Eleven women said that they would be interested in forming a support group in their community.

Reclaiming public spaces

Thirty-five girls from the community of Indira Nagar occupied a space generally used by boys to play matches of Kabaddi (a local ball game). During the campaign, several girls of Indira Nagar spoke about feeling unsafe in Karkare Garden – an open space located near their community. When discussed further, girls opened up about how they did not feel welcome there, and how it was mostly populated by boys. Many girls spoke about experiencing harassment in the area after dark, especially.

One way to create safe spaces for girls and woman is to increase access to these spaces. The moment it stops being a space only for men and boys, women and girls will start to feel more comfortable there. This is especially the case with public spaces where, even though girls have a right to occupy these spaces, they often do not have access to them due to fear of sexual violence or societal pressures. Keeping this in mind, we used the girls' love for the sport of Kabaddi to occupy Karkare Garden in large numbers. Since most of the girls had just finished their exams, they looked forward to some much-deserved fun in the sun. Before going to the garden, we had a short orientation of the reason for this activity. Most of the girls spoke of the importance of sport for health and to build confidence. The discussion led to conversation about how girls are not encouraged to play outside. They are often limited to school grounds or the streets right near their house. Formal sports are also often out of reach for girls. The reasons they gave ranged from not having enough time away from housework to not being allowed by family to participate. During this discussion we also talked about how men playing sports are given much more importance than women playing the same sport (citing examples of the lack of attention given to the women's cricket World Cup that had taken place recently) and how in many sports women do not get the recognition they deserve.

After reaching the garden, we noticed that, besides the girls we were with, there were no other girls in the area. The girls picked a nice spot where there was shade, and we requested the boys playing nearby to give us some space – and they readily obliged. We divided the girls into two groups: the older girls and the younger girls. Each group then had their match of Kabaddi. During the match, a few young boys gathered to cheer on the girls and watched them with great admiration. After four high-energy rounds, the girls insisted on playing a game of Kho-Kho, which is a local version of a 'tag' game, before we called it a day.

After the game we talked with the girls some more and asked them how they felt about the day. One girl spoke about an increase in confidence. She did not think she could play Kabaddi before but, after playing, she saw herself as a pretty decent player. Other girls spoke about how much fun it was to be playing in a large group. We then asked the girls if they would come here again on their own to play a game – to which all the girls gave a loud and confident 'Yes!'

Key challenges
Lack of experience/exposure

Many young girls were inexperienced with being in male-dominated public spaces, and boys were unaccustomed to having them there. The girls lamented how abusive the boys playing in the park could be when the girls happened by. The park was a male-dominated space by tradition, but it was in no way formally declared as such. When it was all boys, the boys acted inappropriately towards the girls. But, when the girls actually entered the park and played just as the boys did, the boys gained respect and completely altered their approach to interaction. Aside from women and girls who felt threatened in various public spaces, there was little awareness or effort to address challenges in those spaces. As a result, the onus is upon the girls to navigate treacherous public spaces. As such, males in the community paid little mind and put little effort into altering those spaces.

Cultural barriers

The primary cultural barrier within this setting was the passivity of many in the community with regard to addressing the perils the girls faced. The girls' parents, rather than being advocates, tended to put the onus and responsibility on the girls themselves instead of advocating for change on their behalf. Moreover, the broader culture saw little priority in redressing issues of sexual harassment and assault, figuring this was just 'how things are'. Education, awareness and exposure can radically change this.

Discussion

This collection of three case studies raises clarity as to the dynamics of the conditions that generate abuse and harassment of women and girls in public spaces (the 'commons'), but they also suggest some creative, simple, but highly successful interventions. There are four issues that undergird the oppressive conditions women and girls face in the commons: (1) a trust deficit that hinges on ensconced sexism and puts the burden of adapting to the abusive conditions on the people being victimized; (2) a lack of awareness among women/girls and men/boys as to what sexual abuse in public spaces is and what impact it has upon women and girls; (3) infrastructure issues that create opportunity for perpetrating violence and harassment; and (4) the widespread loitering of men in public spaces that exists in many parts of the world.

Of these, the trust deficit is probably the most complex and significant. If we were to advise that survivors of domestic violence try harder not to 'bother' their abuser, that suggestion would be rightfully disparaged. But, in public spaces around the world – and particularly in the Global South, that is what we are asking girls and women to do. Women are expected to look out for their own safety and essentially 'adapt' to abusive conditions (Madan and Valla, 2016). The attitude of many – men and women – is that this is just simply 'how things are'. As such, parents often will restrict their daughters to the home, precluding them from attending school or work. That has profound effects on the life experience and opportunity structure of girls and women (Neupane and Chesney-Lind, 2013).

One of the best ways to redress this trust deficit, as Safecity has been learned in its efforts across many cultures and communities, is to deploy discussion-based workshops in communities so that everyone can explore and consider what constitutes abuse. Also of very significant impact is people's stories. Hearing about what happens to girls and women and how these experiences impact them undoubtedly changes hearts and minds as stories engage empathy – and it helps girls and women exorcise the shame that they carry. Talking boxes turn out to be very effective, especially with younger girls or literacy-challenged locations; developing a means of creating talking booths where women and girls can enter something akin to a photo booth to share their story would also be helpful, especially in literacy-challenged areas. These could be solar powered for areas without electricity. Too often, we have learned, women and girls carry shame that is not theirs but that of their abuser(s).

Knowing what issues are happening where is a tremendous tool for effectively addressing infrastructure issues such as toilets and lighting. Having incidents noted on a map allows even a street-level view, which makes it easier to change these conditions. These would seem like banal matters, but they create opportunity for perpetrators (Gaynair, 2013). In the more industrialized, largely northern part of the planet, but also in other parts of the world, some women who are more affluent have increasingly retreated from the commons into private spaces, such as their offices, expensive restaurants, malls and clubs as a strategy for avoiding the risk of sexual harassment or assault. They move from one private space to the next, often in secured private cars or cabs. The larger, open world does not touch them. But this is not a solution available to most women and girls on the planet. They must engage the commons and its various risks.

Finally, loitering stands out as a particularly serious issue as it is relevant in *all* three cases across varying cultures and communities. Tea stalls, parks and even mosques can become sites of male privilege when there are typically only men present (Phadke et al, 2011). Men feel empowered then to do as they like. But the simple strategy of *drawing attention* to such places and the inappropriate behaviour being demonstrated problematizes the issue for the men present. Posting murals or signs or having a bunch of girls go to a male-dominated park to play Kabaddi games are very simple and inexpensive interventions, but they work surprisingly effectively. Essentially, these approaches allow women and girls to challenge norms and, as such, reclaim public spaces for all (Neupane and Chesney-Lind, 2013).

Conclusion

Case studies like these offer in-depth, culturally sensitized insight into complex but *very common* social problems. By looking at such an issue globally, we can better understand some of the underlying challenges. And in many under-resourced places in the world, people's perspectives – especially of youth – offers profound insights into innovative and wildly creative interventions that are cheap but effective. And *that* is how we change the world so that *all people* have access to the commons.

Notes

1   https://safecity.in
2   Details about this case can be found at: https://safecity.in/wp-content/uploads/2017/06/Lal-Kuan-Campaign-Casebook.pdf
3   Details about this case can be found at: https://aspennewvoices.medium.com/how-safecity-is-helping-women-and-girls-speak-out-and-protect-others-bd5b0b29a73e
4   See: https://www.youtube.com/watch?v=upHt6i3r-6g
5   Details about this case can be found at: https://safecity.in/wp-content/uploads/2019/03/Bandra-Plot-Casebook.pdf and at: https://safecity.in/wp-content/uploads/2019/02/Casebook_Indira-Nagar.pdf

References

Allen, H. and Vanderschuren, M. (2016) *Safe and Sound: International Research on Women's Personal Safety on Public Transport*, FIA Foundation Research Paper No 6, London: FIA Foundation. Available from: https://www.fiafoundation.org/media/224027/safe-and-sound-report.pdf [Accessed 8 June 2021].

Gaynair, G. (2013) 'ICRW survey: 95 percent of women and girls consider New Delhi unsafe', International Center for Research on Women, 4 February. Available from: http://www.icrw.org/media/news/icrw-survey-95-percent-women-and-girls-consider-new-delhi-unsafe [Accessed 8 June 2021].

Madan, M. and Nalla, M.K. (2016) 'Sexual harassment in public spaces: examining gender differences in perceived seriousness and victimization', *International Criminal Justice Review*, 26(2): 80–97.

Neupane, G. and Chesney-Lind, M. (2013) 'Violence against women on public transport in Nepal: sexual harassment and the spatial expression of male privilege', *Journal of Comparative and Applied Criminal Justice*, 38(1): 22–38.

Phadke, S., Khan, S. and Ranade, S. (2011) *Why Loiter? Women and Risk on Mumbai Streets*, New York: Penguin.

14

'It's Not Your Fault': Place, Promises to the Future and Honouring the Memory of Eurydice Dixon

Claire Loughnan

Introduction

On 13 June 2018, while returning home after performing at the Melbourne Comedy Festival, 22-year-old Eurydice Dixon was sexually assaulted and murdered. Eurydice had lived in Carlton, a suburb in inner Melbourne, and been a student at a high school located close to my workplace. She was an emerging comedian, and a partner, daughter, sister and friend. Reflecting on this moment has had a special significance for me. My children attended school with her and her brother, and they were profoundly saddened by this loss. As young adults, they took seriously their commitment to the vigil for Eurydice which was held on the dark, cold evening of 18 June 2018. The four of us made our way there, both together and separately, where thousands of others gathered in the darkness, or in spaces illuminated by the lights of the sports field on which Eurydice was found. Disturbingly, I recalled cautioning my daughters some years earlier against walking through these same parklands, alone and at night. Yet such parental cautioning both defies understanding and undermines the freedom and agency of women: why should women not enjoy public space without fear, and without feeling that it is incumbent upon them to ensure their own safety? (Pain, 1997; Vera-Gray and Kelly, 2020).[1]

My concern here though, is less with how public spaces are experienced and perceived as places of violence (important though this is) but more with how they are transformed into impermanent yet compelling sites of public mourning and memorialization of violence against women (Bold et al, 2002). My own location meant that I was regularly transiting the site, on my way to work nearby. The place where Eurydice was assaulted and murdered was also close to the school that she, and my own children, had attended. I could avoid travelling that way, but I chose not to. I was drawn to the way that people, from local and afar –friends, strangers, parents and children – participated in public displays of mourning. They brought candles, flowers, notes and cards, objects, mementoes. In their messages, they conveyed more than their sorrow: this site revealed a localized politics of resistance to the ongoing violence against women. Although not new – there have been extensive examples before and since of such memorials (Ansell, 2019; Siganto, 2020), witnessing this was an intimate and unsettling experience for me.

I begin this chapter by describing Eurydice's assault and death before turning to the public displays of mourning which followed and examining the forms that this mourning took.[2] I explore how this site of public mourning might function to generate a future justice. I conclude by reflecting on what this might mean for those who were close and dear to Eurydice, and upon how the sadness for their loss is both affirmed and eclipsed in such moments.

'She blew me a kiss and said she was going for a walk'

Eurydice Dixon was stalked for up to four kilometres, before being attacked by Jaymes Todd in the grounds of Princes Park, in the suburb of Parkville, in Melbourne, Australia (Cooper, 2018; Jaymes Todd v the Queen, 2019). She was developing her skills as a stand-up comedian and had been performing in the annual Melbourne Comedy Festival at the Highlander Bar, in Highlander Lane, Melbourne. At this last gig, she joked about the ongoing failure to deliver equal rights to women (Cooper, 2018; Palin, 2018). She left the venue at about 10.30 pm and farewelled her boyfriend at Flinders Street in the central business district, just after 11 pm. She was looking forward to the walk home, something she did regularly. Her boyfriend, Tony Magnuson, recounted that Eurydice 'was happy and content. She gave me a hug, blew me a kiss and said she was going for a walk' (Palin, 2018). It seemed that she was unaware that she was being followed (Cooper, 2018). She walked up Swanston Street, towards Elizabeth Street, then onto Royal Parade, Carlton, several kilometres from where she had farewelled Magnuson. Just before the attack, she texted Magnuson from the park, to say that she was nearly home (Cooper, 2018; Razak, 2019).

After stalking her for about an hour, Todd sexually assaulted and murdered Eurydice on one of the soccer pitches, at the southern end of the park

(Cooper, 2018). He was later sentenced to life imprisonment and failed in a 2020 Supreme Court appeal against this sentence. The court's statement described the attack as exceedingly callous, reflecting the attitudes of the local community when it declared:

> A young woman should be able to walk home alone after a night out without any fear of being harmed, let alone subjected to a vile sexual attack and killed. She should not have to be looking over her shoulder to see if anyone is following her. Her heart should not have to skip a beat when she hears approaching steps from behind. Tragically, this case shows that women still cannot have confidence that they can walk in public places at night without potentially attracting the attention of predators. (Jaymes Todd v the Queen, 2019: 17–18)

The park where Eurydice was attacked comprises sports fields, children's playgrounds and a football oval, and extends at its northern end to a bowling green and more public spaces where people regularly picnic and exercise, attracting runners and walkers who follow the circuit of the park. Opposite the area where Eurydice was attacked is the Melbourne cemetery, from which one can see the blue haze of the Dandenong Ranges in the distance. In the absence of green space at the nearby Princes Hill Secondary College – which Eurydice had attended some years before – Princes Park also functions as the grounds for its secondary students. Here students spend their recess and lunch hours and take physical education classes. Princes Park is beautiful, but I have always felt unnerved by its darkness at night, a feeling which I must admit is fuelled by the dominant narrative of the 'stranger' and by a long-term, embodied awareness of my personal fragility as a woman which I find hard to cast away.[3] I fully endorse the view that women should be safe in all places, and that it ought never be incumbent upon us to be responsible for our own safety: safety should be a *given*. However, decades of moving through public spaces with an acute awareness of the unwanted male gaze is hard to shake off and it shapes my movements even as an older woman, who will continue to cross the street when it seems wise to do so. Reluctantly, it has sometimes shaped the messages I pass to my own daughters, even when I have an ethical and political objection to the terms of these messages.

How public space is experienced also changes with time and context: there is often a distinctly temporal dimension to safety (Pain, 1997: 238). Those spaces which are experienced or perceived as relatively safe during the day, might not be so at night (Miranda and van Nes: 2020: 2) So too, are 'vibrant' spaces often perceived to be safer (Miranda and van Nes: 2020: 2, 4) although this is not straightforward, with the 'chaotic and crowded' spaces of music festivals also sites of under-reported sexual violence (Bows et al, 2020; Fileborn et al, 2020: 196). But when we focus predominantly on the spatial characteristics of public spaces, including visibility, land use and the demographics of these sites (Miranda and van Nes, 2020), there is a tendency to reinforce the view that the issue is with the site, and not with the culture enabling such violence (Pain, 1997). Change is accordingly focused on better design, rather than on the more foundational aims of shifting cultural attitudes. Moreover, women typically experience *all* spaces as gendered, whether or not this translates to physical or other forms of violence. 'Avoidance strategies' and limits imposed on women's movement thus undermine the view that the public should be equally accessible to all (Miranda and van Nes, 2020: 28), reinforcing a politics of domination and social control over women (Pain, 1997: 233–234) and a discursively imposed separation between the public and private sphere (Vera-Gray and Kelly, 2020: 266).[4] Yet women retain stronger fears of violence in public spaces (Yates and Ceccato, 2020: 279–280) with safety in public spaces typically achieved as 'embodied work' (Pain, 1991; Pain, 1997; Fileborn, 2014; Fileborn and Vera-Gray, 2017; Vera-Gray, 2017; Vera-Gray and Kelly, 2020: 269). Yet, how might space also offer opportunities for justice?

In seeking justice and in resisting the embodied experiences of fear and harassment, women have fought back through campaigns like Reclaim the Night and Reclaim the Street (Bindel, 2006: Tutton, 2019), and through the #MeToo movement. Similarly, the incidence of online violence against women is being explored not just as a form of violence, but as an opportunity for resistance through online sites (Gjika and Marganski, 2020) and an 'alternative form of justice' (Salter, 2013; Fileborn, 2014: 32) to address the shortcomings of the criminal justice system (McGlynn et al, 2012; Gjika and Marganski, 2020: 165). Justice responses to violence against women have thus increasingly focused on the shortcomings experienced within the criminal justice system, notably for victim survivors of sexual assault, with growing research on alternative avenues for justice for women (Herman, 2005; Powell et al, 2015; Fileborn and Vera-Gray, 2017). In this light, the question posed by Hildur Fjóla Antónsdottir – 'what is the role of space?' – in experiences of justice, is a significant one (2020: 718). As Antónsdottir (2020: 738) observes: 'The creation of just spaces can be understood as a disruption or an intervention in the continuum of injustice. The creation of just spaces relies on the active recognition, solidarity and support of those who count in a given context and who ensure that these spaces are sustainable enough.'

In this chapter I reflect on the diverse forms that the memorialization of the site at Princes Park took, revealing it as a site of resistance, remembering and a future-oriented politics. Although Antónsdottir's (2020: 732) observation that reclaiming of space enables a 'shift in power dynamics' which is directed at *survivors* of sexual violence, it also holds true – though in different ways – in the temporary memorial at Princes Park. This site was not static, with the reclamation of this public space one of ongoing struggle. For example, this dynamic was momentarily disturbed when the soccer pitch was graffitied by an anti-feminist blogger who painted a large penis over the site where Eurydice died (Davey, 2018). Such a rupture in the memorial site was quickly denounced, and the site was soon recovered. However, the incident was a violence that reinforced the violence which had already led to Eurydice's death, by the dishonouring and violation of her memory.

For Vera-Gray (2017: 164) there is a form of alienation that emerges for women, between the body and the space a person occupies, in which neither are experienced as one's own. Fear in public space is a form of social control, which Eurydice sought to disrupt, as her own act of resistance to this control (Fileborn, 2021). In many ways, then, the memorial site at Princes Park asserted a right to public space, affirmed Eurydice's right to be there, in that place, at that time, without fear. Yet as Antónsdottir (2020: 722) argues, the politics of space and women's freedom of movement through it, also requires an examination of justice *in* space for those who have experienced violence. How do individuals seek to remake these spaces as their own? What can we make of memorialization *as* justice (Bold et al, 2002; Schramm, 2011; McDonald, 2020; Steele et al, 2020) not only in Eurydice Dixon's case, but of many others who lost their lives as victims of violence against women.[5]

I ask then: what might public sites of mourning offer, as a source of justice, of resistance and a politics of change? In examining this, I turn to the specific details of the public memorial that emerged incrementally over the weeks following Eurydice's death. In documenting the site, I observed the emergence of many voices, whose messages of support and sympathy were also accompanied by messages of resistance, by a politics of remembrance of sorts, by promises made by parents to honour her in the way that they both cared for, and educated their children. Over the passing weeks, flowers were piled up, candles lit and left burning till they melted to the ground that had held Eurydice. Messages softened in the damp winter weather, and blurred into each other, flowers lost their moisture, and sank to the earth, but the memory of Eurydice and the horror at her death remained gently honoured.[6] What and whose justice is being served in this memorial, for those who do not survive? In exploring this, I collected images of the site over a period of several weeks (Figures 14.1, 14.2 and 14.3), beginning with the vigil in June 2018, until late July 2018, at varying times of the day, on the way to work, and on my way home.[7]

Mourning as a future promise

Two days after her death, a silent vigil was held for Eurydice on the soccer pitch where she died. It was a cold, damp night and the ground was sodden

Figure 14.1: Vigil at Princes Park for Eurydice Dixon, 18 June 2018

Source: Photographs © Claire Loughnan

Figure 14.2: 'Promises to the future': some of the flowers and messages left at the temporary memorial, Princes Park, which honoured the life of Eurydice Dixon

Source: Photographs © Claire Loughnan

Figure 14.3: 'It's not your fault': candles and messages left in the temporary memorial site for Eurydice Dixon

Source: Photographs © Claire Loughnan

underfoot, with large puddles of water. I remember thinking there were so many people, all moving, as in one body in the same direction, all pulled towards the site, coming to pay their respects, to honour her, as well as to honour all those women who have died in this way and all those who continue to die. It was so quiet, so silent. For what seemed like 40 minutes or more (but I cannot recall) people continued to stand in silence. It seemed disrespectful to move or to speak. At the front of the gathering, her family and friends stood holding candles and flowers. Several voices, unaccompanied, sang 'Hallelujah' by Leonard Cohen. In her news report on the vigil, Gay Alcorn (2018) recounted the statements of a student at Eurydice's school, Thea Jones, aged 16:

> [Thea] said she had friends who were in the park on the same night Dixon was killed. Somehow, she hoped the vigil could reclaim the park for everyone. 'I don't want the murder to be what it's remembered by. I want it to be remembered for this', she said, of the estimated 5,000 to 10,000 people, standing together, candles lighting up their faces.

It was clear from her statement, and from the responses of my own children and their friends, that what had happened to Eurydice impacted deeply on their own relationship with Princes Park, transformed from a place of familiarity, connection and joy, into one of grief, anger and solemnity.

The messages left were often acutely personal, frequently addressed directly to Eurydice, and to her family. Statements like 'fly high' and 'no woman deserves to go through what you went through'; 'your life was taken way too soon'; 'you did NOT deserve this', merged together with pages taken from school yearbooks, the lyrics and song score from 'Hallelujah'. Exhortations such as 'No more fear, no more rape. Respect for *ALL*' and #stopviolenceagainstwomen were placed on the site. Others expressed solidarity and grief despite having no personal, direct connection to Eurydice:

> I didn't know you, but I feel like I did. Our lives are very similar. I'm so sorry that this happened to you. I will never see you as a victim. Rather, I will remember you always and what your life could have been. XX I hope this message brings peace to others who are grieving also.

However, there were also other messages that gestured towards a future justice, as a promise. Although there were many statements such as 'you and this crime will *never* be forgotten' there were also calls for what might be described as a call for an alternative justice:

We need to change the way we speak about women as victims waiting for perpetrators and sirens who cause it to happen. We need to challenge that women are mothers and daughters and sisters and wives, above being people. People who occupy and move through space. For our sake, we must reclaim this public space. All public space. And for your sake, all you lost ones, we'll do it in your memory.

Another message simply conveyed the hope that this might 'motivate people to change our society. I hope it was not in vain'. The words left on the site by the Shire of Mitchell, offered a public commitment to something beyond mourning: 'We will remember. We will unite and fight. We will love and respect one another. We will make a difference.'

Others conveyed personal sorrow together with a pledge to make a difference in their own lives:

I'm so sorry we let you down Eurydice. My heart aches for your beautiful life that is senselessly lost. My thoughts will continue to be with you and your loved ones. I will continue to raise the best sons that I can. I am teaching them to love and respect women and girls. I am teaching them to be interested and curious about them. In time, I will teach them to stand up for them, and not to be passive about sexism. I will never stop doing this.

Some messages were a frustrated call for change, accompanied by anger and exasperation that women are still not safe in public spaces, and a future promise:

We all just want to feel safe and be able to do as we wish like something as simply as walking home from work. ... It was not your fault. It's never your fault. I will teach my son and daughter. In your memory. You are enough, you are loved! ... Your legacy will help keep future generations safe.

These pledges to future generations by parents grieving for Eurydice (whether they knew her personally or not) hold the promise of justice, in dismantling the cultural and structural scaffolding that fosters such violence through the personal commitment made by those who visited the site. The site functioned as much more than a makeshift memorial, but as a forum for promises to be made, for and on behalf of future generations of women, and of all of us.[8] One of the most powerful objects left at the site, was the scattering of many small slips of paper, with the words typed on them, 'it's not your fault'. These tiny, narrow pieces of paper that were dropped upon the ground, across flowers, with candles, lay there as a delicate yet emphatic resistance to any suggestion otherwise.

Memorialization, grief and prospective justice

Memorialization, as a form of justice for those subject to diverse harms, has been acknowledged for some time, often as a way of bearing witness, as well as a source of transitional justice (Bold et al, 2002: Moore, 2009; Schramm, 2011). This has tended to focus on a permanent or semi-permanent, formal process for memorialization as justice or with cultural projects dedicated to the memory of past violence (Hirsch and Smith, 2002). Emerging research is pointing to how this is unfolding in relation to institutional sites of violence, such as disability 'care' homes and prisons (Steele et al, 2020). This has followed the growing use of memorials for mass violence like genocide (Moore, 2009). The repurposing of some sites can lead to them functioning as what have been described as Sites of Conscience, a movement that addresses systemic injustice in diverse settings and functions to 'disrupt narratives' that repressed the voices of those subjected to violence in institutional settings (Steele et al, 2020). The focus of this global network – Sites of Conscience – is not simply on preserving memories of the past but working to 'build a better present and future' (Steele et al, 2020: 525–526). In some cases, such memorialization, typically enacted at the site of violence, is achieved through the permanent purposing of a site for future generations to reflect upon (Marcuse, 2010).

On a less formal register, Dave McDonald is exploring how multicoloured ribbons tied onto the fences of churches and other places found to be places of sustained child sexual abuse, act as a present reminder of past acts of violence (McDonald, 2020). These 'loud fences' – a term used to describe the tying of these colourful ribbons to the fences of religious and other institutions responsible for the cover up and complicity in child sexual abuse over many years – have been documented by McDonald to show how telling stories with ribbons function as a public reminder of past harms, while also calling for justice through accountability. The ribbons are often torn down but reappear soon after, as an insistence on naming and shaming as a source of justice and a visible reminder in the presence of such abuse. As he recounts, loud fences 'represent a visual statement of solidarity by the community at large', and thereby suggest, he says, 'new ways of thinking about collective responsibility in the wake of mass harm' (McDonald, 2020).

The temporary, public memorial site for Eurydice Dixon gestures similarly towards other sources of justice for those who cannot access it in the usual forums. It is well established that criminal trials typically offer a limited and traumatic forum for victim survivors to seek justice, with restorative justice proposed as an alternative way of bringing victims and perpetrators together (Jülich, 2006; McGlynn et al, 2012; McSherry and McMillan, 2020). Such recourse is not available to those who did not survive. Here justice is sought on behalf of the victim, by those affected and impacted by the violence. This is a form of community justice, a memorial to the life and violent death of Eurydice, and a future promise to other women. The memorial site for Eurydice Dixon, while impermanent, functioned both to remember her, and as a reminder and promise to future generations.[9]

Such informal practices of honouring the memory of those who have died in horrific circumstances have been evident in other sites such as those of fatal car accidents, bombings, and police killings in the US, which transform the city through the intrusion of private grief into public space (Mchunu, 2020). These informal practices render violence visible in very specific locations, at the scene of the harm, and are generated by a community, rather than by an organization or institution, which might otherwise direct the form that such memorial might take, as McDonald's work on 'loud fences' also shows. In many recent cases of fatal violence against women, communities have come together from far and wide to mourn and pay tribute (Ansell, 2019; *SBS News*, 2020). At the same time, I was left wondering what this might mean for Eurydice's family, and the grief they endured. In the Supreme Court judgment which rejected an appeal by Jaymes Todd, Eurydice was described as 'an aspiring and talented comedian', whose death has been mourned by a 'grieving and loving family. Her death has had a very significant impact on them. Indeed, the impact has been sorely felt by many in the broader community' (Jaymes Todd v the Queen, 2019: 2).

In her victim impact statement, Eurydice's sister, Polly Cotton, reflected that the strongest emotion she experienced was anger, 'seething in anger. My rage is irrational. ... This has shattered and destroyed my family' (Razak, 2019). Her partner, Tony Magnuson, wept as he sat in court, saying that after Eurydice's death he suffered flashbacks, trauma and insomnia (Razak, 2019). In the background of Eurydice's death lies the grief and history of her family. At age seven, her father received a knock at the door to say that her mother had died of a drug overdose in a local shopping centre. After the death of Eurydice's mother, she and her brother continued to live in a local public housing unit in Carlton, with her father taking on the care of Eurydice and her brother: media reports suggested that Eurydice had experienced bullying and had found life 'tough' at times (Palin, 2018).

However, as one of the messages left at the temporary memorial affirmed, 'Eurydice is still a person, her story and who she is should forever be remembered. Not just what happened. She is more than a victim'. The public mourning of Eurydice's violent death has, then, had diverse purposes and effects. It has functioned to affirm her life, to resist the pattern of violence against women, and provided a focal point for a community desirous of change. Her immediate family are both part of this, and yet separate from it in ways that often escape our focus. Although we might be able to imagine their private grief, it is impossible to know if the spatial justice afforded by public mourning provided justice, or at least a salve for the grief endured by

Eurydice's family. We also fail to detect, in these moments, the dimensions of her life with those closest to her. Their suffering is largely hidden from us, but would no doubt remain as palpably endured in each waking moment. In many avenues for alternative modes of justice for those subjected to sexual and other forms of violence, the underlying aim is to ensure that victim survivor stories are heard, that victim survivors can speak about how their abuse made them feel (McGlynn et al, 2012: 218). For Eurydice, there was no such option, and no opportunity for her story to be heard directly by the perpetrator. Yet the aftermath of the violence against her has left traces with those who mourned, whether this is felt 'on individual consciousness' or on 'collective identifications' (Schramm, 2011: 5).

Pierre Nora (1989) alerts us to the modern effects of subjugating memory to the rigid contours of history, through which personal memories, whether individual or collective, are controlled and contained: this process, he argues, undermines the organic fluctuations in, and spontaneity of memory-making.[10] In this process, collective and individual remembering (environments of memory) has been overtaken by 'sites of memory', emerging in the form of archives, documents and physical markers of the past. Against this, he suggests that memory: 'remains in permanent evolution, open to the dialectic of remembering and forgetting, unconscious of its successive deformations, vulnerable to manipulation and appropriation, susceptible to being long dormant and periodically revived' (Nora, 1989: 8).

It is in this light that the temporary memorial at Princes Park – a place for remembering Eurydice Dixon – can be understood as one of justice through memory. The ephemeral, affective traces of those mourning and remembering at that place together yielded the potential for that site to be shaped into a future justice by the memories of all of those who visited it. As Alison Young (2022: 227) remarks, 'the city is a cartography of violence', with such violence often rendered visible by concrete commemorative markers. Yet the city can also be a place of justice, or a place where justice might be sought. In the ostensibly forgotten and ephemeral places of memorialization such as that honouring Eurydice Dixon, what disappears from public space nonetheless endures in individual and collective memories, through a promise to another future.

Conclusion

Memorials like the one at Princes Park constitute an impermanent form of resistance, in concrete terms at least, to the constraints experienced by women in their everyday interactions in space. Despite this, they generated a promise to future justice. As Steele et al (2020) reflect in their work on Sites of Conscience, memorialization can function as a bridge between the present and the future, 'to inform how things can and should be now and into the future' (Steele et al, 2020: 526). This can avoid individualizing injustice and has the potential to be transformative (Steele et al, 2020: 528) with the latter similarly evident in the promises made in the memorial to Eurydice Dixon. Yet the notion of transformative justice has to date been dominated by a focus on post-conflict societies rather than with cases of sexual abuse and violence against women in public spaces (Fileborn and Vera-Gray, 2017: 208–209).

For Eurydice and her family, the memorial is not a permanent, physical site for reflection and resistance to violence against women. Memorializing former sites of violence in this way can yet offer a forum for resisting historical erasure of the violence associated with these sites as well as ensure that the collective or systemic nature of such harms is recognized (Steele et al, 2020: 528; Lloyd et al, 2022). In reflecting on the site and the messages left there, my aim here is to generate an appreciation of how individuals and community responded to her death. What might this reflect for future justice is something beyond a 'cultural countermemory' (Bold et al, 2002), which could nonetheless contest the repression of memories of violence against women. Like more permanent Sites of Conscience, the park memorial to Eurydice Dixon challenged violence, including to women and others subjected to sexual violence. It did so not through formal processes but through the personal, intimate interactions enacted at the site. In the sense described by Steele et al (2020: 550) regarding Sites of Conscience, it is in 'this very place of inordinate pain and loss, that we can best put justice to work and make use of past wrongs for future good'. In honouring the memory of Eurydice, there was a commitment to another future, which lies not just in the spatiality of the site, but is transported into the spaces of the private homes and lives of those who make that commitment to a future justice. Each person takes home their own piece of memory, their own promise to the future.

Notes
[1] This also perpetuates the narrative of 'stranger danger' despite most sexual violence being perpetrated by individuals who are known to women. Shortly after Eurydice Dixon was assaulted and murdered, the local police (Victoria Police) issued a statement warning women to take greater care in their movements through public space. This statement was subject to significant criticism since it reflected a persistent tendency to blame women's movements and conduct for the violence against them, rather than ensuring that this responsibility lies squarely with the perpetrator and with a culture which facilitates such violence. The Premier of Victoria, Daniel Andrews, countered this narrative, posting on Twitter that 'women don't need to change, men do' (*SBS News*, 2018). Yet as I write, the exposure of a culture of abuse, assault and disrespect for women within Australia's halls of government, in Parliament House, in Canberra, Australia, is renewing public debate on the ongoing lack of respect for women, including in the highest offices of the country. See Albeck-Ripka (2021).

2   There was also a vigil at the Highlander Bar, where Eurydice performed her last gig. Fellow comedians, and those close to Eurydice, including her boyfriend, Tony Magnuson, attended and paid tribute to her life. See Schembri (2018).

3   For an exploration of the embodied experiences of street harassment and movement through public space, see Bianca Fileborn's (2021) application of Sara Ahmed's analysis of how experiences of street harassment, for example, are experienced cumulatively in ways that shift the way we inhabit our bodies.

4   It also reinforces the view that women are most at risk in public spaces, which overlooks the reality of sexual and other forms of violence against women in the home (see Pain, 1997: 243) Despite this, evidence points to women being 'more fearful in public than private space' (Yates, and Ceccato, 2020: 279).

5   Less than a year later, La Trobe University student Aya Maasarwe was found dead in suburban Bundoora, in Melbourne Australia. Similarly, a makeshift memorial, filled with messages, flowers and tributes, began to emerge at the site where she was found. See Ansell (2019).

6   Some days after the vigil, Andrew Nolch, an 'anti-feminist blogger' defaced the area by spray-painting a 25-metre penis on the site where Eurydice died. He was charged with criminal damage. The site was restored. See Sweeney (2019).

7   I have selected images that reflect these calls to justice as well as expressions of sorrow and grief, photos taken during June and July, 2018, at varying times of day.

8   Questions remain about what is to be made of such impermanent memorials, questions also raised in relation to temporary memorials created in the aftermath of other forms of violence. What is the afterlife of the archive of such sites? See Wood (2018).

9   Against this, there have been other proposals for permanent memorials, especially in relation to family violence. See, for example, Siganto (2020) and SBS News (2020).

10   Thank you to Alison Young for referring me to this work by Pierre Nora.

Acknowledgements

I wish to extend my thanks to the editors, Bianca Fileborn and Hannah Bows, for their helpful feedback on this chapter, and to Alison Young (2022) for her insights arising from her work on memorialization in response to loss of life in the Grenfell Tower fire.

References

Albeck-Ripka, L. (2021) 'She made a "soul-destroying" rape claim. Then 3 others came forward', *New York Times*, 24 February. Available from: https://www.nytimes.com/2021/02/24/world/australia/australia-parliament-house-rape-claim.html [Accessed 28 February 2021].

Alcorn, G. (2018) 'Eurydice Dixon vigil: silence and song as mourners come to remember and reclaim', *The Guardian*, 18 June. Available from: https://www.theguardian.com/australia-news/2018/jun/18/eurydice-dixon-vigil-silence-and-song-as-mourners-come-to-remember-and-reclaim [Accessed 16 February 2021].

Ansell, B. (2019) 'Aya Maarsarwe's alleged killer charged with murder and rape' *Nine News*, 19 January. Available from: https://www.9news.com.au/national/aiia-maasarwe-student-chose-melbourne-over-new-york-because-it-was-safer/97874cc2-696b-4482-88ac-4bbaeb0cb6f9 [Accessed 16 January 2021].

Antónsdottir, H.F. (2020) 'Injustice disrupted: experiences of just spaces by victim-survivors of sexual violence', *Social & Legal Studies*, 29(5): 718–744.

Bindel, J. (2006) 'Marching to freedom', *The Guardian*, 22 November. Available from: https://www.theguardian.com/society/2006/nov/22/publicvoices.crime [Accessed 16 January 2021].

Bold, C., Knowles, R. and Leach, B. (2002) 'Feminist memorializing and cultural countermemory: the case of Marianne's Park', *Signs*, 28(1): 125–148.

Bows, H., King, H. and Measham, F. (2020) 'Conceptualising safety and crime at UK music festivals: a gendered analysis', in L. Platt and R. Finkel (eds) *Gendered Violence at International Festivals: An Interdisciplinary Perspective*, Abingdon: Routledge, pp 86–103.

Cooper, A. (2018) 'Jaymes Todd stalked Eurydice Dixon for hour before murder, court papers reveal', *The Age*, 8 November. Available from: https://www.theage.com.au/national/victoria/jaymes-todd-stalked-eurydice-dixon-for-hour-before-murder-court-papers-reveal-20181108-p50eva.html [Accessed 16 January 2021].

Davey, M. (2018) 'Eurydice Dixon: memorial to murdered comedian vandalised', *The Guardian*, 18 June. Available from: https://www.theguardian.com/australia-news/2018/jun/18/eurydice-dixon-memorial-to-murdered-comedian-vandalised [Accessed on 20 January 2021].

Fileborn, B. (2014) 'Online Activism and Street Harassment', *Griffith Journal of Law and Human Dignity*, 21(1): 32–51.

Fileborn, B. (2021) 'Embodied geographies: navigating street harassment', in J. Berry, T. Moore, N. Kalms and G. Bawden (eds) *Contentious Cities: Design and the Gendered Production of Space*, Abingdon: Routledge.

Fileborn, B. and Vera-Gray, F. (2017) '"I want to be able to walk the street without fear": transforming justice for street harassment', *Feminist Legal Studies*, 25(2): 203–227.

Fileborn, B., Wadds, P. and Tomsen, S. (2020) 'Sexual harassment and violence at Australian music festivals: reporting practices and experiences of festival attendees', *Australian and New Zealand Journal of Criminology*, 53(2): 194–212.

Gjika, A. and Marganski, A.J. (2020) 'Silent voices, hidden stories: a review of sexual assault (non)disclosure literature, emerging issues and call to action', *International Journal for Crime, Justice and Social Democracy*, 9(4): 163–176.

Herman, J. (2005) 'Justice from the victim's perspective', *Violence Against Women*, 11(5): 571–602.

Hirsch, M. and Smith, V. (2002) 'Feminism and cultural memory: an introduction', *Signs*, 28: 1–19.

Jaymes Todd v The Queen (2019) S EAPCR 2019 0186, Court of Appeal, Melbourne. Available from: https://www.supremecourt.vic.gov.au/sites/default/files/2020-03/todd_v_the_queen_2020_vsca_46_-_judgment.pdf [Accessed 27 April 2022].

Jülich, S. (2006) 'Views of justice among survivors of historical child sexual abuse: implications for restorative justice in New Zealand', *Theoretical Criminology*, 10(1): 125–138.

Lloyd, J. and Steele, L. (2022) 'Place, memory, and justice: critical perspectives on sites of conscience', *Space and Culture*, 25(2): 144–160.

Marcuse, H. (2010) 'Holocaust memorials: the emergence of a genre', *American Historical Review*, 115(1): 53–89.

McDonald, D. (2020) 'Telling stories with ribbons: Ballarat, loud fence and the aftermath of institutional child sexual abuse', *Narrative Network blog*, University of Melbourne, 12 August. Available from: https://blogs.unimelb.edu.au/narrative-network/2020/08/12/telling-stories-with-ribbons/ [Accessed 28 February 2021].

McGlynn, C., Westmarland, N. and Godden, N. (2012) ' "I just wanted him to hear me": sexual violence and the possibilities of restorative justice', *Journal of Law and Society*, 39(2): 213–240.

Mchunu, K. (2020) 'Roadside death memorials revisited: mourning in public spaces', *Cogent Arts and Humanities*, 7(1): art 1792154. Available from: https://doi.org/10.1080/23311983.2020.1792154 [Accessed 16 January 2021].

McSherry, B. and McMillan, N. (2020) ' "What I had to say mattered": how can we provide justice for sexual assault victims beyond criminal trials?', *The Conversation*, 2 December. Available from: https://theconversation.com/what-i-had-to-say-mattered-how-can-we-provide-justice-for-sexual-assault-victims-beyond-criminal-trials-150075 [Accessed 20 January 2021].

Miranda, J.V. and van Nes, A. (2020) 'Sexual violence in the city: space, gender and occurrence of sexual violence in Rotterdam', *Sustainability*, 12(18): art 7609. Available from: https://doi.org/10.3390/su12187609 [Accessed 27 April 2022].

Moore, L.M. (2009) '(Re)covering the past: remembering trauma: the politics of commemoration at sites of atrocity', *Journal of Public and International Affairs*, 20: 47–64.

Nora, P. (1989) 'Between memory and history: *Les Lieux de Mémoire*', *Representations*, 26: 7–24.

Pain, R. (1991) 'Space, sexual violence and social control: integrating geographical and feminist analyses of women's fear of crime', *Progress in Human Geography*, 15(4): 415–431.

Pain, R.H. (1997) 'Social geographies of women's fear of crime', *Transactions of the Institute of British Geographers*, 22(2): 231–244.

Palin, M. (2018) 'Eurydice's tragic family past', *Gladstone Observer*, 16 June. Available from: https://web.archive.org/web/20180616141223/https://www.gladstoneobserver.com.au/news/eurydice-dixons-family-speaks-about-her-horrific-m/3443693/ [Accessed 19 January 2021].

Powell, A. (2015) 'Seeking rape justice: formal and informal responses to sexual violence through technosocial counter-publics', *Theoretical Criminology*, 19(4): 571–588.

Razak, I. (2019) 'Eurydice Dixon's sister and boyfriend face her killer, Jaymes Todd, in Supreme Court hearing', *ABC News*, 15 August. Available from: https://www.abc.net.au/news/2019-08-15/eurydice-dixons-killer-jaymes-todd-faces-victorian-supreme-court/11415748 [Accessed 28 February 2021].

Salter, M. (2013) 'Justice and revenge in online counter-publics: emerging responses to sexual violence in the age of social media', *Crime, Media, Culture: An International Journal*, 9(3): 225–242.

SBS News (2018) '"Women don't need to change, men do": Premier reacts to Eurydice Dixon's murder', 16 June. Available from: https://www.sbs.com.au/news/women-don-t-need-to-change-men-do-premier-reacts-to-eurydice-dixon-s-murder [Accessed 22 April 2021].

SBS News (2020) '"We are a nation in pain": tears and anger at Brisbane vigil for Hannah Clarke and her three children', 23 February. Available from: https://www.sbs.com.au/news/article/we-are-a-nation-in-pain-tears-and-anger-at-brisbane-vigil-for-hannah-clarke-and-her-three-children/sc2kqsf47 [Accessed 27 April 2022].

Schembri, J. (2018) 'Eurydice Dixon – post-gig interviews with friends', 14 July. Available from: https://www.jimschembri.com/eurydice-dixon-tribute-gig-highlander-bar-tuesday-3-july/ [Accessed 24 February 2021].

Schramm, K. (2011) 'Introduction: Landscapes of Violence: Memory and Sacred Space', *History and Memory*, 23(1): 5–22.

Siganto, T. (2020) 'Brisbane City Council creates park memorial for Hannah Clarke and her children', *ABC News*, 11 August. Available from: https://www.abc.net.au/news/2020-08-11/brisbane-reserve-memorial-for-hannah-clarke-and-children/12546730 [Accessed 15 January 2021].

Steele, L., Djuric, B., Hibberd, L. and Yeh, F. (2020) 'Parramatta female factory precinct as a site of conscience: using institutional pasts to shape just legal futures', *UNSW Law Journal*, 43(2): 521–551.

Sweeney, L.K. (2019) 'Man who vandalised Eurydice Dixon memorial continues with appeal', *The Age*, 1 February. Available from: https://www.theage.com.au/national/victoria/man-who-vandalised-eurydice-dixon-memorial-continues-with-appeal-20190201-p50v2p.html [Accessed 16 January 2021].

Tutton, M. (2019) 'Street harassment of young girls should not be "normal": I won't rest until it is illegal', *The Guardian*, 10 October. Available from: https://www.theguardian.com/commentisfree/2019/oct/10/street-harassment-young-girls-illegal-abuse-public [Accessed 19 January 2021].

Vera-Gray, F. (2017) *Men's Intrusion, Women's Embodiment: A Critical Analysis of Street Harassment*, Abingdon: Routledge.

Vera-Gray, F. and Kelly, L. (2020) 'Contested gendered space: public sexual harassment and women's safety work', *International Journal of Comparative and Applied Criminal Justice*, 44(4): 265–275.

Wood, P. (2018) 'What should happen to makeshift memorials at terror attack sites?' *ABC News Breakfast*, 27 February. Available from: https://www.abc.net.au/news/2018-02-27/what-should-happen-to-memorials-at-terror-attack-sites/9483872 [Accessed 20 January 2021].

Yates, A. and Ceccato, V. (2020) 'Individual and spatial dimensions of women's fear of crime: a Scandinavian case', *International Journal of Comparative and Applied Criminal Justice*, 44(4): 277–292.

Young, A. (2022) 'The time of ghosts: sites of violence, environments of memory', in M. Fiddler, T. Kindynis and T. Linneman (eds) *Ghost Criminology: The Afterlife of Crime and Punishment*, New York: NYU Press, 227–252.

15

Resisting Violence Through the Arts: Theatre and Poetry as Spaces for Speaking Out and Seeking Change

Amelia Walker and Corinna Di Niro

Introduction

Writing in the wake of the Second World War and the Nazi Holocaust, Hannah Arendt connected power with the 'space of appearance' (1998 [1958]: 199). Potentially present whenever people assemble for 'speech and action', so that 'the public realm can be organized' (1998 [1958]: 199), such spaces feed 'the lifeblood of the human artifice', setting 'the scene of action and speech' by sustaining a 'web of human affairs and relationships and the stories engendered by them' (1998 [1958]: 204). In present times, recent decades of increasingly dominant 'strong-man politics', 'resurgent ethnic nationalism', 'alt-right politics' and resultant suffering (Damian Martin and Schmidt, 2019: 1) have sparked renewed interest in Arendtian thought among thinkers and activists seeking to 'rethink the space of appearance' in order to resist right-wing totalitarianism and revitalize 'the power and effect of public demonstrations for our time' (Butler, 2011).

Reflecting Arendt's attitude to theatre as 'the political art par excellence' (1998 [1958]: 188), these Arendtian re-turns currently inform both practice and research regarding theatre, performance and the creative arts broadly, where 'spaces of appearance' represent 'temporary sites of politics' erupting 'through public speech and action' (Damian Martin and Schmidt, 2019: 5) to facilitate dialogic 'praxis as a political, and hence civic responsibility' (2019: 2). For example, Luke Matthews applies Arendt's 'space of appearance' to the '"theatre of absence"' (2019: 109–110) and

Sevi Bayraktar works on '"choreopolitics": 'choreographic practices of dissenters' that 'enable political action at moments of extreme coercion' (2019: 92). Diana Damian Martin similarly calls dance a medium for 'hopeful acts in troubled times', championing arts-based 'process[es] of appearance' as modes of 'political engagement' (2019: 33–34), thereby aligning with artist, writer and researcher Jenny Odell's treatment of spaces of appearance as 'incubation spaces' for 'empathy, responsibility, and political innovation' (Odell, 2019: 180). These Arendtian-informed contributions to creative arts research extend the broader scholarly literatures connecting arts practices and arts-based research with social and political change (Campbell and Farrier, 2016; Conroy and Batty, 2020; Harper, 2020).

This chapter articulates the politically engaged creative arts scholarship described thus far with feminist and queer work on space and gender-based violence (GBV) (Tyler and Cohen, 2010; Paul, 2011a, 2011b; Fileborn and Vera-Gray, 2017; Pearce et al, 2019). Space represents overlapping physical and virtual realms of work, socializing and domestic life in which conventionally defined boundaries of the so-called public and private increasingly blur and intermingle as technology, culture, the environment and other aspects of life continue to develop and change (Tyler and Cohen, 2010; Fileborn and Vera-Gray, 2017). GBV includes but exceeds physical violence, also encompassing social, structural and systemic problems – for instance, many workplaces systemically fail women by not providing adequate maternity leave, which compromises careers and exacerbates financial barriers to exiting violent relationships (Tomlinson et al, 2018).

Following Tanusree Paul (2011b) and Bianca Fileborn (2016), we recognize that GBV requires study with attention to how spaces influence ongoing (re)constructions of both gender and violence, which in turn act on and remake the spaces they form part of and thus partly form. For instance, 'masculine spaces' both arise from and reinstate conditions that render women and LGBTQIA+ people more likely to experience violence and less likely to gain fair hearing when speaking out against injustices (Paul, 2011a, 2011b). However, while space can 'contain, confine and define', it simultaneously provides scope for 'imagining – and building, practicing, and embodying – different, often undeterminable, potentialities' (Pearce et al, 2019). People interact with and in spaces via 'active and strategic choices' (Fileborn, 2016: 1108). In queer performance, this includes 'play[ing] out other possibilities and experiment[ing] with modes of being' beyond those of normative settings (Campbell and Farrier, 2016: 9).

This chapter sprang from our desires to demonstrate how arts-based practices offer spaces of appearance for addressing GBV. The next section describes our reflective writing-based research processes, which combined elements of established collaborative arts-based methodologies that similarly entail co-researchers sharing and comparing related-but-distinct lived experiences via processes of writing, reading and reflection (Sawyer and Norris, 2015; Park and Wilmes, 2019). The next section also discusses the initially troublesome surprises our research processes brought us, which reflect how writing occurs at 'the hinge between the conscious and unconscious' (Hecq 2015: 44). We set out to demonstrate radical potentials of burlesque and performance poetry, but our accounts illuminated problems inherent across both spaces, in particular their tendencies to manifest as 'masculine spaces', that is, spaces that sustain cultural ideologies conducive to reinstatement of gender-based inequalities (GBI) and thus of GBV. In line with collaborative writing-based arts research methodologies (Sawyer and Norris, 2015; Park and Wilmes, 2019), that our research did not prove what we hoped it would does not undermine, but actually supports, the validity of the findings this chapter presents: our processes challenged our initial assumptions, forcing us to think beyond bias and thus to conceive issues previously ignored. The ways in which spaces of burlesque and poetry sustain masculine economies conducive to GBI, and thus GBV, are unravelled in this chapter's three analysis sections, each of which focuses on a specific tendency dominant throughout both burlesque and performance poetry as per our experiences of these spaces. The first tendency is towards binary conceptions of gender. The second is commodification. The third involves aesthetic conventions that govern legibility in the burlesque and poetry spaces. Following discussion of these insights, a final section draws our findings together to indicate need for ongoing inquiry focused on transforming arts spaces. Our chapter concludes by mapping scope for continuing such explorations.

Currere, encounter, side–by–side analysis ... and surprises: our collaborative arts-based approach

The findings and recommendations our chapter presents arose through reflective writing-based processes that combined elements of established methodologies including duoethnography and co/autoethnography, both of which entail co-researchers sharing and comparing related-but-distinct lived experiences (Sawyer and Norris, 2015; Park and Wilmes, 2019). Such approaches argue the research value of personal biography or lived experience as *currere* (curricula of life and learning through it), for biodata aids recognition of how one's previous beliefs were culturally formed, and thus of potential cultural forces to consider when revising one's stance and initiating new courses of action, including further courses of writing, reflection and inquiry (Sawyer and Norris, 2015). When two or more sets of personal accounts are combined, the knowledge-generative potentials expand further still, for this process stages a critical encounter via which themes and divergences across accounts become explorable as data of shared cultural forces (Sawyer and Norris, 2015; Park and Wilmes, 2019).

For Sawyer and Norris, co-research relies on 'the inquirers' examination of difference as a means toward their reconceptualization of perception and meaning' (2015: 2). While we share some similarities in gender (female-assigned and identifying), age (approximately 40), career (arts-practitioners and early-career academics), and personal experiences (of GBV – though under very distinct personal situations), differences include our cultural backgrounds (Italian-Australian versus Scottish/Irish-Australian), our relationship histories (primarily heterosexual dating versus queer relationships with people of multiple genders), and our arts practices (theatre versus poetry, or in this case, burlesque versus live performance poetry). Our accounts cover similar time ranges (2007/2010 to present) in Australian contexts but span different cities (Adelaide and Melbourne). While the creative performances we discuss both entailed redress to gender-based injustices, their specific foci were distinct (parodying injustices of heterosexual dating through burlesque versus a fraught attempt to apply principles of *écriture féminine* in queer performance poetry).

Our research process involved two main steps. First, we penned individual accounts of our respective arts practices – theatre, and in this case, specifically burlesque (Di Niro), and poetry, specifically live performance poetry (Walker). Di Niro wrote of *iSize*, a one-woman theatre show Di Niro created and performed in Adelaide during 2010. *iSize* sought to raise awareness of gendered inequalities in heterosexual dating. Walker's account considered open mic and slam poetry practices in Australian cities (especially but not exclusively Adelaide and Melbourne) from 2000 onwards, including backyard performances in Melbourne circa 2007. After penning these accounts, our second step was analysing them for themes. Inspired by Jacques Derrida (1986 [1974]), we employed parallel text and side-by-side re-view, which reveals connections less evident via linear reading. For practical reasons, it is not feasible to present the parallel accounts in their entirety, but a sense is offered in Box 15.1.

Already, it becomes evident how our processes unsettled the assumptions with which we began. Initially, we wanted to demonstrate how burlesque and poetry can facilitate spaces of appearance in which to challenge GBV. But we independently penned accounts indicating the frequently masculine nature of these spaces. For instance, building on Mulvey (1998), Di Niro proceeded to reflect on how:

twenty years later, this gendered power imbalance was still being replicated. ... The Adelaide burlesque scene circa 2010 could be considered a 'masculine territory' that reproduced gendered 'binaries of space' entailing 'public' and 'productive' roles for men and 'private', 'reproductive', or in this case sexually servient roles for women, both of which strongly reflect and reinstate 'asymmetrical power relations' (Paul, 2011b: 413). This scenario sat at odds with discourses of a 'neo-burlesque' claiming to 'unite the radicalism of feminism with provocative sexual display'. (Nally, 2009: 621)

Walker's account of a former lover saying 'You write like a man' proceeded towards recognition of the words' ongoing sting as symptomatic of uneasy truths:

Box 15.1: Sample of parallel text and side-by-side re-view

iSize and Miss Direction: inequalities of gender in Burlesque performance (Di Niro)	Writing like a man? performance poetry's predictable (gendered) aesthetics (Walker)
It was 2010 and Adelaide's burlesque scene was at its highest. I was a big player in that space. I hosted monthly burlesque-themed life drawing events, judged burlesque comps, reviewed shows and performed. However, I never liked the burlesque scene here. It was very focused on objectifying women, encouraging them to strip for applause by a mostly male audience, and did little to subvert the patriarchy – a difficult pill for me, a feminist, to swallow. The objectifying gaze has been an area of research since at least 1964, when Jacques Lacan made it a focus of his psychoanalytic inquiries. Lacan's account of the gaze recasts 'central Freudian concepts, such as Scopophilia, Voyeurism and Fetishism' to describe 'the lack that constitutes castration anxiety resulting from the awareness that one can be viewed' (Sorrentino, 2014). Reconsidering this idea through a feminist lens, Laura Mulvey later posed that, 'in a world ordered by sexual imbalance, pleasure in looking has been split between active/male and passive/female', relegating women to a 'traditional exhibitionist role' of being 'simultaneously looked at and displayed, with their appearance coded for strong visual and erotic impact so that they can be said to connote to-be-looked-at-ness' (1998: 272).	'You write like a man', P sneered. It was 2007 and we were falling apart – as lovers, and as creative collaborators working together on queer arts and performance events run in the lounge-rooms, kitchens and backyards of anyone whose arms we managed to twist. P's words shocked me into silence as I absorbed the brutal flipside of what had attracted me to her in the first place: her ability to instill wild heights of emotion, among other things, through little more than the inflection of a syllable, the crafting of a phrase. Words, as Judith Butler (1997) reminds us, really do *matter* – they *make things happen*, including sublime, ineffable, sometimes painful things. Damn. Why did I write that? I had no plans to write that. I planned to write about performance poetry as a radical egalitarian space in and through which creative acts and dialogues can undo the sociopolitical structures that sustain conditions amenable to GBV.

Thirteen years on, P's words still smart. Why? Because I grasp why she said them, what she meant. ... This undermines what I thought I wanted to write about performance poetry as a space in which I – a queer bisexual woman and domestic violence survivor – strive to challenge GBV and related issues. ... I acknowledge P's point: I often did and still do write like that.

These subversions of our expectations do not undermine but actually affirm the validity of our inquiries. In writing-based research, putting one's perspective on paper enables critical and reflective questioning of that perspective – and thereby, *shifts* of perspective via reflexive intervention in response to what writing reveals (Park and Wilmes, 2019: 153). This is because writing occurs at conscious/unconscious 'hinge[s]' where 'seemingly erratic and apparently irrational elements' bubble and overspill (Hecq, 2015: 44). Writing thus tells us things we don't necessarily want, but need, to know.

The emphasis on masculine spaces prevalent across both our accounts led us to shift our focus towards understanding how and why spaces of burlesque and poetry frequently manifest in the troublesome ways they do. Using our side-by-side analysis strategy, we recognized three themes prevalent across both our accounts: binary gender, commodification and aesthetic conventions governing legibility. The next three sections of this paper address these in turn.

Analysis Part 1: Binary conceptions of gender in spaces of burlesque and poetry

This first of three analysis sections focuses on how (mis)conceptions of gender as binary serve the ongoing remanifestation or maintenance of burlesque and poetry as masculine spaces. Binary gender for us represents the cultural myth of there being but two genders: male and female, and of these essentially entailing certain biologically determined qualities defining people's strengths, weaknesses and suitability for social and professional roles. As the earlier writings of French feminist theorist Hélène Cixous demonstrated, binary gender connects with broader patterns of binary logic or dichotomous thinking in Western culture, writing and philosophy including 'active/passive', 'culture/nature', 'head/heart', and 'day/night', among others (1994: 37). This scenario disadvantages women, who are perceived as weak, erratic, hormonally driven and thus primarily suited to child-rearing rather than professional, artistic and/or intellectual careers. Binary gender erases queer people by discouraging possibilities of rejecting, combining or exceeding dichotomous constraints.

The force of binary gender is evident in both our accounts via reactions to women who behaviourally cross into purportedly masculine territories.

Di Niro described how *iSize* deployed a character called Miss Direction as a device for inverting the scenario critiqued by Mulvey (1998) and turning the objectifying gaze onto men. As Di Niro's account replays, this character: 'embodied an array of hetero-male qualities and behaviours. ... Miss Direction not only unwelcomely gazed at male audience members, but brought them onstage, publicly displaying them as her personal toys'. Di Niro staged *iSize* to emphasize how its point explicitly wasn't that women ought to treat men atrociously, but rather to discourage such behaviours in any context: 'Space played a crucial role. It needed to be manipulated. It needed to be blurred. A careful balancing act was required: I wanted my male audience members to feel safe when being taken from their comfort space to the vulnerable space of the stage.'

Despite these measures, the character of Miss Direction was misunderstood by some: 'feedback later showed that *iSize* was typically well-received by females and tolerated by men. Even in the context of theatre, as an imagined space, male audience members could not see the show for what it was – a tongue in cheek role reversal'.

In one performance, a male audience member initially agreed to participate in an onstage routine, then became publicly recalcitrant, attempting to wreck the performance. Reviewer Jade O'Donahue wrote of how this man's antics 'made Miss Direction's point perfectly, that the double standard still well and truly exists' (2010). By Di Niro's evaluation, the incident demonstrated: 'how male dominance over public spaces is not merely achieved through their numerical appropriation of space, but largely through assertive and aggressive behaviour which intimidates and embarrasses women' (Paul, 2011a: 251).

That binary gender arose in Di Niro's account is partly explainable because *iSize* explicitly confronted male/female power dynamics in heterosexual dating. Walker's account, however, discussed LGBTQIA+ cultures: even those who believe they challenge normative gender may unknowingly reflect and reinstate it. Walker likewise described negative consequences for women behaving in purportedly masculine ways. While Di Niro staged this deliberately via character, receiving external pushback from heterosexual men, Walker's gender transgressions were accidental, via writing 'like a man'. The consequences show queer internalization of heteronormative gender restrictions:

> P's critique ironically reinscribed the very gender system we as queer arts-makers both sought to undermine ... entailed the problematic suggestion that men's and women's orgasms are biologically-prescribed, that a normative model exists for each, and that this gendered model should extend to the prescription of additional practices, such as writing. ... This reminds me that women and LGBTQIA+ people

can, knowingly and unknowingly, participate in and sustain the very systems that continue our oppression.

This reflects queer internalization of gender norms by Walker's former lover 'P'. Also evident were Walker's own self-punishing guilt, shame and failure: 'my writing fails – *I fail* – in my efforts to produce "*écriture féminine*" (Cixous, 1994): feminine writing that unsettles dominant masculine conventions'. However, and more encouragingly, the processes of writing and reflecting on these words enabled Walker to recognize those assumptions as problematic misinterpretations of Cixousian theory:

> as I write this, I wonder, why should I want to 'succeed' at *écriture féminine*? It's contradictory, given the binary value judgements underscoring failure and success ... the idea of feminine versus masculine writing is similarly binary and reductive, eclipsing that combine and/or exceed these tendencies. ... I still *do* want to redress my tendencies towards dominant poetic tropes and techniques. But knee-jerking towards 'feminine' styles as the binary anecdote is equally problematic.

Hence our accounts show not only how binary gender helps maintain burlesque and poetry as masculine spaces, but also how writing-based research can initiate shifts beyond existing limits.

Analysis Part 2: Commodification and the masculine economy

Commodification reflects a masculine economy driven by hierarchical competition. This theme was recurrent across both our accounts, leading us to recognize commodification as a second factor contributing to maintenance of burlesque and poetry as masculine spaces. Commodification in burlesque has already been discussed by Sarah French, for whom neo-burlesque presents 'a troubling example of the dual commodification of performance and the female body in neoliberal times' (2017: 161). French's point is reflected in Di Niro's account through comments about how: '"the male gaze creates the possibility for treating a woman's body, body parts, or sexual functions as separated out from her person" (Bareket et al, 2018: 6) while the "trophy wife" indicates a woman "viewed as an accessory of their husband"' (Meszaros, 2017: 239).

Commodification's connections with a masculine space become evident when Di Niro depicts Adelaide's circa-2010 burlesque scene as: 'a masculine space in which it was impossible for a show like iSize to truly succeed "under the overarching hegemony of a patriarchal society"' (Paul, 2011b: 418).

In Walker's account, commodification arose via consideration of Karma R. Chávez's (2010) critique of poetry slams – competitions where poets vie for prizes, sometimes including large monetary prizes. Walker observed how even poets at non-competitive open-mic events frequently compete: 'for symbolic recognition, cultural capital, and respect or indeed power'.

This led towards further interrogation of how poems themselves, as textual spaces structured through metre, pauses, repetition and other devices, can: 'often be masculine spaces ... reflective and reinstative of a masculine economy and the ideals on which such economies run'. This insight pushed Walker towards a 'new question': 'how can I re-engage with poetry's spaces – its physical and virtual (online) performance spaces, and poems as formal spaces and performances in themselves – to make the queer arts activism I initially sought to discuss here more possible after all?'

Again, our accounts thus not only helped us recognize commodification as a factor that maintains burlesque and poetry as masculine spaces, but also helped us begin to think beyond this troubling situation.

Analysis Part 3: Aesthetic conventions governing legibility

The third of three themes we identified across our accounts as factors supporting the maintenance of burlesque and poetry as masculine spaces involved aesthetic conventions governing legibility. By this we mean the formal theatrical, poetic and other devices via which audiences and participants recognize and make sense of performances. This became evident through our side-by-side analysis when we noticed Mulvey's (1998) work on the male gaze beside Butler's notion of how words 'matter' (1997). While we recognize that tensions between these theories developed in different contexts for different issues, both use psychoanalytic theory to consider which social persons can and cannot legibly make their concerns heard. In Arendtian terms, both thus regard who can and cannot gain access to space(s) and appearance(s).

Both our accounts reflected how legible appearance in performance spaces often relies on devices steeped in dominant Western conventions of theatre and poetics. Di Niro explained how:

> To make the men fit her Ken-inspired fantasies, Miss Direction gave her first male a hat, made the second strap foam muscles onto his arms, and demanded that the third remove his shirt. I intentionally left the shirt removal request for last as this follows the classic comedic rule of three or the comic triple – 'the offer, the advance and the twist' – in which the third element evokes the biggest reaction and reveals the biggest elements of surprise. (Firth, 2009: 7)

Evoking a different rule of three, Walker similarly relayed use of an Aristotelian three-act structure: 'a rising conflict approach that I fall into habitually because it's incredibly common, or arguably the norm, in performance poetry as in theatre and other narrative forms it typically meets expectations and rouses a good response'. The masculine implications of three-act devices emerge through Walker's recount of P's critique: ' "Your poems are all like bloody male orgasm – a little peak, then backing away – another peak, and again, away – and then – oh my, my, oh yes, oh no – the fucking CLIMAX!!! ... And then? Your poems mumble and fall the fuck asleep." '

This connection sparked the reflections relayed in the previous section of poems themselves as masculine textual spaces, additionally leading Walker to perceive her tendency towards producing such poems as reflective of demands shaped by the masculine space of the poetry performance culture: 'In order to appear and bear voice in this [masculine] space, I find myself stylistically pandering to masculine aesthetics ... even when I'm writing about GBV or other purportedly feminist and/or queer issues.'

These revelations led us to recognize a key challenge for feminist, queer and allied practitioners attempting to address issues of GBI and GBV through burlesque and poetry: to appear and gain legible hearing within performance spaces, it frequently seems necessary to deploy aesthetic strategies of the masculine economy – for instance via 'writing like a man' and/or female characters either pandering to the male gaze or themselves displaying masculine tendencies – but doing so risks re-citing masculinity's dominance and maintaining masculine spaces where GBI persists, facilitating GBV. To activate meaningful change through burlesque and/or performance poetry, it thus seems necessary to transform the spaces of these practices themselves and the aesthetic expectations governing legibility therein. These tasks are hefty: there are no quick or simple solutions and attempts at subversion may be quickly reabsorbed into the oppressive status quo. Nonetheless, the capacities that writing-based reflection has shown us for recognizing and thinking beyond such problems spur us to retain optimism. We recognize strong scope for further inquiry, recommended directions for which we outline in this chapter's next, final section.

Scope for further inquiry

We began these inquiries believing in the radical potentials of burlesque and live performance poetry, among other arts practices, for activating spaces of appearance and affecting change around GBI and GBV. Through writing-based inquiry, we have come to a more reserved perspective: we retain our passions for performance arts and the communities they sustain, but recognize that problematically masculine tendencies dominate performance spaces, governing speech, appearance and scope for meaningful dialogues towards change. In a sense, it feels we have gone backwards. However, if we have, backwards was an important direction for travelling; it enables avoidance of false turns and stumbles we might otherwise have taken.

Sometimes, identifying and unpacking problems is itself a useful contribution that deepens awareness of challenges and snares, allowing for more insightful, strategic and effective ways forward. This chapter has identified problems of burlesque and performance poetry as masculine spaces and has unpacked three contributing factors: binary gender, commodification and aesthetic conventions. We take neither the risk nor indulgence of imagining any easy or fast solutions.

Conclusion

Our key recommendation is for further inquiry into how theatre-makers, poets and other arts practitioners may strategically transform creative spaces and conventions to increase scope for using these spaces to address injustices. To guide inquiry, the following sub-recommendations reflect themes from our shared accounts that seem worthy of further exploration. They also reflect this chapter's limitations as latent potentials ongoing research can continue pushing beyond:

- Because binary gender, commodification and aesthetic conventions all contribute to reproducing burlesque and performance poetry as masculine spaces, these three issues represent important sites for inquiry into how to transform these and related arts spaces towards more egalitarian possibilities of gender relation and articulation.
- Attempts at subversion are easily co-opted into the dominant framework (for instance, as in cases of slam poetry and neo-burlesque), and so we encourage cautious avoidance of overconfidence and suggest that the task of transforming spaces be viewed as an ongoing process involving repeated revision of approaches over time.
- One strategy that seems worthy of extended exploration is that of shifting perspectives by playing with spaces of arts practice and performance themselves, including the embodied performance space (for instance, by blurring conventional audience/performer zones) and the textual or conceptual spaces (such as poetics and narrative structure) to enact metaphoric play with and in spaces of culture and thought.
- Perspective shifts may also be possible by working across multiple media and contexts (for instance, we have here considered burlesque and poetry through a mixture of reflective prose and academic writing) and collaborating or otherwise interacting with fellow arts-makers and/or researchers whose fields and practices differ from one's own.

- Our inquiry was limited to burlesque and poetry in Australian contexts across a time frame of 2007 to the present; there remains need to consider additional practices across a wider range of geographic and temporal scenarios.
- We were also limited by the lived experiences to which we bear and lack access; need remains for appropriately resourced practitioners to explore how attempts to transform arts spaces and/or address GBV through arts practices differ when connected with issues of racism, cissexism, ableism, fat-shaming, body-shaming, ageism and/or neurotypical privilege, among additional intersecting modes of injustice.
- All this ongoing work can benefit from constant critical self-reflection and reflexive response through practices including but not limited to collaborative writing-based inquiry through methods such as those our chapter enacts.

References

Arendt, H. (1998 [1958]) *The Human Condition* (2nd edn), Chicago: University of Chicago Press.

Bayraktar, S. (2019) 'Choreographies of dissent and the politics of public space in state-of-emergency Turkey', *Performance Philosophy*, 5(1): 90–108.

Bareket, O., Shnabel, N., Abeles, D., Gervais, S. and Yuval-Greenberg, S. (2018) 'Evidence for an association between men's spontaneous objectifying gazing behavior and their endorsement of objectifying attitudes toward women', *Sex Roles*, 81: 245–256.

Butler, J. (1997) *Excitable Speech: A Politics of the Performative*, New York: Routledge.

Butler, J. (2011) 'Bodies in alliance and the politics of the street', *Transversal Texts blog*, September. Available from: https://transversal.at/transversal/1011/butler/en [Accessed 6 November 2020].

Campbell, A. and Farrier, S. (eds) (2016) *Queer Dramaturgies: International Perspectives on Where Performance Leads Queer*, Basingstoke: Palgrave Macmillan.

Chávez, K.R. (2010) 'Poetic polemics: a (queer feminist of color) reflection on a gay slam poet', *Text and Performance Quarterly*, 30(4): 444–452.

Cixous, H. (1994) *The Hélène Cixous Reader*, ed S. Sellers, London: Routledge.

Conroy, C.M. and Batty, C. (2020) 'Writing the organisational crisis: embodied leadership engaged through the lens of a playscript', *New Writing*, 17(4): 414–427.

Damian Martin, D. (2019) 'Hopeful acts in troubled times: thinking as interruption and the poetics of nonconforming criticism', *Performance Philosophy*, 5(1): 25–41.

Damian Martin, D. and Schmidt, T. (2019) 'Sites of appearance, matters of thought: Hannah Arendt and performance philosophy', *Performance Philosophy*, 5(1): 1–7.

Derrida, J. (1986 [1974]) *Glas*, J.P. Leavy Jr and R. Rand (trans), Lincoln: University of Nebraska Press.

Fileborn, B. (2016) 'Doing gender, doing safety? Young adults' production of safety on a night out', *Gender, Place & Culture*, 23(8): 1107–1120.

Fileborn, B. and Vera-Gray, F. (2017) '"I want to be able to walk the street without fear": transforming justice for street harassment', *Feminist Legal Studies*, 25(2): 203–207.

Firth, C. (2009) 'How to write comedy: the complete and utter guide to writing comedy', *Australian Author*, 41(3): 6–9.

French, S. (2017) 'Neoliberal postfeminism, neo-burlesque, and the politics of affect in the performances of Moira Finucane', in E. Diamond, D. Varney and C. Amich (eds) *Performance, Feminism and Affect in Neoliberal Times*, London: Palgrave Macmillan, pp 161–173.

Harper, G. (2020) 'Why our responses matter', *New Writing*, 17(4): 355.

Hecq, D. (2015) *Towards a Poetics of Creative Writing*, Bristol: Multilingual Matters.

Matthews, L. (2019) 'Heiner Goebbels's *Sifters Dinge* and the Arendtian public sphere', *Performance Philosophy*, 5(1): 109–127.

Meszaros, J. (2017) 'American men and romance tourism: searching for traditional trophy wives as status symbols of masculinity', *Women's Studies Quarterly*, 45(1): 225–242.

Mulvey, L. (1998) 'Visual pleasure and narrative cinema', in L. Goodman and J. de Gay (eds) *The Routledge Reader in Gender and Performance*, London: Routledge, pp 270–275.

Nally, C. (2009) 'Grrrly hurly burly: neo-burlesque and the performance of gender', *Textual Practice*, 23(4): 621–643.

Odell, J. (2019) *How to Do Nothing: Resisting the Attention Economy*, Carlton, VIC: Black.

O'Donahue, J. (2010) '*iSize*: a double shot of burlesque served straight up, with a twist' [theatre review]. Available from: https://stagesecrets.com.au/three-d-radio-isize-adelaide-cabaret-fringe-festival/ [Accessed 13 May 2022].

Park, J.C. and Wilmes, S.E.D. (2019) 'A critical co/autoethnographic exploration of self: becoming science education researchers in diverse cultural and linguistic landscapes', in J. Bazzul and C. Siry (eds) *Critical Voices in Science Education Research: Narratives of Hope and Struggle*, Cham: Springer, pp 141–156.

Paul, T. (2011a) 'Public spaces and everyday lives: gendered encounters in the metro city of Kolkata', in S. Raju and K. Lahiri-Dutt (eds) *Doing Gender, Doing Geography: Emerging Research in India*, New Delhi: Routledge, pp 248–267.

Paul, T. (2011b) 'Space, gender, and fear of crime: some explorations from Kolkata', *Gender, Technology and Development*, 5(3): 411–435.

Pearce, S., Urry, K., Sultan, A. and Challans, B. (2019) 'Locating the self: the sticky, shifting processes of knowledge-making, boundary-tracing and coming home', *Writing from Below: Space and Place*, 4(3). Available from: https://writingfrombelow.org/space-and-place/editorial-locating-self/ [Accessed 6 November 2020].

Sawyer, R. and Norris, J. (2015) 'Duoethnography: a retrospective 10 years after', *International Review of Qualitative Research*, 8(1): 1–4.

Sorrentino, S. (2014) 'Femininity as masquerade in "Untitled Film Stills 1977–1980" by Cindy Sherman', *Subverting the Male Gaze*, 7 November. Available from: https://curatingthecontemporary.org/2014/11/07/subverting-the-male-gaze-femininity-as-masquerade-in-untitled-film-stills-1977-1980-by-cindy-sherman/ [Accessed 11 May 2022].

Tomlinson, M., Enders, J. and Naidoo, R. (2018) 'The Teaching Excellence Framework: symbolic violence and the measured market in higher education', *Critical Studies in Education*, 61(5): 627–642.

Tyler, M. and Cohen, L. (2010) 'Spaces that matter: gender performativity and organizational space', *Organization Studies*, 31(2): 175–198.

Index

References to figures appear in *italic* type; those in **bold** type refer to tables.
References to endnotes show both the page number and the note number (231n3).